LET ME ENJOY
THE EARTH

LET ME ENJOY THE EARTH

Thomas Hardy and Nature

Joanna Cullen Brown

Allison & Busby
Published by W. H. Allen

An Allison & Busby book
Published in 1990 by
W. H. Allen & Co. Plc
Sekforde House
175/9 St John Street
London EC1V 4LL

Copyright © 1990 Joanna Cullen Brown

Typeset by Avocet Robinson, Buckingham
Printed in Great Britain by
Butler & Tanner Ltd, Frome & London

ISBN 0 85031 875 0

For

Enid, Rowena, Patrick, Margaret and George

Let me enjoy the earth no less
Because the all-enacting Might
That fashioned forth its loveliness
Had other aims than my delight.

Contents

═══

ACKNOWLEDGEMENTS

My thanks are due to the following for permission to quote:

Oxford University Press for *The Collected Letters of Thomas Hardy*, ed. Purdy & Millgate (1978–87); Michael Millgate, *Thomas Hardy: A Biography* (1982);

Macmillan Publishers Ltd, for *The Literary Notebooks of Thomas Hardy*, ed. Lennart Björk; F. E. Hardy, *The Life of Thomas Hardy; Personal Notebooks of Thomas Hardy*, ed. R. H. Taylor; Dennis Taylor, *Hardy's Poetry, 1860–1928; Thomas HArdy's Personal Writings*, ed. Harold Orel.

Grafton Books, a division of the Collins Publishing Group, for Jean Brooks' *Thomas Hardy: The Poetic Structure*;

Barrie & Jenkins Ltd for Cynthia Asquith's *Portrait of Barrie*;

J. S. Cox, The Toucan Press, for *Materials for the Study of the Life, Times and Works of Thomas Hardy*;

Dr Desmond Flower for Newman Flower's *Just As It Happened*;

Unwin Hyman Ltd for Roger Robinson's essay on Darwin in *Thomas Hardy: The Writer & His Background*, ed. Norman Page;

the Trustees of Miss E. A. Dugdale for the facsimile extract from Hardy's letter to Mrs Henniker.

I am greatly indebted, not only to Thomas Hardy, whose works are the main text of this book, but to all the Hardy scholars whose writings have enriched my understanding and enjoyment, many of which are quoted or recommended here. I should like to thank Dr James Gibson for help readily given over the years; Mr Roger Peers, the Curator of the Dorset County Museum, Dorchester, for help with manuscripts there and for supplying me with many armfuls of Hardy's own books to study; the library staff of the Dorset County Library, Dorchester, and Avon County Central Library, Bristol, for their ever courteous assistance; Mrs Sarah McBride for her efficiency and patience in the selection of photographs; and as always Bernard, *animae dimidium meae*.

THOMAS HARDY AND NATURE

INTRODUCTION

To begin with a phrase like *Thomas Hardy and Nature* gives very little clue as to where we shall end. Though he could write brilliantly about 'the moods of the air, and earth, and sky', and how for the countryman 'sun, rain, wind, snow, dawn, darkness, mist, are to him, now as ever, personal assistants and obstructors, masters and acquaintances . . .', he was really much more interested in town and country people alike, and in

> The eternal question of what Life was,
> And why we were there, and by whose strange laws
> That which mattered most could not be.[1]

Figures in a Wessex Landscape told a tale of the lives of people in rural Dorset in the nineteenth century: their work and entertainments, their loves, their insecurities and sufferings, their relationship to the past. In this companion volume the spotlight turns even more on to Hardy himself, with all his compelling contradictions – and paradoxically, though starting from the natural world, on to what it means in this universe 'to be human now'.

The book divides into three main parts. The first is of Hardy's amazing descriptions of the natural world, which show his detailed observations of what can actually happen in land and sky and water and light. Yet they are far more than mere descriptions, for they are turned with a poet's eye, turned and crafted not only with the insight of an artist, but with the preoccupations of a thinking and feeling human being. So the second part leads on to the connections Hardy made between men and women and their setting: the reality that surrounds us and governs our physical existence, which is inevitably the world of natural laws. (Throughout the book, for convenience, I distinguish as Hardy did, despite his acceptance of Darwinian theory, between humankind and the rest of nature.) The third part grows from the two that precede it, in looking more precisely at what Hardy thought – or felt – about Nature's part in the ordering of the universe and the living of human life.

Questions need to be asked. Was Hardy a true countryman, or only a bogus landscape artist whose canvases lacked essential authentic detail? What was his own relationship with Nature – or, in his words, 'what we call Nature'? How can his own complex and ambivalent attitude to it be reconciled and understood, as it veered like the winds of heaven between love and disapproval, joy, pity and despair; as he saw Nature, often

1

beautiful, but uncaring, the impotent vassal of 'the Great Face behind',[2] and a part of all the paradoxes of the universe?

In one sense Hardy took the countryside for granted: like Christopher Julian, who found 'the landscape . . . something necessary to the tone, but not regarded.'[3] The town boy, said the poet in a conversation with William Archer, 'will rush to pick a flower which the country boy does not seem to notice. But it is part of the country boy's life. It grows in his soul – he does not want it in his buttonhole.'[4]

This seems to me to be the heart of Hardy's own instinctive feeling (although nothing is simple). The deep country in which he spent his formative years grew in his soul; and, combined with his subtle mind, and his extraordinary gift for observation, and for seeing as an artist sees, it flowered into marvellous evocations of the natural scene.

Yet these evocations are not made for their own sake. Their purpose is almost always to illuminate in some way the lives of the women and men he is creating; and to draw out from a scene its most significant features, as a painter composes his picture. ('Art', noted Hardy, 'is a disproportioning . . . of realities, to show more clearly the features that matter in those realities . . .'[5]) So like any artist he will alter details, and from the strict naturalist's point of view he sometimes appears to make slight mistakes – like, for example, describing flowers blooming together which usually do so a few weeks apart.[6]

These 'mistakes' usually arise from something far more significant than mere cataloguing or simple description: the deep and complex connections he makes between the natural environment and the person who lives in it. For example, the moon becomes for him a many-sided metaphor,[7] accompanying, revealing, concealing the different phases of a person's life. Often the beginning of a new experience of love is shadowed by 'a slim young moon'. Thus preoccupied with the deeper meaning of life, Hardy first wrote in *Under the Greenwood Tree* about Dick's interesting new condition of infatuation, with the new moon rising in the spring evening – instead of setting. (Correspondents were quick to correct him.[8]) Subsequently he made very few of these 'mistakes', even for a greater artistic purpose; but, if he was not using it in his writing, accurate, or scientifically expressed natural detail for its own sake was often unimportant to him. So he could write to Mrs Henniker at Christmas about the suffering of the blackbirds and thrushes in his frosted garden, adding: 'We, like you, have plenty of tits. Florence knows their varieties better than I do.' Indeed, George Gissing, visiting him in September 1895, found several surprises, and wrote to his brother afterwards: 'I find that he does not know the flowers of the field!'[9] (This however proves nothing. Hardy was so reticent, and so accustomed to the Socratic ironic approach, that he was quite capable of obscuring anything he wished. Charles Morgan's remarkable description of the poet's visit to Oxford in 1920 included these words:

> He was not simple; he had the formal subtlety peculiar to his own generation; there was something deliberately 'ordinary' in his demeanour which was a concealment of extraordinary fires.[10])

Yet the natural world was clearly of fundamental importance to him, and daily affected his life. At least in his last years, every day before breakfast at Max Gate – the home in which he lived from 1885 to his death in early 1928 – he would walk to the gate and, looking south towards the Hardy monument on the down, assess the day's weather and then walk round the garden before starting work. The gardener, Mr Bertie Stephens, kept in his mind's eye after the poet's death 'a never-to-be-forgotten picture of an aged old gentleman who was still keenly interested in nature and still studying for his books'. Mr Stephens told how he was never allowed to trap or shoot the animals and birds that damaged the fruit and vegetables there; and when questioned added: 'I think there is no doubt [Mr Hardy] was happiest and got greater contentment when he was alone with nature. He always appeared to be very contented watching the birds, such as blackbirds, thrushes and blue tits, in his own garden.' The parlourmaid, Miss E. E. Titterington, said of him: 'His conversations were often about the Dorset countryside and birds; he was a great nature-lover and we maids had to feed the birds daily.' One of the many visitors to Max Gate testified that 'a gleam of real pleasure and genuine pride came into his face when we began to talk about his beloved countryside.'[11]

But all Hardy's writings show this awareness of nature and its mark in ordinary life. Perhaps of particular significance are his letters and surviving notes.

> [1897] *February 10.* In spite of myself I cannot help noticing countenances and tempers in objects of scenery, e.g., trees, hills, houses.[12]

On 8 June 1875 he wrote enthusiastically to R. D. Blackmore, congratulating him on his novel *Lorna Doone:*

> . . . I cannot help writing just one line to tell you how astonished I was to find what it contained – exquisite ways of describing things which are more after my own heart than the "presentations" of any other writer that I am acquainted with. . . . Little phases of nature which I though nobody had noticed but myself were continually turning up in your book – for instance, the marking of a heap of sand into little pits by the droppings from trees was a fact I should unhesitatingly have declared unknown to any other novelist till now. A kindred sentiment between us in so many things is, I suppose, partly because we both spring from the West of England. . . .[13]

And in March 1909 he wrote to Edward Clodd:

> The raw east wind has reduced my mind no less than my body to a sterile greyness, out of which not a single thought will sprout.

In a hasty note to the same recipient the previous year he had written:

> Yes: that theory of consciousness in plants is an arresting one: but I have always known it intuitively, & hate maiming trees on that account.[14]

3

Much of what he knew 'intuitively' must have derived from his early surroundings. Not only did his home back on to the heath, and his daily walk to school lead across fields, making every tree and incline familiar: his father was a keen countryman, 'an open-air liver' who liked 'going alone into the woods or on the heath . . . with a telescope . . . or, in the hot weather, lying on a bank of thyme or camomile with the grasshoppers leaping over him.'[15] Thomas not only absorbed his surroundings, but he habitually noted them throughout his life. They could not always be called the notes of a conventional naturalist – in his twenties he was trying to take down the exact song of the nightingale – but if not expressed in scientific terms they were actual descriptions of the sounds or colours of a storm, or how light shone through rain or trees.[16] Even when living in London in 1880 he notes near Rotten Row the sparrow at sunset who 'descends from the tree amid the stream of vehicles, and drinks from the little pool left by the watering-cart'.[17] Back in Dorset at Christmas 1883, he is writing in amusing detail about what he called 'The Birds' Bedroom' in the plantation at Bockhampton (page 22). An entry for early November, 1905, shows how meticulously he noted 'the order in which the leaves fall this year' (page 33); and in January, 1920 (when in his eightieth year) he notes evocatively: 'Coming back from Talbothays by West Stafford Cross I saw Orion upside down in a pool of water under an oak.'[18] He tells how in his wanderings he would make notes on large dead leaves or white wood chips left by the wood-cutters; and many an observation of tiny details was later turned into a poem or used in a narrative description. ('Now Hardy possessed an intense power of observation', wrote his friend Hermann Lea. 'He continually took me aback by later reference to some quite trivial thing which I had cursorily noticed but which he had microscopically investigated – that, too, in what had seemed to me a merely passing glance.' And Mr H. L. Voss, frequently his chauffeur, said: 'He was a very interesting companion to have with you on a motor tour . . . He didn't miss a detail.'[19] So observed details abound. In *The Trumpet-Major*'s mill the fine dusting of flour everywhere is just enough, but not too much, to support a delicate growth of lichen indoors on the window-sills. In the woods, as Fitzpiers leaves Grace after Giles's death, the only sounds she can hear are

> the tiny cracklings of the dead leaves which, like a feather-bed, had not yet done rising to their normal level where indented by the pressure of her husband's receding footsteps.

The bobbing leaf he saw one day, imprisoned in a spider's web, became in "Last Week in October" the leaf

> That stays there dangling when the rest pass on;
> Like a suspended criminal hangs he, mumming
> In golden garb, while one yet green, high yon
> Trembles, as fearing such a fate for himself anon.[20]

He observes that Egdon produced 'strange amber-coloured butterflies . . . which were never seen elsewhere'; and Venn and Wildeve are able to gamble grotesquely on its darkened slopes by the light – of all things – of a handful of glow-worms, because, at this their most brilliant season, Hardy knew that 'it is possible on such nights to read the handwriting of a letter by the light of two or three.'

Hardy knew this probably less from personal observation than from the story told by his grandfather of an almost surreal adventure that had befallen him on the heath. His grandson related to Alfred Pope (who in turn read the account to a meeting of the Dorset Natural History and Antiquarian Field Club on 13 February 1912)[21] how one June midnight early in the century the first Thomas Hardy had been crossing the heath when he became aware of two men following him. Fearing robbery, and recognising his vulnerability, he determined to play upon the men's natural superstition. So, rolling a furze-faggot on to the path and sitting on it, he stuck two fir fronds into his hair to simulate horns, and added round the brim of his hat some glow-worms which he had seen and picked up in the grass earlier that night. Then taking a letter from his pocket, he settled down to read it by their light. The men drew nearer, then suddenly took to their heels. The rumour soon spread that the devil had been seen at midnight near 'Greenhill Pond', reading a list of his victims by glow-worm light.

Hardy not only remembered family stories such as this. He also cared enough about natural detail to make notes in his own words from naturalists' writings, like those from J. G. Wood's *Insects at Home* (1872) quoted on page 34, or the following:

> *Beautiful* beetle – gold-green above, shining copper green below – the common green tiger-beetle, or sparkler.
>
> G. J. Wood

> *The nearer the lovelier.* The head of this beetle seems (when casually observed,) to be merely dull green, but under a powerful light, & lens, it blazes with gem-like hues. almost dazzling in their splendour. ib.[22]

Hardy's enjoyment is obvious; and suitably mulled over by him, the tiger-beetle reappeared in *The Return of the Native* (see p 193)

> There was a certain obscurity in Eustacia's beauty, and Venn's eye was not trained. In her winter dress, as now, she was like the tiger-beetle, which, when observed in dull situations, seems to be of the quietest neutral colour, but under a full illumination blazes with dazzling splendour.

Compared with the fruits of his own observation, however, the use of such learnt information is very small. The poet's own gifts and opportunities gave him the intimate knowledge and feeling for birds and insects, horses, trees, stars and weather phenomena evident throughout his writings, (even, and in fact deliberately, in unlikely parts of *The Dynasts*).

The longer evocations of nature in his novels are unforgettable – descriptions like that of the looming storm in *Far from the Madding Crowd;* the moment in *The Hand of Ethelberta* when 'a zinc sky met a leaden sea . . . the low wind groaned and whined, and not a bird sang'; the sorrowful decay of the woodlands in autumn, with their rotting fungi hanging like the lobes of lungs from the ageing bark; the 'great and particular glory of the Egdon waste', its 'Titanic form', its lashing tempests full of the 'wild rhetoric of night', when 'the storm was its lover and the wind its friend'; the 'oozing fatness and warm ferments of the Froom Vale, at a season when the rush of juices could almost be heard below the hiss of fertilization.' The same power of natural description is in countless poems, many of which – like "Once at Swanage", "The Later Autumn", "Night-Time in Mid-Fall", "An Unkindly May", "Snow in the Suburbs", "Summer Schemes", "The Five Students" and so on – are on these pages.

These evocations are stamped with the unmistakable hallmark of personal experience. Nowhere is this more felt than in the luminous description of Gabriel Oak's pause under the stars, when

> to persons standing alone on a hill during a clear midnight such as this, the roll of the earth eastward is almost a palpable movement. . . . Whatever may be its origin, the impression of riding along is vivid and abiding.

Each star is lovingly differentiated, from 'the restless Pleiades' to Orion, 'which gorgeous constellation never burnt more vividly than now, as it soared forth above the rim of the landscape.'

Light (and shadow, with all its Gothic connotations) was particularly sensitively felt by Hardy, as may be seen on almost every page. When Thomasin and her aunt went out to cut holly on the heath,

> The open hills were airy and clear, and the remote atmosphere appeared, as it often appears on a fine winter day, in distinct planes of illumination independently toned, the rays which lit the nearer tracts of landscape streaming visibly across those further off; a stratum of ensaffroned light was imposed on a stratum of deep blue, and behind these lay still remoter scenes wrapped in frigid grey.[23]

The watcher on Norcombe hill noted too how 'a difference of colour in the stars – oftener read of than seen in England – was really perceptible here.' Colours, and smells, are all part of the evocation, from poems like "Neutral Tones", or "A Spellbound Palace", to the descriptions of the sky blazing like a foundry, a brilliant landscape behind the sea, or the tweedy shades of Egdon with its flecks of flints and white sand. Unforgettably, Tranter Dewy came out from his Sunday ablutions 'smelling like a summer fog.' Hardy also knew 'all the heavy perfumes of new vegetation not yet dried by hot sun', and those of the cidery Hintocks 'where the dunghills smell of pomace instead of stable refuse as elsewhere'.

Sounds were even more important. ('I know the happenings from their sound . . .'[24]) We are told that Melbury's horses' bells were tuned to two octaves;[25] to Gabriel Oak the first indication of the wind's change in the approaching great storm came from the grating of the weather-vane as it swung round; the time of the oat harvest was characterized not only by the 'monochromatic Lammas sky', but by

> the droning of blue-bottle flies; out-of-doors the whetting of scythes and the hiss of tressy oat-ears rubbing together as their perpendicular stalks of amber-yellow fell heavily to each swath.[26]

In answer to a query, Hardy wrote to his friend Edmund Gosse in February 1903:

> As you probably know, sparrows, starlings, &c., pull out the straw from the eaves of roofs till they have made a sort of tunnel in the thatch, & it is their creeping down from the further end at dawn that makes the tiny trampling – amusingly like that of people coming reluctantly downstairs of a morning.[27]

The unearthly silence of the fog as Poorgrass walked Fanny's coffin through Yalbury Wood was broken only by the tapping of drops on the leaves and the smarter rap of the rain on the coffin. When Tess and Angel Clare stumble in the black night against the first pillar of Stonehenge, he asks:

> "What monstrous place is this?"
> "It hums," said she, "Hearken!"
> He listened. The wind, playing upon the edifice, produced a booming tune, like the note of some gigantic one-stringed harp.

(In an interview about the future of Stonehenge, reported in the *Daily Chronicle*, Hardy asserted that 'if a gale of wind is blowing the strange musical hum emitted by Stonehenge can never be forgotten.'[28]) *The Return of the Native*, a perpetual symphony of the sounds of Egdon Heath, has some remarkable things to say about the 'acoustic pictures' returned to the experienced listener – as the appropriate pages of this book will show.

Many of these passages reveal Hardy's sensitivity to the *differences* between natural things; and this ability to differentiate illustrates the breadth of his observation of the natural world. (His friend J.M.Barrie was to tease him about this: 'Everyone knows that he had an intimacy with trees . . . and . . . the trees had a similar knowledge of him. . . . When he passed through their woods, they could tell him from all other men!') The opening passage of *Under the Greenwood Tree* may be the most well-known instance of such knowledge, but it is far from being the only one. In "The Three Strangers" the sound of music coming from within the cottage is accompanied by the sound of rain landing (differently) on the downland turf, on cabbages in the garden, beehives by the path, and a row of buckets under the eaves. Experienced walkers on the heath could distinguish the faintest foot-track from the 'maiden herbage' by the feel alone; and a practised eye could similarly judge at a distance whether it was furze, or wood, or straw and general waste, that fed the Guy Fawkes bonfires. Giles and Marty, who were especially in tune with nature, could, as they walked through the darkening wood, tell from years of patient experience which species of branch had brushed against their faces.

For them and his other rural characters, Hardy knew that their natural setting was crucial, one of the 'materials of Fiction', which, he said with deceptive simplicity, are 'human nature and circumstances.'[29] Earlier he had written:

> Even imagination is the slave of stolid circumstance; and the unending flow of inventiveness which finds expression in the literature of Fiction is no exception to the general law. It is conditioned by its surroundings like a river-stream.[30]

As the literature, so the people: conditioned by their surroundings, of which the writer must take note. The world, he continues, now seems to want less 'creative fancy' and more 'realism, that is . . . an artificiality distilled from the fruits of closest observation.' We are back to the idea of 'Art is a disproportioning . . .' He makes it clear that by realism he means neither 'copyism' nor 'prurience'; nor just 'photography'.

'A sight for the finer qualities of existence, an ear for the "still sad music of humanity," are not to be acquired by the outer senses alone, close as their powers in photography may be'. The vital qualities are 'a power of observation informed by a living heart.'[31]

Thus it is that although Hardy's natural descriptions may be savoured for themselves alone, they are never (or hardly ever) mere descriptions. They are part of a greater purpose: the exploration of reality, made by the power of observation informed by a living heart.

The natural setting is part of the reality in which humans live. The writer's art (or science) is 'an observative responsiveness to everything within the cycle of suns that has to do with actual life . . .'[32] He often describes daily life in terms of natural phenomena:

> [John's] figure was not much changed from what it had been; but the many sunrises and sunsets which had passed since that day . . . had abstracted some of his angularities . . . and given him a foreign look.

Owen and Cytherea found among the problems after their father's fatal accident that 'Sudden hopes that were rainbows to the sight proved but mists to the touch.' Nature will keep breaking in:

> The instant that he was gone, Festus shook his fist at the evening star which happened to lie in the same direction as that taken by the dragoon.[33]

The natural scene often forms the background against which a woman or man is forever remembered – "The Figure in the Scene", "The Background and the Figure".[34]

> Every woman who makes a permanent impression on a man is usually recalled to his mind's eye as she appeared in one particular scene, which seems ordained to be her special form of manifestation throughout the pages of his memory.

So when Knight thought of Elfride,

8

he pictured with a vivid fancy those fair summer scenes with her. He again saw
her as at their first meeting. . . . How she would wait for him in green places
. . .[35]

In *The Dynasts*, the natural background to the giant cockpit of Napoleonic war is never
forgotten: the French 'lie down . . . in the dripping green wheat and rye', the English
'huddling together on the ploughed mud'. They have battled, says the Chorus of Rumours,

> in equal fence
> With weather and the enemy's violence.[36]

One of Hardy's 'impressions' (for he always denied having any coherent system of
philosophy) actually went further: the setting was in fact not just the background –
but indeed it could be made up of the people. Two poems, "Transformations" (page
291), and "Voices from Things Growing in a Churchyard", play with the idea that the
buried dead grow into flowers and grasses and trees,

> And they feel the sun and rain,
> And the energy again
> That made them what they were!

For Hardy's rural characters, as for all today who live with drought, flood, earthquake
or pollution, Nature was possibly the most important single determining factor in their
lives – which depended on it. In a wider sense, all human life is subject to its laws.
So Nature is closely and functionally integrated into almost all he writes. Clym and Eustacia's
love is shadowed by the moon's eclipse they are watching. In one of his greatest poems,
"At Castle Boterel", rain and darkness become a remarkable image of Time, which first,
by hindsight, clarifies our past experience, and finally obliterates it (page 254). Nature's
power to shape lives is shown in the gearing of *Under the Greenwood Tree* to the seasons,
or *Far from the Madding Crowd* to the work of the farming year; Tess's story marches
with the kind of landscapes in which she lives. One can clearly sense how this artist and
thinker who also harboured Nature under his skin, as it were, really enjoyed crafting
a sensitive impression of some natural scene specifically to enhance the meaning of the
action. Such, for example, is the unprecedented ice and frost that makes Cytherea, on
her wedding morning, wonder if 'this is a scheme of the great Mother to hinder a union
of which she does not approve.' Such is the chapter in *Two on a Tower* where Lady
Constantine's agonised lingering over her reply to Swithin's proposal of marriage is
partnered, time and again, by the winds blustering around them.

> He waited, while the fir-trees rubbed and prodded the base of the tower and
> the wind roared around and shook it; but she could not find words to reply.
> . . . Each was swayed by the emotion within them, much as the candle-flame
> was swayed by the tempest without. It was the most critical moment of their lives.

Such is the poignant scene by the river when Cytherea, married to Manston only a few hours, meets a haggard Edward – through their reflections in the water, from opposite banks: and as they try to clasp hands across it, the river becomes the image of all the obstacles that separate them.[37]

The nature imagery in all Hardy's writing enriches his deeper meaning. The patterns of lines and traceries, dapples and silhouettes, are closely linked with the patterns in which our lives fall, and particularly the meshes of each human mind as it seeks to make sense of life's experiences. The moon has many complex overtones, some with love, some with sterility, some as a kind of representative of the poet's eye itself peering in upon human tragedy. Light and darkness, frost, webs, green leaves and bare trees, colours and seasons and 'the landscape' – a composite image for all that makes up the natural setting – all signify more than themselves alone, all must be 'read' if life is to be understood. When Grace Melbury (caught up in all the socio-economic problems of the lifehold which fundamentally affected so many lives),[38] meets Winterborne just after her father has forbidden her to see him, she is in great perplexity. Giles is working halfway up a tree, and she fails to answer his greeting, and passes on – before thinking better of it.

> She had reached a gate, whereon she had leant sadly and whispered to herself, "What shall I do?"
> A sudden fog came on . . .

Though she returns to talk seriously to Giles, their whole relationship is befogged and obstructed, Giles 'climbing higher into the sky, and cutting himself off more and more from all intercourse with the sublunary world. . . . till the fog and the night had completely inclosed him from her view.'[39] Grace's later moment of enlightenment, or epiphany, comes when she sees her husband ('her Tannhaüser' – he who was enticed to live for many years with the goddess Venus) riding off to his lover on Grace's own white horse, 'distinctly yet' against the deep violet sky. Immediately after, a new light is shed on Giles, approaching up the valley with his cider-apparatus, looking and smelling 'like Autumn's very brother', 'a stray beam of the sun alighting every now and then like a star on the blades of the pomace-shovels.' Grace joins him, in the conviction that with him lies her true happiness, and 'they passed so far round the hill that the whole west sky was revealed. . . . the eye journeying on under a species of golden arcades, and . . .' (The rest of the description comes on page 70) As he lay dying, Giles still had the power of light for her: 'The spirit of Winterborne seemed to keep her company and banish all sense of darkness from her mind.'[40]

  This is not to say that all Hardy's nature images are heavyweights; so many of the short ones are simply an inspired understanding of human and natural likenesses. Granfer Cantle 'began to sing, in the voice of a bee up a flue';[41] Troy dazzled Bathsheba with his swordplay so that she was 'enclosed in a firmament of light, and of sharp hisses, resembling a sky-full of meteors close at hand.'[42] The sea is discerned in its 'rise and fall along the shore . . . like a sort of great snore of the sleeping world' – and, to Knight hanging over the precipice, as 'that unplummeted ocean below and afar – rubbing its restless flank against the Cliff without a Name'; and, in a storm around the chalk-white columns off Old Harry Point, when

> the waves leapt up their sides like a pack of hounds; this, however, though fearful in its boisterousness, was nothing to the terrible games that sometimes went on round the knees of those giants in stone.[43]

Nature is likened to humanity, and humanity to the rest of nature. On that pitiless summer afternoon when Mrs Yeobright walked doggedly over to Alderworth, the stifling images are of human handiwork:

> There lay the cat asleep on the bare gravel of the path, as if beds, rugs, and carpets were unendurable. The leaves of the hollyhocks hung like half-closed umbrellas, the sap almost simmered in the stems, and foliage with a smooth surface glared like metallic mirrors.[44]

The linking of nature and humanity, the essential identity of all living things, was one of Hardy's convictions[45] – though he would probably have called it an 'impression'. It was a part of his intuitive feeling for Nature, but was taken a step further and reinforced by his acceptance of Darwin's revelations. His impressions about Nature were manifold, and as full of contradictions as life.

So, for example, in his constant study of how the human mind fits (or fights) with the world it inhabits, he sees Nature reflecting the moods, joys and tragedies of men and women. Outer weather mirrors the inner. When the rainbow shines, he persuades himself of its 'Proof that earth was made for man.' Henchard, gloomily leaning over the swirling weir after discovering Elizabeth-Jane's true paternity, felt 'the lugubrious harmony of the spot with his domestic situation'. Gabriel Oak, surveying the scene of his disaster, saw 'an oval pond, and over it hung the attenuated skeleton of a chrome-yellow moon. . . . The pool glittered like a dead man's eye.'[46] But equally, Hardy knows that Nature is also indifferent to humanity, which is but an insect crawling over the face of the earth: at other times the sun shines heartlessly and the sky is bright when a man's life is darkened with grief.

Other impressions are illustrated in these pages. Nature, with its ' "appetite for joy" that pervades all creation', is often vitiated, for example, simply by human social laws, like those of class barriers. Nature is the prime material for the artist, who must follow the pattern he or she sees in it, making of it something quite his or her own. Some superior human beings (like Winterborne, Oak, Clym and Marty) can reach a harmonious understanding with Nature which is probably obsolescent, but shows how things might have been if it had not been 'a world conditioned thus.'

Nature is, of course, constantly creative, and can be healing: 'when mere seeing is meditation, and meditation peace'. Swithin found that 'with motion through the sun and air his mood assumed a lighter complexion.'[47] Sometimes Nature is well-ordered and organised: in lashing wind on the heath, 'those gusts which tore the trees merely waved the furze and heather in a light caress. Egdon was made for such times as these.' In winter 'the boughs are specially disencumbered to do battle with the storm'; yet here was evidence of 'the Unfulfilled Intention', for the June evening was all awry, and the trees, 'laden heavily with their new and humid leaves, were now suffering more damage than during the highest winds of winter.' Nature is spoiled, imperfect: 'God's clock-work jolts'.[48]

'God', or what Hardy often called 'The First Cause(s)' is not strictly part of the subject of this book, though elsewhere I have tried to suggest how interesting to contemporary thought is Hardy's theology.[49] But Nature, for him, is the chief functionary of the lord of doom, herself 'the Great Dame whence incarnation flows'.[50] This line comes from a poem whose subtitle is "Nature's Indifference". Witless, blind and groping, capricious or hostile, host to unlovely fungi and putrid decay, 'the seed-field of all . . . cramps', the Mother *(sic)* mourns that the human being has developed further than she had intended, and now 'finds blemish / Throughout my domain.'[51]

Hardy himself certainly found blemish in the evolution of 'the human race [which] is too extremely developed for its corporeal conditions',[52] – with man and woman so finely tuned that they know, and suffer in themselves, the pain of the universe. He expressed this in many a poem and letter as well as that unmistakable authorial comment which makes his novels much more than just stories.

> Melbury perhaps was an unlucky man in having the sentiment which could make him wander out in the night to regard the imprint of a daughter's footstep. Nature does not carry on her government with a view to such feelings; and when advancing years render the opened hearts of those that possess them less dexterous than formerly in shutting against the blast, they must inevitably, like little celandines, suffer 'buffeting at will by rain and storm.'[53]

Yet here is probably the greatest – and truest – paradox. On the one hand Nature will outlast all puny human life. The heath constantly reverts, despite men's efforts, to the savage waste it has been since prehistory; rain and wind, working inexorably on a human tombstone, obliterate all trace of the individual remembered. Chance and the inscrutable forces of heredity, environment, and survival make the human being a mere determined link in the evolutionary chain.

But is this all? And is it borne out by human experience? The answer is a resounding No. It resounds, not because Hardy shouts, for he never does; but because for him all the experience of life shows that such a description is incomplete. The complex nature of human personality, its capacity for joy, suffering, 'lovingkindness' and truth, its spiritual or ethical response to life, need more explanation than mechanical forces alone. Thus the great paradox which Hardy fully accepted both in life and in his own impressions: that despite everything, humanity is worth more than any other aspect of Nature.

> Hence clouds, mists, and mountains are unimportant beside the wear on a threshold, or the print of a hand.[54]

Nature by itself is meaningless, even 'played out as a Beauty': 'I want to see the deeper reality underlying the scenic.' Human associations are a vital part of this deeper reality; and moreover:

> The poetry of a scene varies with the minds of the perceivers. Indeed, it does not lie in the scene at all.[55]

Humanity makes its mark on the landscape; it can even 'shape' it by its own perceptions. Human memory or vision will outlast the worst that Time or natural law can do. So with Hardy's own indelible picture of his first wife, seen after her death as 'a phantom horsewoman', as he had first seen her in life riding the cliffs and shores of Lyonnesse:

> A ghost-girl-rider. And though, toil-tried,
> He withers daily,
> Time touches her not,
> But she still rides gaily
> In his rapt thought
> On that shagged and shaly
> Atlantic spot,
> And as when first eyed
> Draws rein and sings to the swing of the tide.[56]

Hardy doesn't pretend that he knows any answers about life and its inconsistencies. He has, however, an abiding 'impression' about the eternal value of both truth and 'lovingkindness', and of men and women, beleaguered in a framework of natural (and social) laws which often militate against their happiness. 'Life offers – to deny!' In this situation, his own personal response is never cynicism, but a stoic and stubborn reassertion of those values, and an unfailing tenderness for those who suffer. If Nature is 'unmoral' and uncaring, even inimical, the human individual must gather up all its forces and stand for what it believes – and never descend to anything less, (' . . . to model our conduct on Nature's apparent conduct, as Nietzsche would have taught, can only bring disaster to humanity.'[57]) So in poem and story Hardy's love and concern for his characters – like Julie-Jane, and Patty Beech, Tess, Jude, Henchard, the bedridden peasant, the unborn pauper child,[58] and countless others – insists upon their individual right to life and fulfilment, their rebellion against the chance-ruled pain and injustice of the universe.[59] ("The Milkmaid" – page 146, about another rebel – is a delightful example of the wit and self-mockery that is never far below Hardy's surface.)

What makes his view the more poignant is a luminous and unquenchable, though deeply-buried and agnostic, hope. As Tess began to remake her life, the 'spirit within her [which] rose automatically as the sap in the twigs' brought with it 'hope, and the invincible instinct towards self-delight.'[60] It is no accident that his image is from nature. Despite all his contrary 'impressions' of it, it seems as if Hardy's feeling for Nature, implanted in the childhood of this peculiarly receptive mind and heart, and ripening all his days, was part of the deep emotional core of his life. It survived his withered marriage and illuminated the great poems that followed his first wife's death. It is within the context of his feeling for the natural world and its creatures that there seems most often to be expressed the seed of this hope. Spring may be backward,

> Yet the snowdrop's face betrays no gloom
> And the primrose pants in its heedless push,

and somehow in spite of the most unlikely portents, the 'vespering bird' knows that Spring is imminent. The night-creatures who bang at his midnight lamp and smear his 'new-penned line' at first seem

> 'God's humblest, they!' I muse. Yet why?
> They know Earth secrets that know not I.[61]

(The grammatical ambiguity of the last three words hastens to remind us that this poet finds no answer, finds nothing straightforward.) Though here, as in "The Darkling Thrush", he remains excluded, 'unaware', it is as if Nature in some way presents an analogy or parable for humanity, and one in which he would like to share. "Song of Hope" begins:

> O sweet To-morrow! –
>   After to-day
>   There will away
> This sense of sorrow,
> Then let us borrow
> Hope, for a gleaming
> Soon will be streaming,
>   Dimmed by no gray –
>   No gray!

His greatest hope remains for humanity, expressed perhaps most beautifully and cogently in the superb poem "To an Unborn Pauper's Child" (page 297). It is a hope against all the odds, a hope or solace which comes

> Not from noting Life's conditions,
>   . . . . But in cleaving to the Dream,[62]

the dream nourished in the inner light of the imagination, that citadel of each individual woman and man, and above all of the poet.

It is interesting to see how Hardy wished to be remembered. It must be recalled that his first volume of poems was not published until he was fifty-eight. He had a habit of ending each volume with a farewell; and concluding the first (1898) was "I Look

Into My Glass'' – his farewell to youth.[63] In the volume published when he was seventy-four[64] his final choice was ''A Poet''. It invited the reader to come to his graveside ('Some evening, at the first star-ray'), and in assessment of his life, to 'pause and say':

> 'Whatever his message – glad or grim –
> Two bright-souled women clave to him:'
> Stand and say that while day decays;
> It will be word enough of praise,

Had he died in his seventy-eighth year, when *Moments of Vision* appeared, his farewell would have been his first great pastoral poem, ''Afterwards''.[65] In this, when his 'bell of quittance is heard in the gloom', it is not as a Wessex man, or a poet, or a philosopher, that he seeks to be remembered by his fellow-creatures. It is as one who noticed when

> The dewfall-hawk comes crossing the shades to alight
> Upon the wind-warped upland thorn . . .

as one of whom

> When the hedgehog travels furtively over the lawn,
> One may say, 'He strove that such innocent creatures
> should come to no harm . . .'

as one who had an eye for the mysteries of 'the full-starred heavens'.

His next volume (1922) ended with a confession of his life's failure to match St Paul's picture of love in his letter to the Corinthians.[66] *Human Shows* (1925) ended, understandably for a man of eighty-five, with

> Why do I go on doing these things?
> Why not cease?

His last was a posthumous volume. *Winter Words* was prepared by Hardy, but unfinished; there was, for example, no list of contents in the manuscript, which suggests that, as usual, he was leaving his options open. The last two poems, ''We are Getting to the End'', and ''He Resolves to Say No More'', are sober recognitions of the nightmare tendencies of Europe to lurch into war to solve its problems.

(We Are Getting to the End)

> We are getting to the end of visioning
> The impossible within this universe,
> Such as that better whiles may follow worse,
> And that our race may mend by reasoning.

We know that even as larks in cages sing
Unthoughtful of deliverance from the curse
That holds them lifelong in a latticed hearse,
We ply spasmodically our pleasuring.

And that when nations set them to lay waste
Their neighbours' heritage by foot and horse,
And hack their pleasant plains in festering seams,
They may again, – not warely, or from taste,
But tickled mad by some demonic force. –
Yes. We are getting to the end of dreams!

In the last poem, he 'resolves to say no more' not because he is old and tired, but because he sees (only a few years before Hitler's rise to power) how dangerous the apocalyptic dreamer has been in European civilisation, misleading its peoples 'by prophetic passion into war'. (With fine understanding of Hardy's poetry, Dennis Taylor discusses and illuminates this in a way I cannot do here.[67]) The responsibility of the poet is much in Hardy's mind. It is clear, from other comments too,[68] that he is greatly disillusioned by humanity's downward and backward plunge in the 1914–18 War. Yet typically he asserts in the volume's 'introductory note' that 'no harmonious philosophy is attempted in these pages – or in any bygone pages of mine, for that matter.' As usual, he continued to hold contradictory or parallel impressions in tension, wise enough to know that there is nothing simple in 'the truth that shall make you free'.[69] So despite his intellect's forebodings he is still comparing human beings to caged larks, like the Blinded Bird, whose magnanimous spirit was dominant. His heart and imagination's insight continues to include a reference or image from Nature in almost every poem of the volume. One, particularly, seems to pick up a strand never far hidden in his work.

'I AM THE ONE'

I am the one whom ringdoves see
　　Through chinks in boughs
　　When they do not rouse
　　In sudden dread,
But stay on cooing, as if they said:
　　'Oh; it's only he.'

I am the passer when up-eared hares,
　　Stirred as they eat
　　The new-sprung wheat,
　　Their munch resume
As if they thought: 'He is one for whom
　　Nobody cares.'

16

Wet-eyed mourners glance at me
　　　As in train they pass
　　　Along the grass
　　　To a hollowed spot,
And think: 'No matter; he quizzes not
　　　Our misery.'

I hear above: 'We stars must lend
　　　No fierce regard
　　　To his gaze, so hard
　　　Bent on us thus, –
Must scathe him not. He is one with us
　　　Beginning and end.'

I

THE COUNTRY
OF HARDY'S CHILDHOOD

BOCKHAMPTON

The cry of owls was very familiar to me in childhood . . .

Letter to George Gissing. 6 Sept., 1895

June 2, 1840. It was in a lonely and silent spot between woodland and heathland that Thomas Hardy was born . . .

The Life of Thomas Hardy

[1887] In August [Hardy] was back again at Max Gate, and there remarks on the difference between children who grow up in solitary country places and those who grow up in towns – the former being imaginative, dreamy, and credulous of vague mysteries; giving as the reason that 'The Unknown comes within so short a radius from themselves by comparison with the city-bred.'

The Life of Thomas Hardy

At various times as a young man Hardy returned to his parents' home:

[1868] In April he was . . . taking down the exact sound of the song of the nightingale – the latter showing that he must have been living in sylvan shades at his parents', or at least sleeping there, at the time, where nightingales sang within a yard of the bedroom windows in those days, though they do not now.

The Life of Thomas Hardy

1869. Spring. . . . One of those evenings in the country which makes the townsman feel: "I will stay here till I die – I would, that is, if it were not for that thousand pounds I want to make, and that friend I want to envy me."

Memoranda 1

Four in the Morning

At four this day of June I rise:
The dawn light strengthens steadily;
Earth is a cerule mystery,
As if not far from Paradise

At four o'clock

Or else near the Great Nebula,
Or where the Pleiads blink and smile:
(For though we see with eyes of guile
The grisly grin of things by day,

At four o'clock

They show their best.) . . . In this vale's space
I am up the first, I think. Yet, no,
A whistling? and the to-and-fro
Wheezed whettings of a scythe apace

At four o'clock? . . .

– Though pleasure spurred, I rose with irk:
Here is one at compulsion's whip
Taking his life's stern stewardship
With blithe uncare, and hard at work

At four o'clock!

Bockhampton[70]

[1873] *Nov. 4th.* It is raining in torrents. The light is greenish & unnatural, objects being as if seen through water. A roar of rain in the plantation, & a rush near at hand, yet not a breath of wind. A silver fringe hangs from the eaves of the house to the ground. A flash. Thunder.

Memoranda 1

It is possible that this note may have informed the description of the great storm in Far from the Madding Crowd, *which Hardy was writing at the time.*

[1883] *December 23.* There is what we used to call "The Birds' Bedroom" in the plantation at Bockhampton. Some large hollies grow among leafless ash, oak, birch, etc. At this time of the year the birds select the hollies for roosting in, and at dusk noises not unlike the creaking of withy-chairs arise, with a busy rustling as of people going to bed in a lodging-house: accompanied by sundry shakings, adjustings, and pattings, as if they were making their beds vigorously before turning in.

The Life of Thomas Hardy

[1884] *June 2.* At Bockhampton. My birthday – 44. Alone in the plantation, at 9 o'clock. A weird hour: strange faces and figures formed by dying lights. Holm leaves shine like human eyes, and the sky glimpses between the trunks are like white phantoms and cloven tongues. It is so silent and still that a footstep on the dead leaves could be heard a quarter of a mile off. Squirrels run up the trunks in fear, stamping and crying "chut-chut-chut!"

The Life of Thomas Hardy

In 1917 Hardy began work, with his second wife Florence, on The Life *that was to be published as her biography after his death. By the time he came to put in this note, he added: '(There is not a single squirrel in that plantation now.)'*

In the year following this note, Hardy began to write The Woodlanders: *the passage quoted on page 38 shows how the note contributed to the final description.*

THE HEATH

The poet's evocation of Egdon Heath — a principal character in The Return of the Native *— can be read on page 37f. Much of Hardy's writing suggests the memory of the boy's eye view, and the love of what he had known since childhood.*

Along the ridge ran a faint foot-track . . . Those who knew it well called it a path; and, while a mere visitor would have passed it unnoticed even by day, the regular haunters of the heath were at no loss for it at midnight. The whole secret of following these incipient paths, when there was not light enough in the atmosphere to show a turnpike-road, lay in the development of the sense of touch in the feet, which comes with years of night-rambling in little-trodden spots. To a walker practised in such places a difference between impact on maiden herbage, and on the crippled stalks of a slight footway, is perceptible through the thickest boot or shoe.
The Return of the Native

He walked along towards home without attending to paths. If anyone knew the heath well it was Clym. He was permeated with its scenes, with its substance, and with its odours. He might be said to be its product. His eyes had first opened thereon; with its appearance all the first images of his memory were mingled; his estimate of life had been coloured by it; his toys had been the flint knives and arrow-heads which he found there, wondering why stones should 'grow' to such odd shapes; his flowers, the purple bells and yellow furze; his animal kingdom, the snakes and croppers; his society, its human haunters. Take all the varying hates felt by Eustacia Vye towards the heath, and translate them into loves, and you have the heart of Clym. He gazed upon the side prospect as he walked, and was glad.

The Return of the Native

After nightfall Johnny Nunsuch returns alone to his home on the heath:

As soon as the sad little boy had withdrawn from the fire he clasped the money tight in the palm of his hand, as if thereby to fortify his courage, and began to run. There was really little danger in allowing a child to go home alone on this part of Egdon Heath. The distance to the boy's house was not more than three-eighths of a mile, his father's cottage, and one other a few yards further on, forming part of the small hamlet of Mistover

Knap: the third and only remaining house was that of Captain Vye and Eustacia, which stood quite away from the small cottages, and was the loneliest of lonely houses on these thinly populated slopes.

He ran until he was out of breath, and then, becoming more courageous, walked leisurely along, singing in an old voice a little song about a sailor-boy and a fair one, and bright gold in store. In the middle of this the child stopped: from a pit under the hill ahead of him shone a light, whence proceeded a cloud of floating dust and a smacking noise.

Only unusual sights and sounds frightened the boy. The shrivelled voice of the heath did not alarm him, for that was familiar. The thorn-bushes which arose in his path from time to time were less satisfactory, for they whistled gloomily, and had a ghastly habit after dark of putting on the shapes of jumping madmen, sprawling giants, and hideous cripples. Lights were not uncommon this evening, but the nature of all of them was different from this. Discretion rather than terror prompted the boy to turn back instead of passing the light, with a view of asking Miss Eustacia Vye to let her servant accompany him home.

When the boy had reascended to the top of the valley he found the fire to be still burning on the bank, though lower than before. Beside it, instead of Eustacia's solitary form he saw two persons, the second being a man. . . . He finally decided to face the pit phenomenon as the lesser evil. With a heavy sigh he retraced the slope, and followed the path he had followed before.

The light had gone, the rising dust had disappeared – he hoped for ever. He marched resolutely along, and found nothing to alarm him till, coming within a few yards of the sandpit, he heard a slight noise in front, which led him to a halt. The halt was but momentary, for the noise resolved itself into the steady bites of two animals grazing.

'Two he'th-croppers down here,' he said aloud. 'I have never known 'em come down so far afore.'

The animals were in the direct line of his path, but that the child thought little of; he had played round the fetlocks of horses from his infancy. On coming nearer, however, the boy was somewhat surprised to find that the little creatures did not run off, and that each wore a clog,[71] to prevent his going astray; this signified that they had been broken in. He could now see the interior of the pit, which being in the side of the hill, had a level entrance. In the innermost corner the square outline of a van appeared, with its back towards him. A light came from the interior, and threw a moving shadow upon the vertical face of gravel at the further side of the pit into which the vehicle faced.

The child assumed that this was the cart of a gipsy, and his dread of those wanderers reached but to that mild pitch which titillates rather than pains. Only a few inches of mud wall kept him and his family from being gipsies themselves. He skirted the gravel-pit at a respectful distance, ascended the slope, and came forward upon the brow, in order to look into the open door of the van and see the original of the shadow.

The picture alarmed the boy. . . . [He] knew too well for his peace of mind upon whose lair he had lighted. Uglier persons than gipsies were known to cross Egdon at times, and a reddleman was one of them.

'How I wish 'twas only a gipsy!' he murmured.

The boy is discovered, and the reddleman, in conversation, relieves him of his horrid apprehensions about 'the children's bogey': a reddleman, though luridly coloured, is only an ordinary man:

"Yes, that's what I be. Though there's more than one. You little children think there's only one cuckoo, one fox, one giant, one devil, and one reddleman, when there's lots of us all."

The Return of the Native

Boys Then And Now

'More than one cuckoo?'
And the little boy
Seemed to lose something
Of his spring joy.

When he'd grown up
He'd told his son
He'd used to think
There was only one

Who came each year
With the trees' new trim
On purpose to please
England and him:

And his son – old already
In life and its ways –
Said yawning: 'How foolish
Boys were in those days!'

To dwell on a heath without studying its meanings was like wedding a foreigner without learning his tongue. The subtle beauties of the heath were lost to Eustacia; she only caught its vapours. An environment which would have made a contented woman a poet, a suffering woman a devotee, a pious woman a psalmist, even a giddy woman thoughtful, made a rebellious woman saturnine.

The Return of the Native

Clym and Eustacia:

"You are lonely here."
"I cannot endure the heath, except in its purple season. The heath is a cruel taskmaster to me."

"Can you say so?" he asked. "To my mind it is most exhilarating, and strengthening, and soothing. I would rather live on these hills than anywhere else in the world."

Thomasin and Damon:

"There's something on your mind – I know there is, Damon. You go about so gloomily, and look at the heath as if it were somebody's gaol instead of a nice wild place to walk in."

He looked towards her with pitying surprise. "What, do you like Egdon Heath?" he said.

"I like what I was born near to: I admire its grim old face."

Thomasin steps out into the din and blackness of Egdon's storm:

She was soon ascending Blooms-End valley and traversing the undulations on the side of the hill. The noise of the wind over the heath was shrill, and as if it whistled for joy at finding a night so congenial as this. Sometimes the path led her to hollows between thickets of tall and dripping bracken, dead, though not yet prostrate, which enclosed her like a pool. When they were more than usually tall she lifted the baby to the top of her head, that it might be out of the reach of their drenching fronds. On higher ground, where the wind was brisk and sustained, the rain flew in a level flight without sensible descent, so that it was beyond all power to imagine the remoteness of the point at which it left the bosoms of the clouds. Here self-defence was impossible, and individual drops stuck into her like the arrows into Saint Sebastian.[72] She was enabled to avoid puddles by the nebulous paleness which signified their presence, though beside anything less dark than the heath they themselves would have appeared as blackness.

Yet in spite of all this Thomasin was not sorry that she had started. To her there were not, as to Eustacia, demons in the air, and malice in every bush and bough. The drops which lashed her face were not scorpions, but prosy rain; Egdon in the mass was no monster whatever, but impersonal open ground. Her fears of the place were rational, her dislikes of its worst moods reasonable. At this time it was in her view a windy, wet place, in which a person might experience much discomfort, lose the path without care, and possibly catch cold.

The Return of the Native

Greenhill Pond, by Captain Vye's house, was 'bearded all round by heather and rushes'. Only a few minutes' walk on to the heath behind Hardy's birthplace lies another, Rushy Pond, which appears in a poem on page 55 and in the story "The Withered Arm":

Though the date was comparatively recent, Egdon was much less fragmentary in character than now. The attempts – successful and otherwise – at cultivation on the lower slopes, which intrude and break up the original heath into small detached heaths, had not been carried far; Enclosure Acts had not taken effect, and the banks and fences which now exclude the cattle of those villagers who formerly enjoyed rights of commonage thereon, and the carts of those who had turbary privileges which kept them in firing all the year round, were not erected. Gertrude, therefore, rode along with no other obstacles than the prickly furze bushes, the mats of heather, the white water-courses, and the natural steeps and declivities of the ground. . . . It was . . . nearly eight o'clock when she drew rein to breathe her bearer on the last outlying high point of heath-land towards Casterbridge, previous to leaving Egdon for the cultivated valleys.

She halted before a pool called Rushy-Pond, flanked by the end of two hedges; a railing ran through the centre of the pond, dividing it in half. Over the railing she saw the low green country; over the green trees the roofs of the town; over the roofs a white flat façade, denoting the entrance to the county jail.

The Withered Arm

RAINBARROW

These ancient tumuli (properly 'Rainbarrows') stand out on the ridge only a short walk from Hardy's birthplace. He knew them well, and in a scene set there in The Dynasts *he writes of 'the personality of the spot.' Here stood a beacon in the Napoleonic wars[73]; here was the focal point of* The Return of the Native, *'the pole and axis of this heathery world', and a place of frequent reference in Hardy's writings.*

It is probably with an echo of his own childhood that Hardy makes Nicholas Long, the returning emigrant of "The Waiting Supper", look across to 'his native vale', the Frome valley, from the height of Rainbarrow — 'a point where, in his childhood, he had believed people could stand and see America.'

The Sheep-Boy

A yawning, sunned concave
Of purple, spread as an ocean wave
Entroughed on a morning of swell and sway
After a night when wind-fiends have been heard to rave:
Thus was the Heath called 'Draäts', on an August day.

Suddenly there intunes a hum:
This side, that side, it seems to come.
From the purple in myriads rise the bees
With consternation mid their rapt employ.
So headstrongly each speeds him past, and flees,
As to strike the face of the shepherd-boy.
Awhile he waits, and wonders what they mean;
Till none is left upon the shagged demesne.

To learn what ails, the sheep-boy looks around;
     Behind him, out of the sea in swirls
     Flexuous and solid, clammy vapour-curls
Are rolling over Pokeswell Hills to the inland ground.

     Into the heath they sail,
     And travel up the vale
Like the moving pillar of cloud raised by the Israelite:-
In a trice the lonely sheep-boy seen so late ago,
     Draäts'-Hollow in gorgeous blow,
     And Kite-Hill's regal glow,
Are viewless – folded into those creeping scrolls of white.
On Rainbarrows

THE FROME VALLEY: 'the Vale of Great Diaries':

This lush valley, on which Hardy must often have looked down from Rainbarrows as a child, was also one he visited to the end of his life. At eighty-two he was still cycling there from Max Gate to visit his brother and sister at West Stafford. In some of his stories Hardy shows an intimate knowledge of its water-courses, and how a young man could walk through the river above a fall and thread his way across the 'carriers' in a stream-riddled field; and how a careless step meant a watery death.[74]

Tess Durbeyfield gazed upon the vale from Egdon Heath as she arrived from Marlott to begin work at the dairy farm:

It was intrinsically different from the Vale of Little Dairies, Blackmoor Vale. . . . The world was drawn to a larger pattern here. The enclosures numbered fifty acres instead of ten, the farmsteads were more extended, the groups of cattle formed tribes hereabout; there only families. These myriads of cows stretching under her eyes from the far east to the far west outnumbered any she had ever seen at one glance before. The green lea was speckled as thickly with them as a canvas by Van Alsloot or Sallaert with burghers. The ripe hues of the red and dun kine absorbed the evening sunlight, which the white-coated animals returned to the eye in rays almost dazzling, even at the distant elevation on which she stood.

   The birds's-eye perspective before her was not so luxuriantly beautiful, perhaps, as that other one which she knew so well; yet it was more cheering. It lacked the intensely blue atmosphere of the rival vale, and its heavy soils and scents; the new air was clear, bracing, ethereal. The river itself, which nourished the grass and cows of these renowned dairies, flowed not like the streams in Blackmoor. Those were slow, silent, often turbid; flowing over beds of mud into which the incautious wader might sink and vanish unawares. The

Froom waters were clear as the pure River of Life shown to the Evangelist,[75] rapid as the shadow of a cloud, with pebbly shallows that prattled to the sky all day long. There the water-flower was the lily; the crowfoot here.

Tess of the d'Urbervilles

In the last summer of his life, at eighty-seven, Hardy was still writing of valley and heath.

Seeing the Moon Rise

We used to go to Froom-hill Barrow
    To see the round moon rise
    Into the heath-rimmed skies,
Trudging thither by plough and harrow
Up the pathway, steep and narrow,
    Singing a song.
Now we do not go there. Why?
    Zest burns not so high!

Latterly we've only conned her
    With a passing glance
    From window or door by chance,
Hoping to go again, high yonder
As we used, and gaze, and ponder,
    Singing a song.
Thitherward we do not go:
    Feet once quick are slow!

August 1927

II

HARDY

AS NATURAL OBSERVER

. . . Much of Wordsworth . . . is oppressive because the poet has not seen nature with intensity either in relation to his poem, to himself, or to other human beings; but has accepted her as something in herself so desirable that description can be used in flat stretches without concentration. Tennyson is, of course, the master of the Victorian poets who carried descriptive writing to such a pitch that if their words had been visible the black birds would certainly have descended upon their garden plots to feed upon the apples and plums. Yet we do not feel that this is poetry so much as something fabricated by an ingenious craftsman for our delight. Of the moderns Mr Hardy is without rival in his power to make Nature do his will, so that she neither satiates nor serves as a curious toy, but appears at the right moment to heighten, charm or terrify, because the necessary fusion has already taken place. The first step towards this absorption is to see things with your own eyes.

Times Literary Supplement, 26 May 1921, copied into Memoranda II

*　　　*　　　*

Countrymen [are] born, as may be said, with only an open door between them and the four seasons.

Interlopers at the Knap

Thomas Hardy's earliest years were spent in deep country: he could not help being formed by it, and taking Nature for granted as the background to human life.

He would make notes for his writing while out of doors:

So Hardy went on writing *Far from the Madding Crowd* – sometimes indoors, sometimes out – when he would occasionally find himself without a scrap of paper at the very moment that he felt volumes. In such circumstances he would use large dead leaves, white chips left by the wood-cutters, or pieces of stone or slate that came to hand.

The Life of Thomas Hardy

Hardy's father was a keen naturalist, and his son made notes all his life about natural phenomena:[76]

[1905] *First week in November.* The order in which the leaves fall this year is: Chestnuts; Sycamores; Limes; Hornbeams; Elm; Birch; Beech.

[1917] *June 9.* It is now the time of long days, when the sun seems reluctant to take leave of trees at evening – the shine climbing up the trunks, reappearing higher, and still fondly grasping the treetops till long after.

The Life of Thomas Hardy

(*Throwing away glory.*) *Shedding wings.* Ants, at the end of their flight, *unhitch* their wings and run away, leaving them lying on the ground, apparently quite pleased at being rid of their beautiful wings.

G.J.Wood, ''Ants''.

The old ways. Many successive generations of ants continue to use the same track they have once taken to. I have been shown ant-roads by old men who stated they have been familiar with them from their earliest recollections.[77]

Moonlight. The Hornet works all night if the moon shines. ib.

Literary Notebook I

[1875] *Nov, 28.* I sit under a tree, and feel alone: I think of certain insects around me as magnified under the microscope: creatures like elephants, flying dragons, etc. And I feel I am by no means alone.

  29. He has read well who has learnt that there is more to read outside books than in them.

The Life of Thomas Hardy

Hardy was a poet: he used his gifts of observation and perception, and his skill with words, to describe and interpret the whole sweep of the natural world.

Night on Norcombe Hill

It was nearly midnight on the eve of St Thomas's, the shortest day in the year. A desolating wind wandered from the north over the hill . . .

  The hill was covered on its northern side by an ancient and decaying plantation of beeches, whose upper verge formed a line over the crest, fringing its arched curve against the sky, like a mane. To-night these trees sheltered the southern slope from the keenest blasts, which smote the wood and floundered through it with a sound as of grumbling, or gushed over its crowning boughs in a weakened moan. The dry leaves in the ditch simmered and boiled in the same breezes, a tongue of air occasionally ferreting out a few, and sending them spinning across the grass. A group or two of the latest in date amongst the dead multitude had remained till this very mid-winter time on the twigs which bore them, and in falling rattled against the trunks with smart taps.

  Between this half-wooded half-naked hill, and the vague still horizon that its summit indistinctly commanded, was a mysterious sheet of fathomless shade — the sounds from which suggested that what it concealed bore some reduced resemblance to feature here. The thin grasses, more or less coating the hill, were touched by the wind in breezes of differing powers, and almost of differing natures — one rubbing the blades heavily, another raking them piercingly, another brushing them like a soft broom. The instinctive act of humankind was to stand and listen, and learn how the trees on the right and the trees on the left wailed or chaunted to each other in the regular antiphonies of a cathedral choir; how hedges and other shapes to leeward then caught the note, lowering it to the tenderest sob; and how the hurrying gust then plunged into the south, to be heard no more.

The sky was clear — remarkably clear — and the twinkling of all the stars seemed to be but throbs of one body, timed by a common pulse. The North Star was directly in the wind's eye, and since evening the Bear had swung round it outwardly to the east, till he was now at a right angle with the meridian. A difference of colour in the stars — oftener read of than seen in England — was really perceptible here. The sovereign brilliance of Sirius pierced the eye with a steely glitter, the star called Capella was yellow, Aldebaran and Betelgueux shone with a fiery red.

To persons standing alone on a hill during a clear midnight such as this, the roll of the world eastward is almost a palpable movement. The sensation may be caused by the panoramic glide of the stars past earthly objects, which is perceptible in a few minutes of stillness, or by the better outlook upon space that a hill affords, or by the wind, or by the solitude; but whatever be its origin the impression of riding along is vivid and abiding. The poetry of motion is a phrase much in use, and to enjoy the epic form of that gratification it is necessary to stand on a hill at a small hour of the night, and, having first expanded with a sense of difference from the mass of civilized mankind, who are dreamwrapt and disregardful of all such proceedings at this time, long and quietly watch your stately progress through the stars. After such a nocturnal reconnoitre it is hard to get back to earth, and to believe that the consciousness of such majestic speeding is derived from a tiny human frame. . . .

[Gabriel] stood and carefully examined the sky, to ascertain the time of night from the altitudes of the stars.

The Dog-star and Aldebaran, pointing to the restless Pleiades, were half-way up the Southern sky, and between them hung Orion, which gorgeous constellation never burnt more vividly than now, as it soared forth above the rim of the landscape. Castor and Pollux with their quiet shine were almost on the meridian: the barren and gloomy Square of Pegasus was creeping round to the north-west; far away through the plantation Vega sparkled like a lamp suspended amid the leafless trees, and Cassiopeia's chair stood daintily poised on the uppermost boughs.

'One o'clock,' said Gabriel.

Being a man not without a frequent consciousness that there was some charm in this life he led, he stood still after looking at the sky as a useful instrument, and regarded it in an appreciative spirit, as a work of art superlatively beautiful.

Far from the Madding Crowd

The brooding Heath:

A Saturday afternoon in November was approaching the time of twilight, and the vast tract of unenclosed wild known as Egdon Heath embrowned itself moment by moment. Overhead the hollow stretch of whitish cloud shutting out the sky was as a tent which had the whole heath for its floor.

The heaven being spread with this pallid screen and the earth with the darkest vegetation, their meeting-line at the horizon was clearly marked. In such contrast the heath wore the appearance of an instalment of night which had taken up its place before its astronomical hour was come: darkness had to a great extent arrived hereon, while day stood distinct

35

in the sky. Looking upwards, a furze-cutter would have been inclined to continue work; looking down, he would have decided to finish his faggot[78] and go home. The distant rims of the world and of the firmament seemed to be a division in time no less than a division in matter. The face of the heath by its mere complexion added half an hour to evening; it could in like manner retard the dawn, sadden noon, anticipate the frowning of storms scarcely generated, and intensify the opacity of a moonless midnight to a cause of shaking and dread.

In fact, precisely at this transitional point of its nightly roll into darkness the great and particular glory of the Egdon waste began, and nobody could be said to understand the heath who had not been there at such a time. It could best be felt when it could not clearly be seen, its complete effect and explanation lying in this and the succeeding hours before the next dawn: then, and only then, did it tell its true tale. The spot was, indeed, a near relation of night, and when night showed itself an apparent tendency to gravitate together could be perceived in its shades and the scene. The sombre stretch of rounds and hollows seemed to rise and meet the evening gloom in pure sympathy, the heath exhaling darkness as rapidly as the heavens precipitated it. And so the obscurity in the air and the obscurity in the land closed together in a black fraternization towards which each advanced half-way.

The place became full of a watchful intentness now; for when other things sank brooding to sleep the heath appeared slowly to awake and listen. Every night its Titanic form seemed to await something; but it had waited thus, unmoved, during so many centuries, through the crises of so many things, that it could only be imagined to await one last crisis – the final overthrow.

It was a spot which returned upon the memory of those who loved it with an aspect of peculiar and kindly congruity. Smiling champaigns of flowers and fruit hardly do this, for they are permanently harmonious only with an existence of better reputation as to its issues than the present. Twilight combined with the scenery of Egdon Heath to evolve a thing majestic without severity, impressive without showiness, emphatic in its admonitions, grand in its simplicity. . . . Only in summer days of highest feather did its mood touch the level of gaiety. Intensity was more usually reached by way of the solemn than by way of the brilliant, and such a sort of intensity was often arrived at during winter darkness, tempests, and mists. Then Egdon was aroused to reciprocity; for the storm was its lover, and the wind its friend. Then it became the home of strange phantoms; and it was found to be the hitherto unrecognized original of those wild regions of obscurity which are vaguely felt to be compassing us about in midnight dreams of flight and disaster, and are never thought of after the dream till revived by scenes like this.

It was at present a place perfectly accordant with man's nature – neither ghastly, hateful, nor ugly: neither commonplace, unmeaning, nor tame; but, like man, slighted and enduring; and withal singularly colossal and mysterious in its swarthy monotony. As with some persons who have long lived apart, solitude seemed to look out of its countenance. It had a lonely face, suggesting tragical possibilities.

This obscure, obsolete, superseded country figures in Domesday. Its condition is recorded therein as that of heathy, furzy, briary wilderness – 'Bruaria'. . . . The untameable,

Ishmaelitish[79] thing that Egdon now was it always had been. Civilization was its enemy; and ever since the beginning of vegetation its soil has worn the same antique brown dress, the natural and invariable garment of the particular formation. In its venerable one coat lay a certain vein of satire on human vanity in clothes. A person on a heath in raiment of modern cut and colours has more or less an anomalous look. We seem to want the oldest and simplest human clothing where the clothing of the earth is so primitive.

To recline on a stump of thorn in the central valley of Egdon, between afternoon and night, as now, where the eye could reach nothing of the world outside the summits and shoulders of heathland which filled the whole circumference of its glance, and to know that everything around and underneath had been from prehistoric times as unaltered as the stars overhead, gave ballast to the mind adrift on change, and harassed by the irrepressible New. The great inviolate place had an ancient permanence which the sea cannot claim. Who can say of a particular sea that it is old? Distilled by the sun, kneaded by the moon, it is renewed in a year, in a day, or in an hour. The sea changed, the fields changed, the rivers, the villages, and the people changed, yet Egdon remained.

The Return of the Native

In complete contrast:

Snow in the Suburbs

Every branch big with it,
Bent every twig with it;
Every fork like a white web-foot;
Every street and pavement mute:
Some flakes have lost their way, and grope back upward, when
Meeting those meandering down they turn and descend again.
The palings are glued together like a wall,
And there is not waft of wind with the fleecy fall.

A sparrow enters the tree,
Whereon immediately
A snow-lump thrice his own slight size
Descends on him and showers his head and eyes,
And overturns him,
And near inurns him,
And lights on a nether twig, when its brush
Starts off a volley of other lodging lumps with a rush,

The steps are a blanched slope,
Up which, with feeble hope,
A black cat comes, wide-eyed and thin;
And we take him in.

37

[Grace] skimmed up the garden-path, through the gap in the hedge, and into the mossy cart-track under the trees which led into the depths of the woods.

The leaves overhead were now in their latter green – so opaque, that it was darker at some of the densest spots than in winter time, scarce a crevice existing by which a ray could get down to the ground. But in open places she could see well enough. Summer was ending: in the daytime singing insects hung in every sunbeam: vegetation was heavy nightly with globes of dew; and after showers creeping damps and twilight chills came up from the hollows.

The plantations were always weird at this hour of eve – more spectral far than in the leafless season, when there were fewer masses and more minute lineality. The smooth surfaces of glossy plants came out like weak, lidless eyes: there were strange faces and figures from expiring lights that had somehow wandered into the canopied obscurity; while now and then low peeps of the sky between the trunks were like sheeted shapes, and on the tips of boughs sat faint cloven tongues.[80]

The Woodlanders

Ethelberta rides to Corvsgate Castle:

This was, first by a path on the shore where the tide dragged huskily up and down the shingle without disturbing it, and thence up the steep crest of land opposite, whereon she lingered awhile to let the ass breathe. On one of the spires of chalk into which the hill here had been split was perched a cormorant, silent and motionless, the wings spread out to dry in the sun after his morning's fishing, their white surface shining like mail. Retiring without disturbing him and turning to the left along the lofty ridge which ran inland, the country on each side lay beneath her like a map, domains behind domains, parishes by the score, harbours, fir-woods, and little inland seas mixing curiously together. Thence she ambled along through a huge cemetery of barrows, containing human dust from prehistoric times.

Standing on the top of a giant's grave in this antique land, Ethelberta lifted her eyes to behold two sorts of weather pervading Nature at the same time. Far below on the right hand it was a fine day, and the silver sunbeams lighted up a many-armed inland sea which stretched round an island with fir-trees and gorse, and amid brilliant crimson heaths wherein white paths and roads occasionally met the eye in dashes and zig-zags like flashes of lightning. Outside, where the broad Channel appeared, a berylline and opalized variegation of ripples, currents, deeps, and shallows, lay as far under the sun as a New Jerusalem, the shores being of gleaming sand. Upon the radiant heather bees and butterflies were busy, she knew, and the birds on that side were just beginning their autumn songs.

On the left, quite up to her position, was dark and cloudy weather, shading a valley of heavy greens and browns, which at its farther side rose to meet the sea in tall cliffs, suggesting even here at their back how terrible were their aspects seaward in a growling south-west gale. Here grassed hills rose like knuckles gloved in dark olive, and little plantations between them formed a still deeper and sadder monochrome. A zinc sky met a leaden sea on this hand, the low wind groaned and whined, and not a bird sang.

The ridge along which Ethelberta rode – Nine-Barrow Down by name – divided these two climates like a wall; it soon became apparent that they were wrestling for mastery immediately in her pathway. The issue long remained doubtful, and this being an imaginative hour with her, she watched as typical of her own fortunes how the front of battle swayed – now to the west, flooding her with sun, now to the east, covering her with shade: then the wind moved round to the north, a blue hole appeared in the overhanging cloud, at about the place of the north star; and the sunlight spread on both sides of her.

The Hand of Ethelberta

The Wind's Prophecy

I travel on by barren farms,
And gulls glint out like silver flecks
Against a cloud that speaks of wrecks,
And bellies down with black alarms,
I say: 'Thus from my lady's arms
I go; those arms I love the best!'
The wind replies from dip and rise,
'Nay; toward her arms thou journeyest.'

A distant verge morosely gray
Appears, while clots of flying foam
Break from its muddy monochrome,
And a light blinks up far away.
I sigh: 'My eyes now as all day
Behold her ebon loops of hair!'
Like bursting bonds the wind responds,
'Nay, wait for tresses flashing fair!'

From tides the lofty coastlines screen
Come smitings like the slam of doors,
Or hammerings on hollow floors,
As the swell cleaves through caves unseen.
Say I: 'Though broad this wild terrene,
Her city home is matched of none!'
From the hoarse skies the wind replies:
'Thou shouldst have said her sea-bord one.'

The all-prevailing clouds exclude
The one quick timorous transient star;

The waves outside where breakers are
Huzza like a mad multitude.
'Where the sun ups it, mist-imbued,'
I cry, 'there reigns the star for me!'
The wind outshrieks from points and peaks:
'Here, westward, where it downs, mean ye!'

Yonder the headland, vulturine,
Snores like old Skrymer in his sleep,
And every chasm and every steep
Blackens as wakes each pharos-shine.
'I roam, but one is safely mine,'
I say, 'God grant she stay my own!'
Low laughs the wind as if it grinned:
'Thy Love is one thou'st not yet known.'
Rewritten from an old copy.

This poem, whose full import is not clearly conveyed, is a vivid description of Hardy's drive from Launceston to St Juliot for his first meeting with Emma Gifford on March 7, 1870. (The lady with the 'ebon loops of hair' was perhaps Jane Nicholls, with whom his love-affair was just painfully ending.[81]) To a man of his aesthetic and visual sensitivity, this encounter with the North Cornish coast was sensational: it not only affected his courtship and marriage, but it became the seed of some of his greatest work.

The place is pre-eminently (for one person at least) the region of dream and mystery. The ghostly birds, the pall-like sea, the frothy wind, the eternal soliloquy of the waters, the bloom of dark purple cast that seems to exhale from the shoreward precipices, in themselves lend to the scene an atmosphere like the twilight of a night vision.

A Pair of Blue Eyes, 1895 Preface

*   *   *

From these passages of general natural description we move to Hardy's observations of the detailed features of nature:

. . . the seasons in their moods, morning and evening, night and noon, winds in their different tempers, trees, waters and mists, shades and silences, and the voices of inanimate things.

Tess of the d'Urbervilles

A Sign-Seeker (stanzas I-V)

I mark the months in liveries dank and dry,
The noontides many-shaped and hued;

40

I see the nightfall shades subtrude,
And hear the monotonous hours clang negligently by.

I view the evening bonfires of the sun
On hills where morning rains have hissed;
The eyeless countenance of the mist
Pallidly rising when the summer droughts are done.

I have seen the lightning-blade, the leaping star,
The cauldrons of the sea in storm,
Have felt the earthquake's lifting arm,
And trodden where abysmal fires and snow-cones are.

I learn to prophesy the hid eclipse,
The coming of eccentric orbs;
To mete the dust the sky absorbs,
To weigh the sun, and fix the hour each planet dips.

I witness fellow earth-men surge and strive,
Assemblies meet, and throb, and part;
Death's sudden finger, sorrow's smart;
 — All the vast various moils that mean a world alive. . . .

LIGHT

Overarching all his descriptions is Hardy's feeling for light — and its concomitant darkness and shadow. In The Life *he several times expresses his admiration for the work of J. M. W. Turner, writing of him in January 1889, after a visit to the Royal Academy,*

What he paints chiefly is *light as modified by objects.*

Hardy shared with Turner a preoccupation with light. Differences between lights in nature, reflections, changes and contrasts are everywhere noticed.

[1876] May. In an orchard at Closeworth. Cowslips under trees. A light proceeds from them, as from Chinese lanterns or glow worms.

The Life of Thomas Hardy

Tess and Angel Clare meet in the early light of day:

The gray half-tones of daybreak are not the gray half-tones of the day's close, though the degree of their shade may be the same. In the twilight of the morning light seems active, darkness passive; in the twilight of evening it is the darkness which is active and crescent, and the light which is the drowsy reverse. . . . The spectral, half-compounded, aqueous light which pervaded the open mead, impressed them with a feeling of isolation, as if they were Adam and Eve. . . .

The mixed, singular, luminous gloom in which they walked along together to the spot where the cows lay, often made him think of the Resurrection hour. . . . Whilst all the landscape was in neutral shade his companion's face, which was the focus of his eyes, rising above the mist stratum, seemed to have a sort of phosphorescence upon it. She looked ghostly, as if she were merely a soul at large. In reality her face, without appearing to do so, had caught the cold gleam of the day from the north-east; his own face, though he did not think of it, wore the same aspect to her.

Tess of the d'Urbervilles

Beside him sat a woman, many years his junior – almost, indeed, a girl. Her face too was fresh in colour, but it was of a totally different quality – soft and evanescent, like the light under a heap of rose petals.

The Withered Arm

Cytherea and Edward settle in the chimney recess to talk:

. . . here they sat down facing each other, on benches fitted to the recesses, the fire glowing on the hearth between their feet. Its ruddy light shone on the underslopes of their faces, and spread out over the floor of the room with the low horizontality of the setting sun, giving to every grain of sand and tumour in the paving a long shadow towards the door.

Desperate Remedies

The dairy workers at Talbothays spread across the field to search for the few garlic plants which are flavouring the milk:

As they crept along, stooping low to discern the plant, a soft yellow gleam was reflected from the buttercups into their shaded faces, giving them an elfish, moonlit aspect, though the sun was pouring on their backs in all the strength of noon.

Tess of the d'Urbervilles

A Countenance

Her laugh was not in the middle of her face quite,
    As a gay laugh springs,
It was plain she was anxious about some things
    I could not trace quite.
Her curls were like fir-cones – piled up, brown –
    Or rather like tight-tied sheaves:
It seemed they could never be taken down. . . .

And her lips were too full, some might say:
I did not think so, Anyway.
The shadow her bottom one would cast
Was green in hue whenever she passed
   Bright sun on midsummer leaves.
Alas, I knew not much of her,
And lost all sight and touch of her!

If otherwise, should I have minded
The shy laugh not in the middle of her mouth quite,
And would my kisses have died of drouth quite
   As love became unblinded?
1884

The dull sky soon began to tell its meaning by sending down herald-drops of rain, and the stagnant air of the day changed into a fitful breeze which played about their faces. The quicksilvery glaze on the rivers and pools vanished; from broad mirrors of light they changed to lustreless sheets of lead, with a surface like a rasp.

Tess of the d'Urbervilles

The sharp contrasts in light made by the lighthouses in "The Wind's Prophecy," and the illumination of windows after dark (in a poem like "In her Precincts")[82] *are also made by nature:*

Eustacia arose, and walked beside him in the direction signified, brushing her way over the damping heath and fern, and followed by the strains of the merrymakers, who still kept up the dance. The moon had now waxed bright and silvery, but the heath was proof against such illumination, and there was to be observed the striking scene of a dark, rayless tract of country under an atmosphere charged from its zenith to its extremities with whitest light. To an eye above them their two faces would have appeared amid the expanse like two pearls on a table of ebony.

The Return of the Native

The moon shone to-night, and its light was not of a customary kind. [Boldwood's] window admitted only a reflection of its rays, and the pale sheen had that reversed direction which snow gives, coming upward and lighting up his ceiling in an unnatural way, casting shadows in strange places, and putting lights where shadows had used to be.

Far from the Madding Crowd

Lying Awake

You, Morningtide Star, now are steady-eyed, over the east,
   I know it as if I saw you;
You, Beeches, engrave on the sky your thin twigs, even the least;
   Had I paper and pencil I'd draw you.

You, Meadow, are white with your counterpane cover of dew,
 I see it as if I were there;
You, Churchyard, are lightening faint from the shade of the yew,
 The names creeping out everywhere.

SHADOW

The importance of shadow as a foil to light, and as an image for the dark areas of life, was appreciated by Hardy, who was nurtured on the shadows of Gothic literature (such as Harrison Ainsworth's and Alexandre Dumas') and Gothic architecture.[83] *He noticed how shadows work – as George Somerset, in* A Laodicean, *observed on Paula's cheek 'the moving shadow of leaves cast by the declining sun'.*

At sunset, Clym looks from his window:

His room overlooked the front of the premises and the valley of the heath beyond. The lowest beams of the winter sun threw the shadow of the house over the palings, across the grass margin of the heath, and far up the vale, where the chimney outlines and those of the surrounding tree-tops stretched forth in long dark prongs . . .

The Return of the Native

Keeper Day (and family) set about taking honey from the hives:

He proceeded to dig two holes in the earth beside the hives, the others standing round in a circle except Mrs Day, who . . . returned to the house. The party remaining were now lit up in front by the lantern in their midst, their shadows radiating each way upon the garden-plot like the spokes of a wheel . . .

Under the Greenwood Tree

A certain nobility of aspect was also imparted to [old William Dewy] by the setting sun, which gave him a Titanic shadow at least thirty feet in length, stretching away to the east in outlines of imposing magnitude, his head finally terminating upon the trunk of a grand old oak-tree.

Under the Greenwood Tree

Knight and Elfride discuss life as they walk together:

They were walking between the sunset and the moonrise. With the dropping of the sun a nearly full moon had begun to raise itself. Their shadows, as cast by the western glare, showed signs of becoming obliterated in the interest of a rival pair in the opposite direction which the moon was bringing to distinctness.

44

'I consider my life to some extent a failure,' said Knight again after a pause, during which he had noticed the antagonistic shadows.

A Pair of Blue Eyes

[1888] *March.* At the Temperance Hotel. The people who stay here appear to include religious enthusiasts of all sorts. They talk the old faiths with such new fervours and original aspects that such faiths seem again arresting. They open fresh views of Christianity by turning it in reverse positions, as Gérôme the painter did by painting the *shadow* of the Crucifixion instead of the Crucifixion itself as former painters had done.

The Life of Thomas Hardy

Evening Shadows

The shadows of my chimneys stretch afar
Across the plot, and on to the privet bower,
And even the shadows of their smokings show,
And nothing says just now that where they are
They will in future stretch at this same hour,
Though in my earthen cyst I shall not know,

And at this time the neighbouring Pagan mound,
Whose myths the Gospel news now supersede,
Upon the greensward also throws its shade,
and nothing says such shade will spread around
Even as to-day when men will no more heed
The Gospel news than when the mound was made.

Stephen Smith watches events in the summer-house from the darkness outside:

The scratch of a striking light was heard, and a glow radiated from the interior of the building. The light gave birth to dancing leaf-shadows, stem-shadows, lustrous streaks, dots, sparkles, and threads of silver sheen of all imaginable variety and transience. It awakened gnats, which flew towards it, revealed shiny gossamer threads, disturbed earthworms. Stephen gave but little attention to these phenomena, and less time. He saw in the summer-house a strongly illuminated picture.

The picture shows his former love Elfride with 'his friend and preceptor' Henry Knight's arm around her:

The flame dwindled down, died away, and all was wrapped in a darkness to which the gloom before the illumination bore no comparison in apparent density. Stephen, shattered in spirit and sick to his heart's centre, turned away. In turning he saw a shadowy outline behind the summer-house on the other side. His eyes grew accustomed to the darkness. Was the form a human form, or was it an opaque bush of juniper?

A Pair of Blue Eyes

Writing in December 1894 to H. Macbeth-Raeburn, who was to make engravings for the Wessex Novels edition of 1895–6, Hardy made some suggestions for the illustrations for A Pair of Blue Eyes:

It will be a pity if you have to do the illustration from photographs only: the coast there is so very picturesque, and has such changing aspects of light and shade that you ought to see it. Photographs, being taken always in fine weather, miss all that is most striking in the scenery there.

Perhaps Hardy's last words should be a poem which considers the vastness of the heavens and, characteristically, the precious worth of humanity; and one of his most brilliant evocations of light and shadow:

In the November bonfires on the heath:

The brilliant lights and sooty shades which struggled upon the skin and clothes of the person standing round caused their lineaments and general contours to be drawn with Düreresque vigour and dash. Yet the permanent moral expression of each face it was impossible to discover, for as the nimble flames towered, nodded and swooped through the surrounding air, the blots of shade and flakes of light upon the countenances of the group changed shape and position endlessly. All was unstable; quivering as leaves, evanescent as lightning. Shadowy eye-sockets, deep as those of a death's head, suddenly turned into pits of lustre: a lantern-jaw was cavernous, then it was shining; wrinkles were emphasized to ravines, or obliterated entirely by a changed ray. Nostrils were dark wells; sinews in old necks were gilt mouldings; things with no particular polish on them were glazed; bright objects, such as the tip of a furze-hook one of the men carried, were as glass; eyeballs glowed like little lanterns. Those whom Nature had depicted as merely quaint became grotesque, the grotesque became preternatural; for all was in extremity.

The Return of the Native

At a Lunar Eclipse

Thy shadow, Earth, from pole to Central Sea,
Now steals along upon the Moon's meek shine
In even monochrome and curving line
Of imperturbable serenity.

How shall I link such sun-cast symmetry
With the torn troubled form I know as thine,
That profile, placid as a brow divine,
With continents of moil and misery?

And can immense Mortality but throw
So small a shade, and Heaven's high human scheme
Be hemmed within the coasts yon arc implies?

Is such the stellar gauge of earthly show,
Nation at war with nation, brains that teem,
Heroes, and women fairer than the skies?

SUNSET AND EVENING

He Prefers Her Earthly

This after-sunset is a sight for seeing,
Cliff-heads of craggy cloud surrounding it,
  – And dwell you in that glory-show?
You may; for there are strange strange things in being,
          Stranger than I know.

Yet if that chasm of splendour claim your presence
Which glows between the ash cloud and the dun,
  How changed must be your mortal mould!
Changed to a firmament-riding earthless essence
          From what you were of old:

All too unlike the fond and fragile creature
Then known to me. . . . Well, shall I say it plain?
  I would not have you thus and there,
But still would grieve on, missing you, still feature
          You as the one you were.

The sun blazed down and down, till it was within half-an-hour of the setting; but the sketcher still lingered at his occupation of measuring and copying the chevroned doorway . . . which formed the tower entrance to an English village church. The graveyard being quite open on its western side, the tweed-clad figure of the young draughtsman, and the tall mass of antique masonry which rose above him to a battlemented parapet, were fired to a great brightness by the solar rays, that crossed the neighbouring mead like a warp of gold threads, in whose mazes groups of equally lustrous gnats danced and wailed incessantly.

He was so absorbed in his pursuit that he did not mark the brilliant chromatic effect of which he composed the central feature, till it was brought home to his intelligence by the warmth of the moulded stonework under his touch when measuring; which led him at length to turn his head and gaze on its cause.

There are few in whom the sight of a sunset does not beget as much meditative melancholy as contemplative pleasure, the human decline and death that it illustrates being too obvious to escape the notice of the simplest observer.

A Laodicean

After the shearing supper:

It was still the beaming time of evening, though night was stealthily making itself visible low down upon the ground, the western lines of light raking the earth without alighting upon it to any extent, or illuminating the dead levels at all. The sun had crept round the tree as a last effort before death, and then began to sink, the shearers' lower parts becoming steeped in embrowning twilight, whilst their heads and shoulders were still enjoying day, touched with a yellow of self-sustained brilliancy that seemed inherent rather than acquired.

The sun went down in an ochreous mist; but they sat, and talked on, and grew as merry as the gods in Homer's heaven. Bathsheba still remained enthroned inside the window . . . from which she sometimes looked up to view the fading scene outside. The slow twilight expanded and enveloped them completely. . . .

Far from the Madding Crowd

It is an evening at the beginning of October, and the mellowest of autumn sunsets irradiates London, even to its uttermost eastern end. Between the eye and the flaming West, columns of smoke stand up in the still air like tall trees. Everything in the shade is rich and misty blue.

A Pair of Blue Eyes

Coming Up Oxford Street: Evening

The sun from the west glares back,
And the sun from the watered track,
And the sun from the sheets of glass
And the sun from each window-brass;
Sun-mirrorings, too, brighten
From show-cases beneath
The laughing eyes and teeth
Of ladies who rouge and whiten.
And the same warm god explores
Panels and chinks of doors;
Problems with chymists' bottles
Profound as Aristotle's
He solves, and with good cause,
Having been ere man was.

48

Also he dazzles the pupils of one who walks west,
A city-clerk, with eyesight not of the best,
Who sees no escape to the very verge of his days
From the rut of Oxford Street into open ways;
And he goes along with head and eyes flagging forlorn,
Empty of interest in things, and wondering why he was born.
As seen 4 July 1872

1873 *Nov. 3.* A sunset. A brazen sun, bristling with a thousand spines, which struck
into & tormented my eyes.
1879 *March 2:* Sunset. Sun a vast bulb of crimson pulp.

Memoranda I

[1877] *End of November.* This evening the west is like some vast foundry where new
worlds are being cast.

The Life of Thomas Hardy

It was an evening of exceptional irradiations, and the west heaven gleamed like a foundry
of all metals common and rare. The clouds were broken into a thousand fragments, and
the margin of every fragment shone.

Two on a Tower

At half-past six the sun settled down upon the levels, with the aspect of a great forge
in the heavens, and presently a monstrous pumpkin-like moon arose on the other hand.

Tess of the d'Urbervilles

The Sun on the Bookcase
(Student's Love-Song: 1870)

Once more the cauldron of the sun
Smears the bookcase with winy red,
And here my page is, and there my bed,
And the apple-tree shadows travel along.
Soon their intangible track will be run,
And dusk grow strong
And they have fled.

Yes: now the boiling ball is gone,
And I have wasted another day. . . .
But wasted – *wasted*, do I say?
Is it a waste to have imaged one
Beyond the hills there, who, anon,
My great deeds done,
Will be mine alway?

49

Evening drew on apace. It chanced to be the eve of St Valentine's . . . and the sun shone low under the rim of thick hard cloud, decorating the eminences of the landscape with crowns of orange fire. As the train changed its direction on a curve, the same rays stretched in through the window, and coaxed open Knight's half-closed eyes.

. . . The train continued rattling on. . . . The yellows of evening had turned to browns, the dusky shades thickened, and a flying cloud of dust occasionally stroked the window – borne upon a chilling breeze which blew from the north-east. The previously gilded but now dreary hills began to lose their daylight aspects of rotundity, and to become black discs vandyked[84] against the sky, all nature wearing the cloak that six o'clock casts over the landscape at this time of the year.

A Pair of Blue Eyes

They came out of church just as the sun went down, leaving the landscape like a platform from which an eloquent speaker has retired, and nothing remains for the audience to do but to rise and go home.

A Pair of Blue Eyes

NIGHT AND DARKNESS

Few evocations of the majesty of night can equal that in Far From The Madding Crowd *when Gabriel Oak stood alone at midnight on Norcombe Hill (page 34); nor those of Egdon Heath in its livery of silver and black (page 43), as a 'confronting pile of firmamental darkness', or in its stormy turbulence when 'during winter darkness . . . the storm was its lover, and the wind its friend'. (p. 35) Hardy was writing about what he knew.*

The darkness thickened rapidly, at intervals shutting down on the land in a perceptible flap, like the wave of a wing.

Interlopers at the Knap

'On a cold and starry Christmas Eve' Dick Dewy walks through the plantation:

The lonely lane he was following connected one of the hamlets of Mellstock parish with Upper Mellstock and Lewgate, and to his eye, casually glancing upward, the silver and black-stemmed birches with their characteristic tufts, the pale grey boughs of beech, the dark-creviced elm, all appeared now as black and flat outlines upon the sky, wherein the white stars twinkled so vehemently that their flickering seemed like the flapping of wings. Within the woody pass, at a level anything lower than the horizon, all was dark as the grave. The copsewood forming the sides of the bower interlaced its boughs so densely, even at this season of the year, that the draught from the north-east flew along the channel with scarcely an interruption from lateral breezes.

After passing the plantation and reaching Mellstock Cross the white surface of the lane revealed itself between the dark hedgerows like a ribbon jagged at the edges; the irregularity being caused by temporary accumulations of leaves extending from the ditch on either side.

. . . Having come more into the open he could now be seen rising against the sky, his profile appearing on the light background like the portrait of a gentleman in black cardboard. It assumed the form of a low-crowned hat, an ordinary-shaped nose, an ordinary chin, an ordinary neck, and ordinary shoulders. What he consisted of further down was invisible from lack of sky low enough to picture him on.

Shuffling, halting, irregular footsteps of various kinds were now heard coming up the hill, and presently there emerged from the shade severally five men of different ages and gaits, all of them working villagers of the parish of Mellstock. They, too, lost their rotundity with the daylight, and advanced against the sky in flat outlines, which suggested some processional design on Greek or Etruscan pottery.

Under the Greenwood Tree

Marty South works long into the night:

The lights in the village went out, house after house, till there only remained two in the darkness. . . .

Eleven, twelve, one o'clock struck; the heap of spars grew higher, and the pile of chips and ends more bulky. Even the light on the hill had now been extinguished; but she still worked on . . . When the clock struck three she arose . . . She wrapped round her a long red woollen cravat and opened the door. The night in all its fullness met her flatly on the threshold, like the very brink of an absolute void, or the ante-mundane Ginnung-Gap believed in by her Teuton forefathers.[85] For her eyes were fresh from the blaze, and here there was no street-lamp or lantern to form a kindly transition between the inner glare and the outer dark. A lingering wind brought to her ear the creaking sound of two overcrowded branches in the neighbouring wood, which were rubbing each other into wounds, and other vocalized sorrows of the trees, together with the screech of owls, and the fluttering tumble of some awkward wood-pigeon ill-balanced on its roosting-bough.

But the pupils of her young eyes soon expanded, and she could see well enough for her purpose. Taking a bundle of spars under each arm, and guided by the serrated line of tree-tops against the sky, she went some hundred yards or more down the lane till she reached a long open shed, carpeted around with the dead leaves that lay about everywhere. Night, that strange personality which within walls brings ominous introspectiveness and self-distrust, but under the open sky banishes such subjective anxieties as too trivial for thought, gave to Marty South a less perturbed and brisker manner now.

The Woodlanders

Nightfall at the allotments:

One fine day Tess and 'Liza-Lu worked on here with their neighbours till the last rays of the sun smote flat upon the white pegs that divided the plots. As soon as twilight succeeded to sunset the flare of the couch-grass and cabbage-stalk fires began to light up the allotments fitfully, their outlines appearing and disappearing under the dense smoke as wafted by the wind. When a fire glowed, banks of smoke, blown level along the ground, would themselves become illuminated to an opaque lustre, screening the work-people from one another; and the meaning of the 'pillar of a cloud', which was a wall by day and a light by night, could be understood.[86]

As evening thickened some of the gardening men and women gave over for the night, but the greater number remained to get their planting done, Tess being among them. . . . It was on one of the couch-burning plots that she laboured with her fork, its four shining prongs resounding against the stones and dry clods in little clicks. Sometimes she was completely involved in the smoke of her fire; then it would leave her figure free, irradiated by the brassy glare from the heap. . . . The women further back wore white aprons, which with their pale faces, were all that could be seen of them in the gloom, except when at moments they caught a flash from the flames.

Westward, the wiry boughs of the bare thorn hedge which formed the boundary of the field rose against the pale opalescence of the lower sky. Above, Jupiter hung like a full-blown jonquil, so bright as almost to throw a shade. A few small nondescript stars were appearing elsewhere. In the distance a dog barked, and wheels occasionally rattled along the dry road.

Still the prongs continued to click assiduously, for it was not late, and though the air was fresh and keen there was a whisper of spring in it that cheered the workers on. Something in the place, the hour, the crackling fires, the fantastic mysteries of light and shade, made others as well as Tess enjoy being there. Nightfall, which in the frost of winter comes as a fiend and in the warmth of summer as a lover, came as a tranquillizer on this March day.

Tess of the d'Urbervilles

Night-Time in Mid-Fall

It is a storm-strid night, winds footing swift
    Through the blind profound;
  I know the happenings from their sound;
Leaves totter down still green, and spin, and drift;
The tree-trunks rock to their roots, which wrench and lift
  The loam where they run onward underground.

The streams are muddy and swollen; eels migrate
    To a new abode;
  Even cross, 'tis said, the turnpike-road;
(Men's feet have felt their crawl, homecoming late):
The westward fronts of towers are saturate,
  Church-timbers crack, and witches ride abroad.

Tree-leaves labour up and down,
　　And through them the fainting light
　　Succumbs to the crawl of night,
　Outside in the road the telegraph wire
　　To the town from the darkening land
Intones to travellers like a spectral lyre
　　Swept by a spectral hand.

A car comes up, with lamps full-glare,
　　That flash upon a tree:
　　It has nothing to do with me,
　And whangs along in a world of its own,
　　Leaving a blacker air;
And mute by the gate I stand again alone,
　　And nobody pulls up there.
October 9, 1924

MOONLIGHT

Tess stay[ed] on till dusk with the body of harvesters. Then they all rode home in one of the largest waggons, in the company of a broad tarnished moon that had risen from the ground to the eastwards, its face resembling the outworn gold-leaf halo of some worm-eaten Tuscan saint.

Tess of the d'Urbervilles

Cytherea and Springrove return on the excursion steamboat:

Night had quite closed in by the time they reached Budmouth harbour, sparkling with its white, red, and green lights in opposition to the shimmering path of the moon's reflection on the other side, which reached away to the horizon till the flecked ripples reduced themselves to sparkles as fine as gold dust.

Desperate Remedies

The mummers make their way through the moonlight:

There was a slight hoar-frost that night, and the moon, though not more than half-full, threw a spirited and enticing brightness upon the fantastic figures of the mumming band, whose plumes and ribbons rustled in their walk like autumn leaves. Their path was not over Rainbarrow now, but down a valley which left that ancient elevation a little to the east. The bottom of the vale was green to a width of ten yards or thereabouts, and the shining facets of frost upon the blades of grass seemed to move on with the shadows of those they surrounded. The masses of furze and heath to the right and left were dark as ever; a mere half-moon was powerless to silver such sable features as theirs.

The Return of the Native

— and the Mellstock quire go their rounds at Christmas:

Just before the clock struck twelve they lighted the lanterns and started. The moon, in her third quarter, had risen since the snowstorm; but the dense accumulation of snow-cloud weakened her power to a faint twilight which was rather pervasive of the landscape than traceable to the sky.

Under the Greenwood Tree

Setting out to shadow Aeneas Manston, Anne Seaway finds that

. . . Since she had come indoors from her walk in the early part of the evening the moon had risen. But the thick clouds overspreading the whole landscape rendered the dim light pervasive and grey: it appeared as an attribute of the air.

Desperate Remedies

Grace runs through the woods to find medical help for Giles:

It was past midnight when Grace arrived opposite her father's house . . . Ever since her emergence from the denser plantations about Winterborne's residence a pervasive lightness had hung in the damp autumn sky in spite of the vault of cloud, signifying that a moon of some age was shining above its arch. The two white gates were distinct, and the white balls on the pillars: and the puddles and damp ruts left by the recent rain had a cold corpse-eyed luminousness.

The Woodlanders

The same deathly image was seen by Gabriel Oak when disaster befell his flock. The moon, which appears also in some seventy poems, is one of Hardy's most potent images, as a later section will show. In The Return of the Native *the eclipse of the moon is gradually developed as an image of the uncertain future of Clym and Eustacia's love, though at first Hardy paints it from his own experience as 'watcher of the skies':*

The low moon was not as yet visible from the front of the house, and Yeobright climbed out of the valley until he stood in the full flood of her light. But even now he walked on, and his steps were in the direction of Rainbarrow.

In half an hour he stood at the top. The sky was clear from verge to verge, and the moon flung her rays over the whole heath, but without sensibly lighting it, except where paths and water-courses had laid bare the white flints and glistening quartz sand, which made streaks upon the general shade. After standing awhile he stooped and felt the heather. It was dry, and he flung himself down upon the barrow, his face towards the moon, which depicted a small image of herself in each of his eyes.

He had often come up here without stating his purpose to his mother; but this was the first time that he had been ostensibly frank as to his purpose while really concealing it. It was a moral situation which, three months earlier, he could hardly have credited of himself. In returning to labour in this sequestered spot he had anticipated an escape from the chafing of social necessities; yet behold they were here also. More than ever he longed to be in some world where personal ambition was not the only recognized form of progress – such, perhaps, as might have been the case at some time or other in the silvery globe when shining upon him. His eye travelled over the length and breadth of that distant country – over the Bay of Rainbows, the sombre Sea of Crises, the Ocean of Storms, the Lake of Dreams, the vast Walled Plains, and the wondrous Ring Mountains – till he almost felt himself to be voyaging bodily through its wild scenes, standing on its hollow hills, traversing its deserts, descending its vales and old sea bottoms, or mounting to the edge of its craters.

While he watched the far-removed landscape a tawny stain grew into being on the lower verge: the eclipse had begun. This marked a preconcerted moment: for the remote celestial phenomenon had been pressed into sublunary service as a lover's signal. Yeobright's mind flew back to earth at the sight; he arose, shook himself, and listened. Minute after minute passed by, perhaps ten minutes passed, and the shadow on the moon perceptibly widened.

The Return of the Native

(This passage is continued on page 221)

The two following poems are likewise far more than merely descriptive, but they also instance Hardy's perception of the moon (or its reflection) as a natural phenomenon.

At Rushy Pond

On the frigid face of the heath-hemmed pond
    There shaped the half-grown moon:
Winged whiffs from the north with a husky croon
    Blew over and beyond.

And the wind flapped the moon in its float on the pool,
    And stretched it to oval form;
Then corkscrewed it like a wriggling worm;
    Then wanned it weariful.

And I cared not for conning the sky above
    Where hung the substant thing,
For my thought was earthward sojourning
    On the scene I had vision of.

Since it was once, in a secret year,
　　I had called a woman to me
From across this water, ardently –
　　And practised to keep her near;

Till the last weak love-words had been said,
　　And ended was her time,
And blurred the bloomage of her prime,
　　And white the earlier red.

And the troubled orb in the pond's sad shine
　　Was her very wraith, as scanned
When she withdrew thence, mirrored, and
　　Her days dropped out of mine.

A Cathedral Façade at Midnight

Along the sculptures of the western wall
　　I watched the moonlight creeping:
It moved as if it hardly moved at all,
　　Inch by inch thinly peeping
Round on the pious figures of freestone, brought
And poised there when the Universe was wrought
To serve its centre, Earth, in mankind's thought.

The lunar look skimmed scantly toe, breast, arm,
　　Then edged on slowly, slightly,
To shoulder, hand, face; till each austere form
　　Was blanched its whole length brightly
Of prophet, king, queen, cardinal in state,
That dead men's tools had striven to simulate;
And the stiff images stood irradiate.

A frail moan from the martyred saints there set
　　Mid others of the erection
Against the breeze, seemed sighings of regret
　　At the ancient faith's rejection
Under the sure, unhasting, steady stress
Of Reason's movement, making meaningless
The coded creeds of old-time godliness.

[1897] *August 10, Salisbury.* Went into the Close late at night, The moon was visible

56

through both the north and south clerestory windows to me standing on the turf on the north side. . . . Walked to the west front, and watched the moonlight creep round upon the statuary of the façade – stroking tentatively and then more and more firmly the prophets, the martyrs, the bishops, the kings, and the queens. . . . Upon the whole the Close of Salisbury under the full summer moon on a windless midnight, is as beautiful a scene as any I know in England – or for the matter of that elsewhere.[87]

The Life of Thomas Hardy

STARS

'When I set out for Lyonnesse'
(1870)

When I set out for Lyonnesse
  A hundred miles away
  The rime was on the spray.
And starlight lit my lonesomeness.
When I set out for Lyonnesse
  A hundred miles away.

What would bechance at Lyonnesse
  While I should sojourn there
  No prophet durst declare
Nor did the wisest wizard guess
What would bechance at Lyonnesse
  While I should sojourn there.

When I came back from Lyonnesse
  With magic in my eyes,
  All marked with mute surmise
My radiance rare and fathomless,
When I came back from Lyonnesse
  With magic in my eyes!

Hardy's Cornish journey in March 1870 – a journey begun in Bockhampton, and ended at St Juliot, by starlight – must have been very like the one he describes as Stephen Smith's:

Scarcely a solitary house or man had been visible along the whole dreary distance of open country they were traversing; and now that night had begun to fall, the faint twilight, which still gave an idea of the landscape to their observation, was enlivened by the quiet appearance of the planet Jupiter, momentarily gleaming in intenser brilliancy in front of them, and by Sirius shedding his rays in rivalry from his position over their shoulders.

A Pair of Blue Eyes

In his next novel, Far from the Madding Crowd, *Hardy lovingly and expertly differentiates each star that Gabriel scanned in the midnight sky. (Page 35). In the next,* The Hand of Ethelberta *he used his knowledge of the stars to make a telling simile for Ethelberta, a woman of strong character*

She mostly was silent as to her thoughts, and she wore an air of unusual stillness. It was the silence and stillness of a starry sky, where all is force and motion.

The Hand of Ethelberta

In all his writing, Hardy showed that awareness of the stars which was never to leave him. In his first published novel, Desperate Remedies, *some of his images may appear conventional or tongue in cheek, but they are apt; they also reveal how naturally the stars came to his mind as an element in comparison:*

The sight of the lithe girl, set off by an airy dress, coquettish jacket, flexible hat, a ray of starlight in each eye and a war of lilies and roses in each cheek, was a palpable pleasure to the mistress of the mansion . . .

Manston came forward from the other room with a candle in his hand, as Owen pushed open the door.

Her frightened eyes were unnaturally large, and shone like stars in the darkness of the background, as the light fell upon them.

The rector of Carriford trotted homewards under the cold and clear March sky, its countless stars fluttering like bright birds.

Desperate Remedies

The opening of Under the Greenwood Tree *(page 101) characteristically describes the stars whose 'flickering seemed like the flapping of wings' – a favourite image in several of the fifty or more poems in which stars, meteors, or comets figure.[88] In every novel there are images or descriptions of the stars; but in 1882 Hardy published* Two on a Tower, *whose very theme and basis was astronomy. It was typical of this wide-ranging mind, cherishing both the scientific and the poetic approach, that he wrote to Edmund Gosse of his aim: 'to make science, not the mere padding of a romance, but the actual vehicle of romance.' (4 December, 1882).*

He slyly describes how he set about researching it:

It was necessary that he should examine an observatory, the story moving in an astronomical medium, and he applied to the Astronomer Royal for permission to see Greenwich. He was requested to state before it could be granted if his application was made for astronomical and scientific reasons or not. He therefore drew up a scientific letter, the gist of which was that he wished to ascertain if it would be possible for him to adapt an old tower, built in a plantation in the West of England for other objects, to the requirements of a telescopic study of the stars by a young man very ardent in that pursuit (this being the imagined situation in the proposed novel). An order to view Greenwich Observatory was promptly sent.

The Life of Thomas Hardy

The hero, Swithin St Cleeve, was a young astronomer whose enthusiasm caused Lady Constantine not only to give him the necessary equipment, but also to love him:

He became quite natural, all his self-consciousness fled, and his eye spoke into hers no less than his lips to her ears, as he said, 'How such a theory can have lingered on to this day beats conjecture! François Arago, as long as forty or fifty years ago, conclusively established the fact that scintillation is the simplest thing in the world, – merely a matter of atmosphere. But I won't speak of this to you now. The comparative absence of scintillation in warm countries was noticed by Humboldt. Then, again, the scintillations vary. No star flaps his wings like Sirius when he lies low! He flashes out emeralds and rubies, amethystine flames and sapphirine colours, in a manner quite marvellous to behold, and this is only *one* star! So, too, do Arcturus, and Capella, and lesser luminaries. . . . But I tire you with this subject?'

'On the contrary, you speak so beautifully that I could listen all day.'

Two on a Tower

'Yes; the scenery is well hung to-night,' she said, looking out upon the heavens.

Then they proceeded to scan the sky, roving from planet to star, from single stars to double stars, from double to coloured stars, in the cursory manner of the merely curious. They plunged down to that at other times invisible multitude in the back rows of the celestial theatre: remote layers of constellations whose shapes were new and singular; pretty twinklers which for infinite ages had spent their beams without calling forth from a single earthly poet a single line, or being able to bestow a ray of comfort on a single benighted traveller.

'And to think,' said Lady Constantine, 'that the whole race of shepherds since the beginning of the world, – even those immortal shepherds who watched near Bethlehem, – should have gone into their graves without knowing that for one star that lighted them in their labours, there were a hundred as good behind trying to do so! . . . I have a feeling for this instrument not unlike the awe I should feel in the presence of a great magician in whom I really believed. Its powers are so enormous, and weird, and fantastical, that I should have a personal fear in being with it alone. Music drew an angel down, said the poet: but what is that to drawing down worlds!'

'I often experience a kind of fear of the sky after sitting in the observing chair a long time,' he answered. 'And when I walk home afterwards I also fear it for what I know is there, but cannot see, as one naturally fears the presence of a vast formless something that only reveals a very little of itself. That's partly what I meant by saying that magnitude which up to a certain point has grandeur, has beyond it ghastliness.'

Thus the interest of their sidereal observations led them on, till the knowledge that scarce any other human vision was travelling within a hundred million miles of their own gave them such a sense of the isolation of that faculty as almost to be a sense of isolation in respect of their whole personality, causing a shudder at its absoluteness. At night, when human discords and harmonies are hushed, in a general sense, for the greater part of twelve hours, there is nothing to moderate the blow with which the infinitely great, the stellar universe, strikes down upon the infinitely little, the mind of the beholder; and this was the case now. Having got closer to immensity than their fellow-creatures, they saw at once its beauty and its frightfulness. They more and more felt the contrast between their own tiny magnitudes and those among which they had recklessly plunged till they were oppressed with the presence of a vastness they could not cope with even as an idea, and which hung about them like a nightmare.

Two on a Tower

Swithin succumbs to a grave illness after his 'New Astronomical Discovery' is forestalled by an American astronomer. It is only the chance news of the appearance of a new comet which restores his will to live:

The crisis passed, there was a turn for the better; and after that he rapidly mended. The comet had in all probability saved his life. The limitless and complex wonders of the sky resumed their old powers over his imagination; the possibilities of that unfathomable blue ocean were endless.

Two on a Tower

Several years later, Swithin is studying the southern skies of South Africa:

It was below the surface that his material lay. There, in regions revealed only to the instrumental observer, were suns of hybrid kind – fire-fogs, floating nuclei, globes that flew in groups like swarms of bees, and other extraordinary sights – which, when decomposed by Swithin's equatorial, turned out to be the beginning of a new series of phenomena instead of the end of an old one.

There were gloomy deserts in those southern skies such as the north shows scarcely an example of; sites set apart for the position of suns which for some unfathomable reason were left uncreated, their places remaining ever since conspicuous by their emptiness.

The inspection of these chasms brought him a second pulsation of the old horror which he had used to describe to Viviette as produced in him by bottomlessness in the north heaven. The ghostly finger of limitless vacancy touched him now on the other side. Infinite deeps in the north stellar region had a homely familiarity about them, when compared with infinite deeps in the region of the south pole. This was an even more unknown tract of the unknown. Space here, being less the historic haunt of human thought than overhead at home, seemed to be pervaded with a more lonely loneliness.

Two on a Tower

In October 1899 Hardy cycled to Southampton to witness the embarkation of troops to South Africa at the onset of the Boer War. Only a month later this fine poem was published – an example not only of the poet's sensitive evocation of place, but of the country boy's natural sense of orientation by the stars:

Drummer Hodge

I

They throw in Drummer Hodge, to rest
  Uncoffined – just as found:
His landmark is a kopje-crest
  That breaks the veldt around;
And foreign constellations west
  Each night above his mound.

II

Young Hodge the Drummer never knew –
  Fresh from his Wessex home –
The meaning of the broad Karoo,
  The Bush, the dusty loam,
And why uprose to nightly view
  Strange stars amid the gloam.

III

Yet portion of that unknown plain
  Will Hodge for ever be;
His homely Northern breast and brain
  Grow to some Southern tree,
And strange-eyed constellations reign
  His stars eternally.

DAWN AND SUNRISE

1873 Dec. 23. Before day. A lavender curtain, with a pale crimson hem, covers the east & shuts out the dawn.

Memoranda I

On the morning appointed for her departure Tess was awake before dawn – at the marginal minute of the dark when the grove is still mute, save for one prophetic bird who sings with a clear-voiced conviction that he at least knows the correct time of day, the rest preserving silence as if equally convinced that he is mistaken.

Tess of the d'Urbervilles

They met daily in that strange and solemn interval, the twilight of the morning, in the violet or pink dawn . . .[89]

Tess of the d'Urbervilles

Stephen . . . turned into the lane. It was so early that the shaded places still smelt like night time, and the sunny spots had hardly felt the sun. The horizontal rays made every shallow dip in the ground to show as a well-marked hollow. Even the channel of the path was enough to throw shade, and the very stones of the road cast tapering dashes of darkness westward, as long as Jael's tent-nail.[90]

A Pair of Blue Eyes

Then the dawn drew on. The full power of the clear heaven was not equal to that of a cloudy sky at noon, when Boldwood arose and dressed himself. He descended the stairs and went out towards the gate of a field to the east, leaning over which he paused and looked around.

It was one of the usual slow sunrises of this time of the year, and the sky, pure violet in the zenith, was leaden to the northward, and murky to the east, where over the snowy down or ewe-lease on Weatherbury Upper Farm, and apparently resting upon the ridge, the only half of the sun yet visible burnt rayless, like a red and flameless fire shining over a white hearthstone. The whole effect resembled a sunset as childhood resembles age.

In other directions the fields and sky were so much of one colour by the snow that it was difficult in a hasty glance to tell whereabouts the horizon occurred: and in general there was here, too, that before-mentioned preternatural inversion of light and shade which attends the prospect when the garish brightness commonly in the sky is found on the earth, and the shades of earth are in the sky. Over the west hung the wasting moon, now dull and greenish-yellow, like a tarnished brass.

Far from the Madding Crowd

The reddleman stands thinking by his van on the heath:

While he stood the dawn grew visible in the north-east quarter of the heavens, which, the clouds having cleared off, was bright with a soft sheen at this midsummer time, though it was only between one and two o'clock.

The Return of the Native

The local people watch all night on the ridge to see the King pass:

Thus they lingered, and the day began to break. . . . Anne in her place and the trumpet-major in his, each in private thought of no bright kind, watched the gradual glory of the east through all its tones and changes. The world of birds and insects got lively, the blue and the yellow and the gold of Loveday's uniform again became distinct; the sun bored its way upward, the fields, the trees, and the distant landscape kindled to flame, and the trumpet-major, backed by a lilac shadow as tall as a steeple, blazed in the rays like a very god of war.

It was half-past three o'clock.

The Trumpet-Major

It was a hazy sunrise in August. The denser nocturnal vapours, attacked by the warm beams, were dividing and shrinking into isolated fleeces within hollows and coverts, where they waited till they should be dried away to nothing.

The sun, on account of the mist, had a curious sentient, personal look, demanding the masculine pronoun for its adequate expression. His present aspect, coupled with the lack of all human forms in the scene, explained the old-time heliolatries in a moment. One could feel that a saner religion had never prevailed under the sky. The luminary was a golden-haired, beaming, mild-eyed, God-like creature, gazing down in the vigour and intentness of youth upon an earth that was brimming with interest for him.

His light, a little later, broke through chinks of cottage shutters, throwing stripes like red-hot pokers upon cupboards, chests of drawers, and other furniture within; and awakening harvesters who were not already astir . . .

Two groups, one of men and lads, the other of women, had come down the lane just at the hour when the shadows of the eastern hedge top struck the west hedge midway, so that the heads of the groups were enjoying sunrise while their feet were still in the dawn.

Tess of the d'Urbervilles

Christopher and Faith see a wonder:

He touched the blind, up it flew, and a gorgeous view presented itself to her eyes. A huge inflamed sun was breasting the horizon beyond a sheet of embayed sea which, to her surprise and delight, the mansion overlooked. The brilliant disc fired all the waves that lay between it and the shore at the bottom of the grounds, where the water tossed the ruddy light from one undulation to another in glares as large and clear as mirrors, incessantly altering them, destroying them, and creating them again; while further off they multiplied, thickened, and ran into one another like struggling armies, till they met the fiery source of them all.

The Hand of Ethelberta

No Hardy description is merely an account of what he sees, but of what he also thinks, feels, and brings to the sight as 'the echo of a great mind'. His own 'idiosyncratic mode of regard'[91] is shown even in his early writing:

From their coaster en route for Plymouth, Knight and Elfride watch the sunrise:

All up the coast, prominences singled themselves out from recesses. Then a rosy sky spread over the eastern sea and behind the low line of land, flinging its livery in dashes upon the thin airy clouds in that direction. Every projection on the land seemed now so many fingers anxious to catch a little of the liquid light thrown so prodigally over the sky, and after a fantastic time of lustrous yellows in the east, the higher elevations along the shore were flooded with the same hues. The bluff and bare contours of Start Point caught the brightest, earliest glow of all, and so also did the sides of its white lighthouse, perched upon a shelf in its precipitous front like a medieval saint in a niche. Their lofty neighbour Bolt Head on the left remained as yet ungilded, and retained its gray.

Then up came the sun, as it were in jerks, just to seaward of the easternmost point of land, flinging out a Jacob's-ladder path of light from itself to Elfride and Knight, and coating them with rays in a few minutes. The inferior dignitaries of the shore – Froward Point, Berry Head, and Prawle – all had acquired their share of the illumination ere this, and at length the very smallest protuberance of wave, cliff, or inlet, even to the uttermost recesses of the lovely valley of the Dart, had its portion; and sunlight, now the common possession of all, ceased to be the wonderful and coveted thing it had been a short half-hour before.

A Pair of Blue Eyes

Among his papers Hardy left several outlines for possible stories. Three were about the Vauxhall fiddler Barthélémon, who composed the poet's favourite 'Morning Hymn'. In July 1921, on the anniversary of Barthélémon's death in 1808, Hardy published in The Times *the following poem, making several drafts of the note he presented with it:*

Barthélémon at Vauxhall

François Hippolite Barthélémon, first-fiddler at Vauxhall Gardens, composed what was probably the most popular morning hymn-tune ever written. It was formerly sung, full-voiced, every Sunday in most churches, to Bishop Ken's words, but is now seldom heard.

He said: 'Awake my soul, and with the sun,' . . .
And paused upon the bridge, his eyes due east,
Where was emerging like a full-robed priest
The irradiate globe that vouched the dark as done.

It lit his face – the weary face of one
Who in the adjacent gardens charged his string,
Nightly, with many a tuneful tender thing,
Till stars were weak, and dancing hours outrun.

And then were threads of matin music spun
In trial tones as he pursued his way:
'This is a morn,' he murmured, 'well begun:
This strain to Ken will count when I am clay!'

And count it did; till, caught by echoing lyres,
It spread to galleried naves and mighty quires.

SUNLIGHT

Knapwater Park is the picture – at eleven o'clock on a muddy, quiet, hazy, but bright morning – a morning without any blue sky, and without any shadows, the earth being enlivened and lit up rather by the spirit of an invisible sun than by its bodily presence.

Desperate Remedies

As the Swancourts, on board the Juliet, *watched the busy wharf-scene:*

. . . they turned to look at the dashes of lurid sunlight, like burnished copper stars afloat on the ripples, which danced into and tantalized their vision . . .

A Pair of Blue Eyes

It was the week after the Easter holidays, and [Dick] was journeying along with Smart the mare and the light spring-cart, watching the damp slopes of the hill-sides as they streamed in the warmth of the sun, which at this unsettled season shone on the grass with the freshness of an occasional inspector rather than as an accustomed proprietor. . . . The distant view was darkly shaded with clouds; but the nearer parts of the landscape were whitely illuminated by the visible rays of the sun streaming down across the heavy grey shade behind . . .

(Dick proceeds to Keeper Day's house in Yalbury Wood)
. . . The sun shone obliquely upon the patch of grass in front, which reflected its brightness through the open doorway and up the staircase opposite, lighting up each riser with a shiny green radiance and leaving the top of each step in shade.

Under the Greenwood Tree

For the observer of Susan Henchard:

The chief – almost the only – attraction of the young woman's face was its mobility. When she looked down sideways . . . she became pretty, and even handsome, particularly that in the action her features caught slantwise the rays of the strongly coloured sun, which made transparencies of her eyelids and nostrils and set fire on her lips.

The Mayor of Casterbridge

Anne looked hither and thither in the bright rays of the day, each of her eyes having a little sun in it, which gave her glance a peculiar golden fire, and kindled the brown curls grouped over her forehead to a yellow brilliancy, and made single hairs, blown astray by the night, look like lacquered wires.

The Trumpet-Major

At the garden-party George Somerset watches Paula approaching him:

[Her] hair hung under her hat in great knots so well compacted that the sun gilded the convexity of each knot like a ball . . .

A Laodicean

Mrs Yeobright, as she walks across the heath, is attacked, and then blessed, by the sun:

The sun had now got far to the west of south and stood directly in her face, like some merciless incendiary, brand in hand, waiting to consume her . . .
(After two hours' walk, she pauses to rest on a patch of thyme)
She leant back to obtain more thorough rest, and the soft eastern portion of the sky was as great a relief to her eyes as the thyme was to her head. While she looked a heron arose on that side of the sky and flew on with his face towards the sun. He had come dripping wet from some pool in the valleys, and as he flew the edges and lining of his wings, his thighs, and his breast were so caught by the bright sunbeams that he appeared as if formed of burnished silver. Up in the zenith where he was seemed a free and happy place . . .

The Return of the Native

Cytherea and Owen are gathered with the Springroves in their cottage:

Whilst they talked, looking out at the yellow evening light that coated the hedges, trees, and church tower, a brougham rolled round the corner of the lane, and came in full view. It reflected the rays of the sun in a flash from its polished panels as it turned the angle, the spokes of the wheels bristling in the same light like bayonets.

Desperate Remedies

The Last Signal
(Oct. 11, 1886)

A MEMORY OF WILLIAM BARNES

Silently I footed by an uphill road
That led from my abode to a spot yew-boughed;
Yellowly the sun sloped low down to westward,
And dark was the east with cloud.

Then, amid the shadow of that livid sad east,
    Where the light was least, and a gate stood wide,
Something flashed the fire of the sun that was facing it,
        Like a brief blaze on that side.

Looking hard and harder I knew what it meant –
    The sudden shine sent from the livid east scene;
It meant the west mirrored by the coffin of my friend there,
        Turning to the road from his green,

To take his last journey forth – he who in his prime
    Trudged so many a time from that gate athwart the land!
Thus a farewell to me he signalled on his grave-way,
        As with a wave of his hand.
Winterborne-Came Path.

The poet William Barnes was Hardy's friend and neighbour, and it was while Hardy walked across the fields to Barnes's funeral that this incident occurred.[92] *The poem is an example of Hardy's interest in hundreds of different metres and rhyme-schemes: close attention to each line's consonant correspondences and the internal rhymes show its link with some of the Welsh bardic metre variations in the system known as 'cynghanedd', or 'harmony'.*

A Spellbound Palace
(Hampton Court)

On this kindly yellow day of mild low-travelling winter sun
        The stirless depths of the yews
        Are vague with misty blues:
Across the spacious pathways stretching spires of shadows run,
And the wind-gnawed walls of ancient brick are fired vermilion.

    Two or three early sanguine finches tune
Some tentative strains, to be enlarged by May or June:
    From a thrush or blackbird
    Comes now and then a word,
While an enfeebled fountain somewhere within is heard.

        Our footsteps wait awhile,
        Then draw beneath the pile,
        When an inner court outspreads
        As 'twere History's own asile,

Where the now-visioned fountain its attenuate crystal sheds
In passive lapse that seems to ignore the yon world's clamorous clutch,
And lays an insistent numbness on the place, like a cold hand's touch.

And there swaggers the Shade of a straddling King, plumed, sworded, with sensual face,
And lo, too, that of his Minister, at a bold self-centred pace:
   Sheer in the sun they pass; and thereupon all is still,
Save the mindless fountain tinkling on with thin enfeebled will.

NOON

The heaviness of noon pervaded the scene, and under its influence the sheep had ceased to feed. Nobody was standing at the Cross, the few inhabitants being indoors at their dinner. No human being was on the down, and no human eye or interest but Anne's seemed to be concerned with it. The bees still worked on, and the butterflies did not rest from roving, their smallness seeming to shield them from the stagnating effect that this turning moment of day had on larger creatures. Otherwise all was still.

The Trumpet-Major

The oat-harvest began, and all the men were afield under a monochromatic Lammas sky, amid the trembling air and short shadows of noon. Indoors nothing was to be heard save the droning of blue-bottle flies; out-of-doors the whetting of scythes and the hiss of tressy oat-ears rubbing together as their perpendicular stalks of amber-yellow fell heavily to each swath. Every drop of moisture not in the men's bottles and flagons in the form of cider was raining as perspiration from their foreheads and cheeks. A drought was everywhere else.

Far from the Madding Crowd

The Sunshade

Ah — it's the skeleton of a lady's sunshade,
   Here at my feet in the hard rock's chink,
   Merely a naked sheaf of wires! —
   Twenty years have gone with their livers and diers
   Since it was silked in its white or pink.

Noonshine riddles the ribs of the sunshade,
   No more a screen from the weakest ray;
   Nothing to tell us the hue of its dyes,
   Nothing but rusty bones as it lies
   In its coffin of stone, unseen till to-day.

Where is the woman who carried that sunshade
   Up and down this seaside place? —
   Little thumb standing against its stem,

Thoughts perhaps bent on a love-stratagem,
Softening yet more the already soft face!

Is the fair woman who carried that sunshade
  A skeleton just as her property is,
  Laid in the chink that none may scan?
  And does she regret — if regret dust can —
  The vain things thought when she flourished this?
Swanage Cliffs

SKIES AND CLOUDS

It was one of those cloudless days which sometimes occur in Wessex and elsewhere between days of cold and wet, as if intercalated by caprice of the weather-god.

Jude the Obscure

More often, Hardy describes every imaginable kind of cloud and sky.

[1870] *August.* In Cornwall. The smoke from a chimney droops over the roof like a feather in a girl's hat.[93] Clouds, dazzling white, retain their shape by the half-hour, motionless, & so far below the blue that one can almost see round them.

Memoranda I

The weather was far different from that of the evening before. The yellow and vapoury sunset which had wrapped up Eustacia from [Clym's] parting gaze had presaged change. It was one of those not infrequent days of an English June which are as wet and boisterous as November. The cold clouds hastened on in a body, as if painted on a moving slide.

The Return of the Native

Within the walls all was silence, chaos, and obscurity, till towards eleven o'clock, when the thick immovable cloud that had dulled the daytime broke into a scudding fleece, through which the moon forded her way as a nebulous spot of watery white, sending light enough, though of a rayless kind, into the castle chambers to show the confusion that reigned there.

A Laodicean

It was the evening of a fine spring day. The descending sun appeared as a nebulous blaze of amber light, its outline being lost in cloudy masses hanging round it like wild locks of hair.

Under the Greenwood Tree

The scene without grew darker; mud-coloured clouds bellied downwards from the sky

69

like vast hammocks slung across it, and with the increase of night a stormy wind arose; but as yet there was no rain.

The Return of the Native

The bonfires going up over the heath lit both land and sky:

These tinctured the silent bosom of the clouds above them and lit up their ephemeral caves, which seemed thenceforth to become scalding caldrons.

The Return of the Native

As Bathsheba sits by the wayside in painful thought:

Above the dark margin of the earth appeared foreshores and promontories of coppery cloud, bounding a green and pellucid expanse in the western sky. Amaranthine glosses came over them then, and the unresting world wheeled her round to a contrasting prospect eastward, in the shape of indecisive and palpitating stars. She gazed upon their silent throes amid the shades of space, but realized none at all. Her troubled spirit was far away with Troy.

Far from the Madding Crowd

With their minds on these things [Giles and Grace] passed so far round the hill that the whole west sky was revealed. Between the broken clouds they could see far into the recesses of heaven as they mused and walked, the eye journeying on under a species of golden arcades, and past fiery obstructions, fancied cairns, logan-stones, stalactites and stalagmites of topaz. Deeper than this their gaze passed thin flakes of incandescence, till it plunged into a bottomless medium of soft green fire.

The Woodlanders

He Prefers Her Earthly *(page 47) is one of Hardy's most beautiful poems with a sky setting; the following illustrates a more prosaic, ironic approach which he knew to be another kind of realism:*

Suspense

A clamminess hangs over all like a clout,
The fields are a water-colour washed out,
The sky at its rim leaves a chink of light,
Like the lid of a pot that will not close tight.

She is away by the groaning sea,
Strained at the heart, and waiting for me:
Between us our foe from a hid retreat
Is watching, to wither us if we meet. . . .

70

But it matters little, however we fare –
Whether we meet, or I get not there;
The sky will look the same thereupon,
And the wind and the sea go groaning on.

RAIN, WIND AND STORM

From a light-hearted note observed in London:

[1874] *August.* A scene in Celbridge Place . . . It rains a little, a very mild moisture, which a duck would call nothing, a dog a pleasure, a cat possibly a good deal . . .

Memoranda I

[1876] *Aug.* Rain: like a banner of gauze waved in folds across the scene.

Memoranda I

The Figure in the Scene

It pleased her to step in front and sit
Where the cragged slope was green,
While I stood back that I might pencil it
With her amid the scene.
Till it gloomed and rained;
But I kept on, despite the drifting wet
That fell and stained
My draught, leaving for curious quizzings yet
The blots engrained.

And thus I drew her there alone,
Seated amid the gauze
Of moisture, hooded, only her outline shown,
With rainfall marked across,
– Soon passed our stay;
Yet her rainy form is the Genius still of the spot,
Immutable, yea,
Though the place now knows her no more, and has known her not
Ever since that day.

From an old note.

[1879] *July.* Rainy sunset: the sun streaming his yellow rays through the wet atmosphere like straying hair. The wet ironwork & wet slates shine.

Memoranda I

The drizzling rain increased, and drops from the trees at the wayside fell noisily upon the hard road beneath them, which reflected from its glassy surface the faint halo of light hanging over the lamps of the adjacent town.

Desperate Remedies

(The same picture of the 'borough lights' in a 'haloed view' was to appear in the poem Hardy wrote after Emma's death, called "Your Last Drive". 'Halo' or 'nimb[us]' is a favourite image.)

[1872] *Oct 30.* Returning from D[orchester]. Wet night. The town, looking back from S[tinsford] Hill, is circumscribed by a halo like an aurora: up the hill comes a broad band of turnpike road, glazed with moisture, which reflects the lustre of the mist.

Memoranda I

One afternoon it was raining in torrents. Such leaves as there were on trees at this time of year – those of the laurel and other evergreens – staggered beneath the hard blows of the drops which fell upon them, and afterwards could be seen trickling down the stems beneath and silently entering the ground. The surface of the mill-pond leapt up in a thousand spirits under the same downfall, and clucked like a hen in the rat-holes along the banks as it undulated under the wind.

The Trumpet-Major

At Higher Crowstairs up on the down:

The level rainstorm smote walls, slopes, and hedges like the clothyard shafts of Senlac and Crecy. Such sheep and outdoor animals as had no shelter stood with their buttocks to the winds; while the tails of little birds trying to roost on some scraggy thorn were blown inside out like umbrellas. The gable end of the cottage was stained with wet, and the eavesdroppings flapped against the wall.

The Three Strangers

The rain came down unmercifully, the booming wind caught it, bore it across the plain, whizzed it against the carriage like a sower sowing his seed.

The Hand of Ethelberta

It was so high a situation, this field, that the rain had no occasion to fall, but raced along horizontally upon the yelling wind, sticking into them like glass splinters till they were wet through. Tess had not known till now what was really meant by that. There are degrees of dampness, and a very little is called being wet through in common talk. But to stand working slowly in a field, and feel the creep of rain-water, first in legs and shoulders, then on hips and head, then at back, front, and sides, and yet to work on till the leaden light diminishes and marks that the sun is down, demands a distinct modicum of stoicism, even of valour.

Tess of the d'Urbervilles

A Wet Night

I pace along, the rain shafts riddling me,
Mile after mile out by the moorland way,
And up the hill, and through the ewe-leaze gray
Into the lane, and round the corner tree;

Where, as my clothing clams me, mire-bestarred,
And the enfeebled light dies out of the day,
Leaving the liquid shades to reign, I say
'This is a hardship to be calendared!'

Yet sires of mine now perished and forgot,
When worse beset, ere roads were shapen here,
And night and storm were foes indeed to fear,
Times numberless have trudged across this spot
In sturdy muteness on their strenuous lot,
And taking all such toils as trifles mere.[94]

Equally Hardy observing the rain could see the funny side — as in a long note of a very wet stay in Weymouth when his mother came to visit in August 1879, with:

. . . the [excursion] steamer-bell ringing persistently, and nobody going on board except an unfortunate boys' school that had come eight miles by train that morning to spend a happy day by the sea. The rain goes into their baskets of provisions, and runs out a strange mixture of cake-juice and mustard-water, but they try to look as if they were enjoying it — all except the pale thin assistant-master who has come with them, and whose face is tragic with his responsibilities . . .

The Life of Thomas Hardy

The note (which he had transferred from his notebook) ends thus:

At Weymouth, contd. Windy: chimney board necessary because of the high winds. Can hear the seven of them growling behind this chimney-board at nights. You open the window; in comes the gale, down falls the chimney-board, open bursts the door. The front door follows suit in bursting open. The carpet rises & falls in billows.

Memoranda I

The young Thomas, in his daily walk from Higher Bockhampton to school in Dorchester, evidently knew all kinds of weather and the different sounds made by the rain falling on different objects or vegetation (page 103). Winds are also personalities to be reckoned with in his writings, their behaviour observed in meticulous detail — as, for example, in the marvellous description of Gabriel's midnight experience on the hill. As usual, Hardy's sharp and careful note-taking, allied with his

73

sensitive imagination and skill with words, brings the reader very close to nature. He knew how a 'neighbouring hill . . . formed variable currents in the wind', and how when 'the night wind died out . . . the quivering little pools in the cup-like hollows of the stones lay still,[95] *He could describe the north wind as:*

that not unacceptable compromise between the atmospheric cutlery of the eastern blast and the spongy gales of the west quarter.

The Woodlanders

As Clym walks on the heath,

Vapours from other continents arrived upon the wind, which curled and parted round him as he walked on.

The Return of the Native

The next scene is a tempestuous afternoon in the following month, and Fancy Day is discovered walking from her father's home towards Mellstock.

A single vast gray cloud covered the country, from which the small rain and mist had just begun to blow down in wavy sheets, alternately thick and thin. The trees of the fields and plantations writhed like miserable men as the air wound its way swiftly among them: the lowest portions of their trunks that had hardly ever been known to move, were visibly rocked by the fiercer gusts, distressing the mind by its painful unwontedness, as when a strong man is seen to shed tears. Low-hanging boughs went up and down; high and erect boughs went to and fro; the blasts being so irregular, and divided into so many cross-currents, that neighbouring branches of the same tree swept the skies in independent motions, crossed each other, or became entangled. Across the open spaces flew flocks of green and yellowish leaves which, after travelling a long distance from their parent trees, reached the ground and lay there with their under-sides upwards.

As the rain and wind increased, and Fancy's bonnet-ribbons leapt more and more snappishly against her chin, she paused on entering Mellstock-Lane to consider her latitude, and the distance to a place of shelter.

Under the Greenwood Tree

No sooner had [Grace] retired to rest that night than the wind began to rise, and after a few prefatory blasts to be accompanied by rain. The wind grew more violent, and as the storm went on it was difficult to believe that no opaque body, but only an invisible colourless thing, was trampling and climbing over the roof, making branches creak, springing out of the trees upon the chimney, popping its head into the flue, and shrieking and blaspheming at every corner of the walls. As in the grisly story, the assailant was a spectre which could be felt but not seen. She had never before been so struck with the devilry of a gusty night in a wood, because she had never been so entirely alone in spirit as she was now.

The Woodlanders

The great storm on the heath begins:

To Clym's regret it began to rain and blow hard as the evening advanced. The wind rasped and scraped at the corners of the house, and filliped the eavesdroppings like peas against the panes. He walked restlessly about the untenanted rooms, stopping strange noises in windows and doors by jamming splinters of wood into the casements and crevices, and pressing together the lead-work of the quarries where it had become loosened from the glass. It was one of those nights when cracks in the walls of old churches widen, when ancient stains on the ceilings of decayed manor-houses are renewed and enlarged from the size of a man's hand to an area of many feet.

The Return of the Native

This passage (which obviously has affinities with the poem "Night-Time in Mid-Fall" on page 52), continues into a long description of the storm in which both Wildeve and Eustacia were to lose their lives.[96] *There are many vivid accounts of storms in Hardy's writings, including one of a storm at sea by the Chesil Beach:*

They started through the twanging and spinning storm. The sea rolled and rose so high on their left, and was so near them on their right, that it seemed as if they were traversing its bottom like the Children of Israel. Nothing but the frail bank of pebbles divided them from the raging gulf without, and at every bank of the tide against it the ground shook, the shingle clashed, the spray rose vertically, and was blown over their heads. Quantities of sea-water trickled through the pebble wall, and ran in rivulets across their path to join the sea within. The 'Island' was an island still.

They had not realized the force of the elements till now. Pedestrians had often been blown into the sea hereabouts, and drowned, owing to a sudden breach in the bank; which, however, had something of a supernatural power in being able to close up and join itself together again after such disruption, like Satan's form when, cut in two by the sword of Michael,

> 'The ethereal substance closed,
> Not long divisible.'[97]

Her clothing offered more resistance to the wind than his, and she was consequently in the greater danger. It was impossible to refuse his proffered aid. First he gave his arm, but the wind tore them apart as easily as coupled cherries.

The Well-Beloved

Perhaps the most detailed observation of a storm, extending over many pages as the story's action develops, comes in Far from the Madding Crowd. *It begins with the presages of storm noted by Gabriel Oak, who fears for the harvested, but still uncovered, wheat:*

One night, at the end of August . . . when the weather was yet dry and sultry, a man stood motionless in the stockyard of Weatherbury Upper Farm, looking at the moon and sky.

The night had a sinister aspect. A heated breeze from the south slowly fanned the summits of lofty objects, and in the sky dashes of buoyant cloud were sailing in a course at right angles to that of another stratum, neither of them in the direction of the breeze below. The moon, as seen through these films, had a lurid metallic look. The fields were sallow with the impure light, and all were tinged in monochrome, as if beheld through stained glass. The same evening the sheep had trailed homeward head to tail, the behaviour of the rooks had been confused, and the horses had moved with timidity and caution.

Thunder was imminent, and, taking some secondary appearances into consideration, it was likely to be followed by one of the lengthened rains which mark the close of dry weather for the season. Before twelve hours had passed a harvest atmosphere would be a bygone thing. . . .

Gabriel proceeded towards his home. In approaching the door, his toe kicked something which felt and sounded soft, leathery, and distended, like a boxing-glove. It was a large toad humbly travelling across the path. Oak took it up, thinking it might be better to kill the creature to save it from pain; but finding it uninjured, he placed it again among the grass. He knew what this direct message from the Great Mother[98] meant. And soon came another.

When he struck a light indoors there appeared upon the table a thin glistening streak, as if a brush of varnish had been lightly dragged across it. Oak's eyes followed the serpentine sheen to the other side, where it led up to a huge brown garden-slug, which had come indoors to-night for reasons of its own. It was Nature's second way of hinting to him that he was to prepare for foul weather.

Oak sat down meditating for nearly an hour. During this time two black spiders, of the kind common in thatched houses, promenaded the ceiling, ultimately dropping to the floor. This reminded him that if there was one class of manifestation on this matter that he thoroughly understood, it was the instincts of sheep. He left the room, ran across two or three fields towards the flock, got upon a hedge, and looked over among them.

They were crowded close together on the other side around some furze bushes, and the first peculiarity observable was that, on the sudden appearance of Oak's head over the fence, they did not stir or run away. They had now a terror of something greater than their terror of man. But this was not the most noteworthy feature: they were all grouped in such a way that their tails, without a single exception, were towards that half of the horizon from which the storm threatened. There was an inner circle closely huddled, and outside these they radiated wider apart, the pattern formed by the flock as a whole not being unlike a vandyked lace collar, to which the clump of furze-bushes stood in the position of a wearer's neck.

This was enough to re-establish him in his original opinion. . . .

. . . Every voice in nature was unanimous in bespeaking change. But two distinct translations attached to these dumb expressions. Apparently there was to be a thunder-storm, and afterwards a cold continuous rain. The creeping things seemed to know all about the later rain, but little of the interpolated thunder-storm; whilst the sheep knew all about the thunder-storm and nothing of the later rain.

This complication of weathers being uncommon, was all the more to be feared. . . .

[Gabriel] went again into the lone night. A hot breeze, as if breathed from the parted lips of some dragon about to swallow the globe, fanned him from the south, while directly opposite in the north rose a grim misshapen body of cloud, in the very teeth of the wind. So unnaturally did it rise that one could fancy it to be lifted by machinery from below. Meanwhile the faint cloudlets had flown back into the south-east corner of the sky, as if in terror of the large cloud, like a young brood gazed in upon by some monster. . . .

. . . Time went on, and the moon vanished not to reappear. It was the farewell of the ambassador previous to war. The night had a haggard look, like a sick thing; and there came finally an utter expiration of air from the whole heaven in the form of a slow breeze, which might have been likened to a death.

Gabriel begins to thatch the ricks for their protection – and the storm erupts:

A light flapped over the scene, as if reflected from phosphorescent wings crossing the sky, and a rumble filled the air. It was the first move of the approaching storm.

The second peal was noisy, with comparatively little visible lightning.

. . . Then there came a third flash. Manoeuvres of a most extraordinary kind were going on in the vast firmamental hollows overhead. The lightning now was the colour of silver, and gleamed in the heavens like a mailed army. Rumbles became rattles. Gabriel from his elevated position could see over the landscape at least half-a-dozen miles in front. Every hedge, bush, and tree was distinct as in a line engraving. In a paddock in the same direction was a herd of heifers, and the forms of these were visible at this moment in the act of galloping about in the wildest and maddest confusion, flinging their heels and tails high into the air, their heads to earth. A poplar in the immediate foreground was like an ink stroke on burnished tin. Then the picture vanished, leaving the darkness so intense that Gabriel worked entirely by feeling with his hands.

He had stuck his ricking-rod, or poniard, as it was indifferently called – a long iron lance, polished by handling – into the stack, used to support the sheaves instead of the support called a groom used on houses. A blue light appeared in the zenith, and in some indescribable manner flickered down near the top of the rod. It was the fourth of the larger flashes. A moment later there was a smack – smart, clear, and short. Gabriel felt his position to be anything but a safe one, and he resolved to descend.

Not a drop of rain had fallen as yet.

Having improvised a lightning conductor, Gabriel resolves to continue thatching:

. . . Before Oak had laid his hands upon his tools again out leapt the fifth flash, with the spring of a serpent and the shout of a fiend. It was green as an emerald, and the reverberation was stunning.

Bathsheba joins him and carries reed-sheaves up the ladder to him:

At her third ascent the rick suddenly brightened with the brazen glare of shining majolica – every knot in every straw was visible. On the slope in front of him appeared two human shapes, black as jet. The rick lost its sheen – the shapes vanished. Gabriel turned his head. It had been the sixth flash which had come from the east behind him, and the two dark forms on the slope had been the shadows of himself and Bathsheba.

Then came the peal. It hardly was credible that such a heavenly light could be the parent of such a diabolical sound.

"How terrible!" she exclaimed, and clutched him by the sleeve. Gabriel turned and steadied her on her aerial perch by holding her arm. At the same moment, while he was still reversed in his attitude, there was more light, and he saw, as it were, a copy of the tall poplar tree on the hill drawn black on the wall of the barn. It was the shadow of that tree, thrown across by a secondary flash in the west.

The next flare came. Bathsheba was on the ground now, shouldering another sheaf, and she bore its dazzle without flinching – thunder and all – and again ascended with the load. There was then a silence everywhere for four or five minutes, and the crunch of the spars, as Gabriel hastily drove them in, could again be distinctly heard. He thought the crisis of the storm had passed. But there came a burst of light.

"Hold on!" said Gabriel, taking the sheaf from her shoulder, and grasping her arm again.

Heaven opened then, indeed. The flash was almost too novel for its inexpressibly dangerous nature to be at once realized, and they could only comprehend the magnificence of its beauty. It sprang from east, west, north, south, and was a perfect dance of death. The forms of skeletons appeared in the air, shaped with blue fire for bones – dancing, leaping, striding, racing around, and mingling altogether in unparalleled confusion. With these were intertwined undulating snakes of green, and behind these was a broad mass of lesser light. Simultaneously came from every part of the tumbling sky what may be called a shout; since, though no shout ever came near it, it was more of the nature of a shout than of anything else earthly. In the meantime one of the grisly forms had alighted upon the point of Gabriel's rod, to run invisibly down it, down into the chain, and into the earth. Gabriel was almost blinded, and he could feel Bathsheba's warm arm tremble in his hand – a sensation novel and thrilling enough; but love, life, everything human, seemed small and trifling in such close juxtaposition with an infuriated universe.

Oak had hardly time to gather up these impressions into a thought, and to see how strangely the red feather of her hat shone in this light, when the tall tree on the hill before mentioned seemed on fire to a white heat, and a new one among these terrible voices mingled with the last crash of those preceding. It was a stupefying blast, harsh and pitiless, and it fell upon their ears in a dead, flat blow, without that reverberation which lends the tones of a drum to more distant thunder. By the lustre reflected from every part of the earth and from the wide domical scoop above it, he saw that the tree was sliced down the whole length of its tall, straight stem, a huge riband of bark being apparently flung off. The other portion remained erect, and revealed the bared surface as a strip of white down the front. The lightning had struck the tree. A sulphurous smell filled the air; then all was silent, and black as a cave in Hinnom.[99]

. . . The darkness was now impenetrable by the sharpest vision. . . . At last he said –

78

"The storm seems to have passed now, at any rate."

"I think so too," said Bathsheba, "Though there are multitudes of gleams, look!"

The sky was now filled with an incessant light, frequent repetition melting into complete continuity, as an unbroken sound results from the successive strokes on a gong.

"Nothing serious," said he. "I cannot understand no rain falling. But Heaven be praised, it is all the better for us. I am going up again."

*   *   *

Tired, Bathsheba retires. Gabriel continues thatching in a reverie:

He was disturbed in his meditation by a grating noise from the coachhouse. It was the vane on the roof turning round, and this change in the wind was the signal for a disastrous rain.

*   *   *

It was now five o'clock, and the dawn was promising to break in hues of drab and ash.

The air changed its temperature and stirred itself more vigorously. Cool breezes coursed in transparent eddies round Oak's face. The wind shifted yet a point or two and blew stronger. In ten minutes every wind of heaven seemed to be roaming at large. Some of the thatching on the wheat-stacks was now whirled fantastically aloft, and had to be replaced and weighted with some rails that lay at hand . . . A huge drop of rain smote his face, the wind snarled round every corner, the trees rocked to the bases of their trunks, and the twigs clashed in strife . . . The rain came on in earnest, and Oak soon felt the water to be tracking cold and clammy routes down his back. Ultimately he was reduced well-nigh to a homogeneous sop, and the dyes of his clothes trickled down and stood in a pool at the foot of the ladder. The rain stretched obliquely through the dull atmosphere in liquid spines, unbroken in continuity between their beginnings in the clouds and their points in him.

Far from the Madding Crowd

She Hears the Storm

> There was a time in former years –
>   While my roof-tree was his –
> When I should have been distressed by fears
>   At such a night as this!
>
> I should have murmured anxiously
>   'The pricking rain strikes cold;
> His road is bare of hedge or tree,
>   And he is getting old.'

But now the fitful chimney-roar,
    The drone of Thorncombe trees,
The Froom in flood upon the moor,
    The mud of Mellstock leaze,

The candle slanting sooty-wick'd,
    The thuds upon the thatch,
The eaves-drops on the window flicked,
    The clacking garden-hatch,

And what they mean to wayfarers,
    I scarcely heed or mind;
He has won that storm-tight roof of hers
    Which Earth grants all her kind.

FOG

                    The rolling brume
That parts, and joins, and parts again below us
In ragged restlessness, unscreens by fits
The quality of the scene . . .

The Dynasts

At dusk Hayward went to the door, where he stood till he heard the voices of his guests from the direction of the low grounds, now covered with their frequent fleece of fog. The voices grew more distinct, and then on the white surface of the fog there appeared two trunkless heads, from which bodies and a horse and a cart gradually extended as the approaching pair rose towards the house.

The Romantic Adventures of a Milkmaid

At daybreak Tess and Angel Clare rise for the skimming and milking:

They could then see the faint summer fogs in layers, woolly, level, and apparently no thicker than counterpanes, spread about the meadows in detached remnants of small extent. On the gray moisture of the grass were marks where the cows had lain through the night – dark-green islands of dry herbage the size of their carcases, in the general sea of dew. From each island proceeded a serpentine trail, by which the cow had rambled away to feed after getting up, at the end of which trail they found her; the snoring puff from her nostrils, when she recognized them, making an intenser little fog of her own amid the prevailing one. . . .

Or perhaps the summer fog was more general, and the meadows lay like a white sea, out of which the scattered trees rose like dangerous rocks. Birds would soar through it into the upper radiance, and hang on the wing sunning themselves, or alight on the wet rails subdividing the mead, which now shone like glass rods. Minute diamonds of moisture from the mist hung, too, upon Tess's eyelashes, and drops upon her hair, like seed pearls.

Tess of the d'Urbervilles

Joseph Poorgrass leads the waggon containing Fanny's coffin to Weatherbury:

The afternoon drew on apace, and, looking to the right towards the sea as he walked beside the horse, Poorgrass saw strange clouds and scrolls of mist rolling over the long ridges which girt the landscape in that quarter. They came in yet greater volumes, and indolently crept across the intervening valleys, and around the withered papery flags of the moor and river brinks. Then their dank spongy forms closed in upon the sky. It was a sudden overgrowth of atmospheric fungi which had their roots in the neighbouring sea, and by the time that horse, man, and corpse entered Yalbury Great Wood, these silent workings of an invisible hand had reached them, and they were completely enveloped, this being the first arrival of the autumn fogs, and the first fog of the series.

The air was as an eye suddenly struck blind. The waggon and its load rolled no longer on the horizontal division between clearness and opacity, but were imbedded in an elastic body of a monotonous pallor throughout. There was no perceptible motion in the air, not a visible drop of water fell upon a leaf of the beeches, birches, and firs composing the wood on either side. The trees stood in an attitude of intentness, as if they waited longingly for a wind to come and rock them. A startling quiet overhung all surrounding things – so completely, that the crunching of the waggon-wheels was as a great noise, and small rustles, which had never obtained a hearing except by night, were distinctly individualized.

Joseph Poorgrass looked round upon his sad burden as it loomed faintly through the flowering laurustinus, then at the unfathomable gloom amid the high trees on each hand, indistinct, shadowless, and spectre-like in their monochrome of grey. He felt anything but cheerful, and wished he had the company even of a child or dog. Stopping the horse he listened. Not a footstep or wheel was audible anywhere around, and the dead silence was broken only by a heavy particle falling from a tree through the evergreens and alighting with a smart rap upon the coffin of poor Fanny. The fog had by this time saturated the trees, and this was the first dropping of water from the overbrimming leaves. The hollow echo of its fall reminded the waggoner painfully of the grim Leveller.[100] Then hard by came down another drop, then two or three. Presently there was a continual tapping of these heavy drops upon the dead leaves, the road, and the travellers. The nearer boughs were beaded with the mist to the greyness of aged men, and the rusty-red leaves of the beeches were hung with similar drops, like diamonds on auburn hair.

Far from the Madding Crowd

The trees fret fitfully and twist,
Shutters rattle and carpets heave,
Slime is the dust of yestereve,
 And in the streaming mist
Fishes might seem to fin a passage if they list.

  But to his feet,
  Drawing nigh and nigher
  A hidden seat,
  The fog is sweet
  And the wind a lyre.

A vacant sameness grays the sky,
A moisture gathers on each knop
Of the bramble, rounding to a drop,
 That greets the goer-by
With the cold listless lustre of a dead man's eye.

  But to her sight,
  Drawing nigh and nigher
  Its deep delight,
  The fog is bright
  And the wind a lyre.

THE FOUR SEASONS

The Five Students

The sparrow dips in his wheel-rut bath,
 The sun grows passionate-eyed,
And boils the dew to smoke by the paddock-path;
 As strenuously we stride, –
Five of us; dark He, fair He, dark She, fair She, I,
 All beating by.

 The air is shaken, the high-road hot,
  Shadowless swoons the day,
The greens are sobered and cattle at rest; but not

We on our urgent way, –
Four of us; fair She, dark She, fair He, I are there,
But one – elsewhere.

Autumn moulds the hard fruit mellow,
And forward still we press
Through moors, briar-meshed plantations, clay-pits yellow,
As in the spring hours – yes,
Three of us; fair He, fair She, I, as heretofore,
But – fallen one more.

The leaf drops: earthworms draw it in
At night-time noiselessly,
The fingers of birch and beech are skeleton-thin,
And yet on the beat are we, –
Two of us; fair She, I. But no more left to go
The track we know.

Icicles tag the church-aisle leads,
The flag-rope gibbers hoarse,
The home-bound foot-folk wrap their snow-flaked heads,
Yet I still stalk the course, –
One of us. . . . Dark and fair He, dark and fair She, gone:
The rest – anon.

The four seasons as an image of the stages of life is a favourite theme with Hardy, as a later look at his imagery will confirm; this poem, however, stands as sensitive natural description. Hardy, bred in the country, was inevitably aware of the seasons and observed them closely, knowledgeably, and idiosyncratically.

Not far from Overcombe Mill:

. . . a steep slope rose high into the sky, merging in a wide and open down, now littered with sheep newly shorn. The upland by its height completely sheltered the mill and village from north winds, making summers of springs, reducing winds to autumn temperatures, and permitting myrtle to flourish in the open air.

The Trumpet-Major

AUTUMN

[1921] *Oct. 18.* In afternoon to Stinsford with F. A matchless Oct. sunshine, mist, & turning leaves.

Memoranda II

A more beautiful October morning . . . never beamed upon the Welland groves. The yearly dissolution of leafage was setting in apace. The foliage of the park trees rapidly resolved itself into the multitude of complexions which mark the subtle grades of decay, reflecting wet lights of such innumerable hues that it was a wonder to think their beauties only a repetition of scenes that had been exhibited there on scores of previous Octobers, and had been allowed to pass away without a single dirge from the imperturbable beings who walked among them. Far in the shadows semi-opaque screens of blue haze made mysteries of the commonest gravel-pit, dingle, or recess.

Two on a Tower

The season was that period in the autumn when the foliage alone of an ordinary plantation is rich enough in hues to exhaust the chromatic combinations of an artist's palette. Most lustrous of all are the beeches, graduating from bright rust red at the extremity of the boughs to a bright yellow at their inner parts; young oaks are still of a neutral green; Scotch firs and hollies are nearly blue; whilst occasional dottings of other varieties give maroons and purples of every tinge.

A Pair of Blue Eyes

It was an afternoon which had a fungous smell out of doors, all being sunless and stagnant overhead and around. The various species of trees had begun to assume the more distinctive colours of their decline, and where there had been one pervasive green were now twenty greenish yellows, the air in the vistas between them being half opaque with blue exhalation.

The Hand of Ethelberta

1917. *Last week in October.* – The trees are undressing, flinging down their brilliant robes and laces on the grass, road, roof, and window-sill. One leaf waltzes down across the panes every second almost. One gets caught in a spider's web, and dangles in the breeze like an executed criminal in raiment of gold.
Note cancelled from The Life of Thomas Hardy.

Last Week in October

    The trees are undressing, and fling in many places –
    On the gray road, the roof, the window-sill –
    Their radiant robes and ribbons and yellow laces;
      A leaf each second so is flung at will,
Here, there, another and another, still and still.

    A spider's web has caught one while downcoming,
    That stays there dangling when the rest pass on;
    Like a suspended criminal hangs he, mumming
      In golden garb, while one yet green, high yon,
Trembles, as fearing such a fate for himself anon.

Autumn had begun to make itself felt and seen in bolder and less subtle ways than at first. In the morning now, on coming downstairs, in place of a yellowish-green leaf or two lying in a corner of the lowest step, which had been the only previous symptoms around the house, [Ethelberta] saw dozens of them playing at corkscrews in the wind, directly the door was opened. Beyond, towards the sea, the slopes and scarps that had been muffled with a thick robe of cliff herbage, were showing their chill grey substance through the withered verdure, like the background of velvet whence the pile has been fretted away. Unexpected breezes broomed and rasped the smooth bay in evanescent patches of stippled shade, and, besides the small boats, the ponderous lighters used in shipping stone were hauled up the beach in anticipation of the equinoctial attack.

The Hand of Ethelberta

It was a yellow, lustrous, late autumn day, one of those days of the quarter when morning and evening seem to meet together without the intervention of a noon.

Desperate Remedies

[1872] *Nov. 13.* The first frost of autumn. Outdoor folk look reflective. The scarlet runners are dishevelled; geraniums wounded in the leaf; open-air cucumber leaves have collapsed like green umbrellas with all the stays broken.

Memoranda I

Autumn drew shiveringly to its end. One day something seemed to be gone from the gardens; the tenderer leaves of vegetables had shrunk under the first smart frost, and hung like faded linen rags; the forest leaves, which had been descending at leisure, descended in haste and in multitudes, and all the golden colours that had hung overhead were now crowded together in a degraded mass underfoot, where the fallen myriads got redder and hornier, and curled themselves up to rot.

The Woodlanders

June Leaves and Autumn

I

Lush summer lit the trees to green;
   But in the ditch hard by
Lay dying boughs some hand unseen
Had lopped when first with festal mien
   They matched their mates on high.
It seemed a melancholy fate
That leaves but brought to birth so late
   Should rust there, red and numb,
In quickened fall, while all their race
Still joyed aloft in pride of place
   With store of days to come.

At autumn-end I fared that way,
　And traced those boughs fore-hewn
Whose leaves, awaiting their decay
In slowly browning shades, still lay
　Where they had lain in June
And now, no less embrowned and curst
Than if they had fallen with the first,
　Nor known a morning more,
Lay there alongside, dun and sere,
Those that at my last wandering here
　Had length of days in store.
19 November 1898

WINTER

Winter had almost come, and unsettled weather made [Elizabeth-Jane] still more dependent upon indoor resources. But there were certain early winter days in Casterbridge – days of firmamental exhaustion which followed angry south-westerly tempests – when, if the sun shone, the air was like velvet.

The Mayor of Casterbridge

The open hills were airy and clear, and the remote atmosphere appeared, as it often appears on a fine winter day, in distinct planes of illumination independently toned, the rays which lit the nearer tracts of landscape streaming visibly across those further off; a stratum of ensaffroned light was imposed on a stratum of deep blue, and behind these lay still remoter scenes wrapped in frigid grey.

The Return of the Native

It was a fine and quiet afternoon, about three o'clock; but the winter solstice having stealthily come on, the lowness of the sun caused the hour to seem later than it actually was, there being little here to remind an inhabitant that he must unlearn his summer experience of the sky as a dial. In the course of many days and weeks sunrise had advanced its quarters from north-east to south-east, sunset had receded from north-west to south-west; but Egdon had hardly heeded the change.

The Return of the Native

But none knew better than Hardy how even greater change could come:

[Eustacia] reached the wicket at Mistover Knap, but before opening it she turned and faced the heath once more. The form of Rainbarrow stood above the hills, and the moon stood above Rainbarrow. The air was charged with silence and frost.

The Return of the Native

Winter brought suffering to man and beast.
Lady Baxby's brother is with the Parliamentary forces in the Civil War:

The first frosts of autumn had touched the grass, and shrivelled the more delicate leaves of the creepers; and she thought of William sleeping on the chilly ground, under the strain of these hardships. Tears flooded her eyes . . .

Anna, Lady Baxby. (A Group of Noble Dames.)

One afternoon it began to freeze, and the frost increased with evening, which drew on like a stealthy tightening of bonds. It was a time when in cottages the breath of the sleepers freezes to the sheets; when round the drawing-room fire of a thick-walled mansion the sitter's backs are cold, even whilst their faces are all aglow. Many a small bird went to bed supperless that night among the bare boughs.

Far from the Madding Crowd

Boldwood was listlessly noting how the frost had hardened and glazed the surface of the snow, till it shone in the red eastern light with the polish of marble; how, in some portions of the slope, withered grass bents, encased in icicles, bristled through the smooth wan coverlet in the twisted and curved shapes of old Venetian glass; and how the footprints of a few birds, which had hopped over the snow whilst it lay in the state of a soft fleece, were now frozen to a short permanency.

Far from the Madding Crowd

Frost always filled Hardy with a dread which caused him to use it as a frequent and potent symbol.[101] *At the same time his sharp mind and observant eye made him analyse factually how snowflakes behave in falling, how*

Brambles, though churlish when handled, are kindly shelter in early winter, being the latest of the deciduous bushes to lose their leaves.

The Return of the Native

– and the successive stages of winter's march:

For dreariness nothing could surpass a prospect in the outskirts of a certain town and military station, many miles north of Weatherbury, at a later hour on this same snowy evening – if that may be called a prospect of which the chief constituent was darkness. . . .

The scene was a public path, bordered on the left hand by a river, behind which rose a high wall. On the right was a tract of land, partly meadow and partly moor, reaching at its remote verge, to a wide undulating upland.

The changes of the seasons are less obtrusive on spots of this kind than amid woodland scenery. Still, to a close observer, they are just as perceptible; the difference is that their media of manifestation are less trite and familiar than such well-known ones as the bursting of the buds or the fall of the leaf. Many are not so stealthy and gradual as we may be apt to imagine in considering the general torpidity of a moor or waste. Winter, in coming to the country hereabout, advanced in well-marked stages, wherein might have been successively observed the retreat of the snakes, the transformation of the ferns, the filling of the pools, a rising of fogs, the embrowning by frost, the collapse of the fungi, and an obliteration by snow.

This climax of the series had been reached to-night on the afore said moor, and for the first time in the season its irregularities were forms without features; suggestive of anything, proclaiming nothing, and without more character than of being the limit of something else − the lowest layer of a firmament of snow. From this chaotic skyful of crowding flakes the mead and moor momentarily received additional clothing, only to appear momentarily more naked thereby. The vast arch of cloud above was strangely low, and formed as it were the roof of a large cavern, gradually sinking in upon its floor; for the instinctive thought was that the snow lining the heavens and that encrusting the earth would soon unite into one mass without any intervening stratum of air at all.

Far from the Madding Crowd

In the light-hearted poem "Snow in the Suburbs" (page 37) Hardy actually spoofs some of his own favourite tragic images − such as the whiteness he always associates with death or tragedy, the webs of fate in which we are entangled, the losing of path or identity in a changing landscape. But his descriptions of the full grip of winter are no joke.

There had not been such a winter for years. It came on in stealthy and measured glides, like the moves of a chess-player. One morning the few lonely trees and the thorns of the hedgerows appeared as if they had put off a vegetable for an animal integument. Every twig was covered with a white nap as of fur grown from the rind during the night, giving it four times its usual stoutness; the whole bush or tree forming a staring sketch in white lines on the mournful gray of the sky and horizon. Cobwebs revealed their presence on sheds and walls where none had ever been observed till brought out into visibility by the crystallizing atmosphere, hanging like loops of white worsted from salient points of the out-houses, posts, and gates.

After this season of congealed dampness came a spell of dry frost, when strange birds from behind the North Pole began to arrive silently on the upland of Flintcomb-Ash; gaunt spectral creatures with tragical eyes − eyes which had witnessed scenes of cataclysmal horror in inaccessible polar regions of a magnitude such as no human being had ever conceived, in curdling temperatures that no man could endure; which had beheld the crash of icebergs and the slide of snow-hills by the shooting light of the Aurora; been half blinded by the whirl of colossal storms and terraqueous distortions; and retained the expression of feature that such scenes had engendered. . . .

Then one day a peculiar quality invaded the air of this open country. There came a moisture which was not of rain, and a cold which was not of frost. It chilled the eyeballs of [Marian and Tess], made their brows ache, penetrated to their skeletons, affecting the surface of the body less than its core. They knew that it meant snow, and in the night the snow came. . . .

The snow had followed the birds from the polar basin as a white pillar of a cloud, and individual flakes could not be seen. The blast smelt of icebergs, arctic seas, whales, and white bears, carrying the snow so that it licked the land but did not deepen on it. They trudged onwards with slanted bodies through the flossy fields, keeping as well as they could in the shelter of hedges, which, however, acted as strainers rather than screens. The air, afflicted to pallor with the hoary multitudes that infested it, twisted and spun them eccentrically, suggesting an achromatic chaos of things.

Tess of the d'Urbervilles

In The Dynasts, *the winter retreat from Moscow of the stragglers of Napoleon's Great Army, and his desertion of them, furnishes Hardy with the opportunity for one of his most curious stories of winter and death. The scene is:*

THE OPEN COUNTRY BETWEEN SMORGONI AND WILNA

The winter is more merciless, and snow continues to fall upon a deserted expanse of unenclosed land in Lithuania. Some scattered birch bushes merge in a forest in the background.

It is growing dark, though nothing distinguishes where the sun sets. There is no sound except that of a shuffling of feet in the direction of a bivouac. Here are gathered tattered men like skeletons. Their noses and ears are frost-bitten, and pus is oozing from their eyes.

These stricken shades in a limbo of gloom are among the last survivors of the French Army. Few of them carry arms. One squad, ploughing through snow above their knees, and with icicles dangling from their hair that clink like glass-lustres as they walk, go into the birch wood, and are heard chopping. They bring back boughs, with which they make a screen on the windward side, and contrive to light a fire. With their swords they cut rashers from a dead horse, and grill them in the flames, using gunpowder for salt to eat them with. Two others return from a search, with a dead rat and some candle ends. Their meal shared, some try to repair their gaping shoes and to tie up their feet, that are chilblained to the bone.

A straggler enters, who whispers to one or two soldiers of the group. A shudder runs through them at his words.

FIRST SOLDIER (*dazed*)
What – gone, do you say ? Gone ?

STRAGGLER
Yes, I say gone!
He left us at Smorgoni hours ago.
The Sacred Squadron even he has left behind.
By this time he's at Warsaw or beyond,
Full pace for Paris.

SECOND SOLDIER (*jumping up wildly*)
Gone ? How did he go?
No, surely ! He could not desert us so!

The soldiers predictably react with 'rage, grief, and despair', some insanely singing and dancing, until:

89

Exhausted, they again crouch round the fire. Officers and privates press together for warmth. Other stragglers arrive, and sit at the backs of the first. With the progress of the night the stars come out in unusual brilliancy, Sirius and those in Orion flashing like stilettos; and the frost stiffens.

The fire sinks and goes out; but the Frenchmen do not move. The day dawns, and still they sit on.

In the background enter some light horse of the Russian army, followed by KUTÚZOF himself and a few of his staff. . . . The whole detachment pauses at the sight of the French asleep. They shout; but the bivouackers give no sign.

KUTÚZOF

Go, stir them up! We slay not sleeping men.

The Russians advance and prod the French with their lances.

RUSSIAN OFFICER

Prince, here's a curious picture. They are dead.

KUTÚZOF (*with indifference*)

Oh, naturally. After the snow was down
I marked a sharpening of the air last night
We shall be stumbling on such frost-baked meats
Most of the way to Wilna.

OFFICER (*examining the bodies*)

They all sit
As if they were living still, but stiff as horns;
And even the colour has not left their cheeks,
Whereof the tears remain in strings of ice. —
It was a marvel they were not consumed:
Their clothes are cindered by the fire in front,
While at their back the frost has caked them hard.

KUTÚZOF

'Tis well. So perish Russia's enemies!

Exeunt KUTÚZOF, his staff, and the detachment of horse in the direction of Wilna; and with the advance of day the snow resumes its fall, slowly burying the dead bivouackers.

The Dynasts

Hardy could see winter as beautiful — 'Watching the full-starred heavens that winter sees' — and as a cosy time domestically: 'Though the winter fire burned brightly' . . .[102] *Yet his association of winter with tragedy and cruelty is far more typical — even in an apparently simple poem like the following. Hardy was, however, never simple. His experiments with the triolet form, where the object is to change the meaning of the opening phrase, by repetition in three different breaks and versions of the line, were part of his constant re-evaluation of meaning and experience. In these few lines he conveys three different characters: two rather sociable birds and one uncompromising stater of facts, – with whose further attitudes and significance he gives the reader (as so often) no help at all.*[103]

Winter in Durnover Field

SCENE. – *A wide stretch of fallow ground recently sown with wheat, and frozen to iron hardness. Three large birds walking about thereon, and wistfully eyeing the surface. Wind keen from north-east: sky a dull grey.*

(Triolet)

Rook. –	Throughout the field I find no grain;
	The cruel frost encrusts the cornland!
Starling. –	Aye: patient pecking now is vain
	Throughout the field, I find . . .
Rook. –	No grain!
Pigeon. –	Nor will be, comrade, till it rain,
	Or genial thawings loose the lorn land
	Throughout the field.
Rook. –	I find no grain:
	The cruel frost encrusts the cornland!

But the winter must move towards spring. In January 1891 Hardy was in London, and saw:

. . . what is called sunshine up here – a red-hot bullet hanging in a livid atmosphere – reflected from window-panes in the form of bleared copper eyes, and inflaming the sheets of plate-glass with smears of gory light. A drab snow mingled itself with liquid horse-dung, and in the river puddings of ice moved slowly on. The steamers were moored, with snow on their gangways. A captain, in sad solitude, smoked his pipe against the bulk-head of the cabin stairs. The lack of traffic made the water like a stream through a deserted metropolis. In the City George Peabody sat comfortably in his easy chair, with snow on the folds of his ample waistcoat, the top of his bare head, and shoulders, and knees.

The Life of Thomas Hardy

The month of February passed with alternations of mud and frost, rain and sleet, east winds and north-westerly gales. The hollow places in the ploughed fields showed themselves as pools of water, which had settled there from the higher levels, and had not yet found time to soak away. The birds began to get lively, and a single thrush came just before sunset each evening, and sang hopefully on the large elm-tree which stood nearest to Mrs Newberry's house. Cold blasts and brittle earth had given place to an oozing dampness more unpleasant in itself than frost; but it suggested coming spring, and its unpleasantness was of a bearable kind.

The Distracted Preacher

How do you know that the pilgrim track
Along the belting zodiac
Swept by the sun in his seeming rounds
Is traced by now to the Fishes' bounds
And into the Ram, when weeks of cloud
Have wrapt the sky in a clammy shroud,
And never as yet a tinct of spring
Has shown in the Earth's apparelling;
    O vespering bird, how do you know,
      How do you know?

How do you know, deep underground,
Hid in your bed from sight and sound,
Without a turn in temperature,
With weather life can scarce endure,
That light has won a fraction's strength,
And day put on some moments' length,
Whereof in merest rote will come,
Weeks hence, mild airs that do not numb;
    O crocus root, how do you know,
      How do you know?
February 1910

It was now the end of March. . . . Now came the days of battle between winter and spring. . . . Though spring was to the forward during the daylight, winter would reassert itself at night, and not unfrequently at other moments. Tepid airs and nipping breezes met on the confines of sunshine and shade; trembling raindrops that were still akin to frost crystals dashed themselves from the bushes as [Somerset] pursued his way from town to castle; the birds were like an orchestra waiting for the signal to strike up, and colour began to enter the country round.

A Laodicean

SPRING

The month of March arrived, and the heath showed its first faint signs of awakening from winter trance. The awakening was almost feline in its stealthiness. The pool outside the bank by Eustacia's dwelling, which seemed as dead and desolate as ever to an observer who moved and made noises in his observation, would gradually disclose a state of great animation when silently watched awhile. A timid animal world had come to life for the season. Little tadpoles and efts began to bubble up through the water, and to race along beneath it; toads made noises like very young ducks, and advanced to the margin in twos and threes; overhead, bumble-bees flew hither and thither in the thickening light, their drone coming and going like the sound of a gong.

The Return of the Native

A Backward Spring

The trees are afraid to put forth buds,
And there is timidity in the grass;
The plots lie gray where gouged by spuds,
    And whether next week will pass
Free of sly sour winds is the fret of each bush
    Of barberry waiting to bloom

Yet the snowdrop's face betrays no gloom,
And the primrose pants in its heedless push,
Though the myrtle asks if it's worth the fight
    This year with frost and rime
    To venture one more time
On delicate leaves and buttons of white
From the selfsame bough as at last year's prime,
And never to ruminate on or remember
What happened to it in mid-December.
April 1917

It was now early spring – the time of going to grass with the sheep, when they have the first feed of the meadows, before these are laid up for mowing. The wind, which had been blowing east for several weeks, had veered to the southward, and the middle of spring had come abruptly – almost without a beginning. It was that period in the vernal quarter when we may suppose the Dryads to be waking for the season. The vegetable world begins to move and swell and the saps to rise, till in the completest silence of lone gardens and trackless plantations, where everything seems helpless and still after the bond and slavery of frost, there are bustlings, strainings, united thrusts, and pulls-all-together, in comparison with which the powerful tugs of cranes and pulleys in a noisy city are but pigmy efforts.

Far from the Madding Crowd

Spring weather came on rather suddenly, the unsealing of buds that had long been swollen accomplishing itself in the space of one warm night. The rush of sap in the veins of the trees could almost be heard. The flowers of late April took up a position unseen, and looked as if they had been blooming a long while, though there had been no trace of them the day before yesterday; birds began not to mind getting wet. In-door people said they had heard the nightingale, to which out-door people replied contemptuously that they had heard him a fortnight before.

The Woodlanders

An Unkindly May

A shepherd stands by a gate in a white smock-frock:
He holds the gate ajar, intently counting his flock.

The sour spring wind is blurting boisterous-wise,
And bears on it dirty clouds across the skies;
Plantation timbers creak like rusty cranes,
And pigeons and rooks, dishevelled by late rains,
Are like gaunt vultures, sodden and unkempt,
And song-birds do not end what they attempt:
The buds have tried to open, but quite failing
Have pinched themselves together in their quailing.
The sun frowns whitely in eye-trying flaps
Through passing cloud-holes, mimicking audible taps.
'Nature, you're not commendable today!'
I think. 'Better to-morrow!' she seems to say.
That shepherd still stands in that white smock-frock,
Unnoting all things save the counting his flock.

'On a thyme-scented, bird-hatching morning in May . . .'[104]

The month was May – the time, morning. Cuckoos, thrushes, blackbirds, and sparrows gave forth a blithe confusion of song and twitter. The road was spotted white with the fallen leaves of apple-blossoms, and the sparkling grey dew still lingered on the grass and flowers. Two swans floated into view . . .

Desperate Remedies

Growth in May

I enter a daisy-and-buttercup land,
   And thence thread a jungle of grass:
Hurdles and stiles scarce visible stand
   Above the lush stems as I pass.

Hedges peer over, and try to be seen,
   And seem to reveal a dim sense
That amid such ambitious and elbow-high green
   They make a mean show as a fence.

Elsewhere the mead is possessed of the neats,
    That range not greatly above
The rich rank thicket which brushes their teats,
    And *her* gown, as she waits for her Love.
Near Chard

The last day of the story is dated just subsequent to that point in the development of the seasons when country people go to bed among nearly naked trees, are lulled to sleep by a fall of rain, and awake next morning among green ones; when the landscape appears embarrassed with the sudden weight and brilliancy of its leaves; when the night-jar comes and strikes up for the summer his tune of one note; when the apple-trees have bloomed, and the roads and orchard-grass become spotted with fallen petals; when the faces of the delicate flowers are darkened and their heads weighed down by the throng of honey-bees, which increase their humming till humming is too mild a term for the all-pervading sound; and when cuckoos, blackbirds, and sparrows, that have hitherto been merry and respectful neighbours, become noisy and persistent intimates.

Under the Greenwood Tree

When the Present has latched its postern behind my tremulous stay,
    And the May month flaps its glad green leaves like wings,
Delicate-filmed as new-spun silk, will the neighbours say,
    'He was a man who used to notice such things'?

Afterwards

'If It's Ever Spring Again'
(Song)

If it's ever spring again,
    Spring again
I shall go where went I when
Down the moor-cock splashed, and hen,
Seeing me not, amid their flounder,
Standing with my arm around her;
If it's ever spring again,
    Spring again,
I shall go where went I then.

If it's ever summer-time,
    Summer-time,
With the hay crop at the prime
And the cuckoos – two – in rhyme,
As they used to be, or seemed to,
We shall do as long we've dreamed to,

If it's ever summer-time,
      Summer-time,
With the hay, and bees achime.

SUMMER

It was the first day of June, and the sheep-shearing season culminated, the landscape, even to the leanest pasture, being all health and colour. Every green was young, every pore was open, and every stalk was swollen with racing currents of juice. God was palpably present in the country, and the devil had gone with the world to town. Flossy catkins of the later kinds, fern-sprouts like bishops' croziers, the square-headed moschatel, the odd cuckoo-pint, – like an apoplectic saint in a niche of malachite, – snow-white ladies' – smocks, the toothwort, approximating to human flesh, the enchanter's night-shade, and the black-petalled doleful-bells, were among the quainter objects of the vegetable world in and around Weatherbury at this teeming time . . .

Far from the Madding Crowd

It was a typical summer evening in June, the atmosphere being in such delicate equilibrium and so transmissive that inanimate objects seemed endowed with two or three senses, if not five. There was no distinction between the near and the far, and an auditor felt close to everything within the horizon. The soundlessness impressed [Tess] as a positive entity rather than as the mere negation of noise.

Tess of the d'Urbervilles

The season developed and matured. Another year's instalment of flowers, leaves, nightingales, thrushes, finches, and such ephemeral creatures, took up their positions where only a year ago others had stood in their place when these were nothing more than germs and inorganic particles. Rays from the sunrise drew forth the buds and stretched them into long stalks, lifted up sap in noiseless streams, opened petals, and sucked out scents in invisible jets and breathings.

Tess of the d'Urbervilles

Proud Songsters

The thrushes sing as the sun is going,
And the finches whistle in ones and pairs
And as it gets dark loud nightingales
      In bushes
Pipe, as they can when April wears,
      As if all Time were theirs.

These are brand new birds of twelvemonths' growing,
Which a year ago, or less than twain,
No finches were, or nightingales,
     Nor thrushes,
But only particles of grain,
     And earth, and air, and rain.

The complexity of Hardy's thought can be seen in many of these passages about the seasons. So many are symbolic of some deeper meaning, even where, as in this poem, they seem perhaps simple. Here the theme is mirrored in the rhyme-scheme (unique in Hardy's thousand poems); the incongruities and counterpoint in life reflected in such incongruities as the nightingale 'piping'; and the whole innocent picture of the natural cycle becomes a meditation on life and love and death.[105] *All the gathered and pondered wisdom of Hardy's long life he distils into such a poem – a poem probably inspired by the re-reading of* Tess *for a new edition.*

The hot weather of July had crept upon them unawares, and the atmosphere of the flat vale hung heavy as an opiate over the dairy-folk, the cows, and the trees. Hot steaming rains fell frequently, making the grass where the cows fed yet more rank, and hindering the late haymaking in the other meads.

Tess of the d'Urbervilles

The July sun shone over Egdon and fired its crimson heather to scarlet. It was the one season of the year, and the one weather of the season, in which the heath was gorgeous. This flowering period represented the second or noontide division in the cycle of those superficial changes which alone were possible here; it followed the green or young-fern period, representing the morn, and preceded the brown period, when the heath-bells and ferns would wear the russet tinges of evening; to be in turn displaced by the dark hue of the winter period, representing night.

The Return of the Native

As Owen and Cytherea move to Budmouth-Regis:

The day of their departure was the most glowing that the climax of a long series of summer heats could evolve. The wide expanse of landscape quivered up and down like the flame of a taper, as they steamed along through the midst of it. Placid flocks of sheep reclining under trees a little way off appeared of a pale blue colour. Clover fields were livid with the brightness of the sun upon their deep red flowers. All waggons and carts were moved to the shade by their careful owners; rain-water butts fell to pieces; well-buckets were lowered inside the covers of the well-hole, to preserve them from the fate of the butts, and, generally, water seemed scarcer in the country than the beer and cider of the peasantry who toiled or idled there.

Desperate Remedies

— and Angel Clare wore a 'cabbage-leaf inside his hat to keep his head cool'. Some of Hardy's most vivid descriptions are of intense summer heat, especially of 'the great valley of purple heath thrilling silently in the sun.'

Thursday, the thirty-first of August, was one of a series of days during which snug houses were stifling, and when cool draughts were treats; when cracks appeared in clayey gardens, and were called 'earthquakes' by apprehensive children; when loose spokes were discovered in the wheels of carts and carriages; and when stinging insects haunted the air, the earth and every drop of water that was to be found.

In Mrs Yeobright's garden large-leaved plants of a tender kind flagged by ten o'clock in the morning; rhubarb bent downwards at eleven; and even stiff cabbages were limp by noon.

She sets out across the heath to visit her son:

The sun had branded the whole heath with his mark, even the purple heath-flowers having put on a brownness under the dry blazes of the few preceding days. Every valley was filled with air like that of a kiln, and the clean quartz sand of the winter water-courses, which formed summer paths, had undergone a species of incineration since the drought had set in.

. . . So she went on, the air around her pulsating silently, and oppressing the earth with lassitude. She looked at the sky overhead, and saw that the sapphirine hue of the zenith in spring and early summer had been replaced by a metallic violet.

In the afternoon she arrives at Alderworth:

She came down the hill to the gate, and looked into the hot garden.

There lay the cat asleep on the bare gravel of the path, as if beds, rugs, and carpets were unendurable. The leaves of the hollyhocks hung like half-closed umbrellas, the sap almost simmered in the stems, and foliage with a smooth surface glared like metallic mirrors. A small apple-tree . . . grew just inside the gate . . . and among the fallen apples on the ground beneath were wasps rolling drunk with the juice, or creeping about the little caves in each fruit which they had eaten out before stupefied by its sweetness.

This passage is continued on page 66. It is not until dusk that Clym finds his mother, prostrate on the heath, and tries to carry her to safety. Hardy notes a last detail:

The air was now completely cool; but whenever he passed over a sandy patch of ground uncarpeted with vegetation there was reflected from its surface into his face the heat which it had imbibed during the day.

The Return of the Native

'Gone,' I call them, gone for good, that group of local hearts and heads;
    Yet at mothy curfew-tide,
And at midnight when the noon-heat breathes it back from walls and leads,
They've a way of whispering to me – fellow-wight who yet abide . . .

Friends Beyond

Summer Schemes

When friendly summer calls again,
    Calls again
Her little fifers to these hills,
We'll go – we two – to that arched fane
Of leafage where they prime their bills
Before they start to flood the plain
With quavers, minims, shakes, and trills.
    ' – We'll go,' I sing; but who shall say
    What may not chance before that day!

And we shall see the waters spring,
    Waters spring
From chinks the scrubby copses crown;
And we shall trace their oncreeping
To where the cascade tumbles down
And sends the bobbing growths aswing,
And ferns not quite but almost drown.
    ' – We shall,' I say; but who may sing
    Of what another moon will bring!

It was a morning of the latter summer-time; a morning of lingering dews, when the grass is never dry in the shade. Fuchsias and dahlias were laden till eleven o'clock with small drops and dashes of water, changing the colour of their sparkle at every movement of the air; and elsewhere hanging on twigs like small silver fruit. The threads of garden-spiders appeared thick and polished. In the dry and sunny places dozens of long-legged crane-flies whizzed off the grass at every step the passer took.

Under the Greenwood Tree

It was just that stage in the slow decline of the summer days, when the deep, dark, and vacuous hot-weather shadows are beginning to be replaced by blue ones that have a surface and substance to the eye.

Desperate Remedies

[Anne] went on into the garden amid the September sunshine, whose rays lay level across the blue haze which the earth gave forth. The gnats were dancing up and down in airy companies, the nasturtium flowers shone out in groups from the dark hedge over which they climbed, and the mellow smell of the decline of summer was exhaled by everything.

The Trumpet-Major

At the Royal Academy

These summer landscapes – clump, and copse, and croft –
Woodland and meadowland – here hung aloft,
Gay with limp grass and leafery new and soft,

Seem caught from the immediate season's yield
I saw last noonday shining over the field,
By rapid snatch, while still are uncongealed

The saps that in their live originals climb;
Yester's quick greenage here set forth in mime
Just as it stands, now, at our breathing-time.

But these young foils so fresh upon each tree,
Soft verdures spread in sprouting novelty,
Are not this summer's though they feign to be.

Last year their May to Michaelmas term was run,
Last autumn browned and buried every one,
And no more know they sight of any sun.

SOUNDS, SCENTS, AND COLOURS

SOUNDS

1897. *January 27*. To-day has length, breadth, thickness, colour, smell, voice. As soon as it becomes *yesterday* it is a thin layer among many layers, without substance, colour, or articulate sound.

The Life of Thomas Hardy

The faint sounds heard only accentuated the silence. The rising and falling of the sea, far away along the coast, was the most important. A minor sound was the scurr of a distant night-hawk. Among the minutest where all were minute were the light settlement of gossamer fragments floating in the air, a toad humbly labouring along through the grass near the entrance, the crackle of a dead leaf which a worm was endeavouring to pull into the earth, a waft of air, getting nearer and nearer, and expiring at [Stephen's] feet under the burden of a winged seed.

A Pair of Blue Eyes

To dwellers in a wood almost every species of tree has its voice as well as its feature. At the passing of the breeze the fir-trees sob and moan no less distinctly than they rock; the holly whistles as it battles with itself; the ash hisses amid its quiverings; the beech rustles while its flat boughs rise and fall. And winter, which modifies the note of such trees as shed their leaves, does not destroy its individuality.

Under the Greenwood Tree

Dick said nothing; and the stillness was disturbed only by some small bird that was being killed by an owl in the adjoining wood, whose cry passed into the silence without mingling with it.

Under the Greenwood Tree

[1871] *March.* Lonely places in the country have each their own peculiar silences.

Memoranda I

Growing up in a deeply rural world lacking today's volume of motor and other noises, Hardy had listened to the natural sounds of his surroundings. He knew about the 'lispings of the sea' and its 'canine crunching of pebbles'; how the dust of the roads deadened footfalls; how a silk dress scratched over stubble; how bark-ripping sounded rather like the quack of a duck; how in the solitude of a wood one could hear the slight rustle of a nearby eft coming out to take the sun; and how often after dark 'only the distant fall of water disturbed the stillness of the manorial precincts'. He was in addition (as hundreds of his poems show) unusually sensitive to sound and its interpretation. His favourite Bible passage was 'that magnificent climax of the wind, the earthquake, the fire, and the still small voice'; and it is frequently that 'The whole proceeding had been depicted by sounds.'[106]

The three adventuresome boys at West Poley begin yet again to divert the stream in its underground cavern:

Steve took the spade, and Job the pickaxe. First they finished what Job had begun – the turning of the stream into the third tunnel or crevice, which led to neither of the Poleys. This done, they set to work jamming stones into the other two openings, treading earth and clay around them, and smoothing over the whole in such a manner that nobody should notice they had ever existed. So intent were we on completing it that – to our utter disaster – we did not notice what was going on behind us.

I was the first to look round, and I well remember why. My ears had been attracted by a slight change of tone in the purl of the water down the new crevice discovered by Job, and I was curious to learn the reason of it. The sight that met my gaze might well have appalled a stouter and older heart than mine . . .

Our Exploits at West Poley

Similarly he often uses sounds to set the scene.[107] *When Pitt rises to address the Commons, the stage directions read:*

During the momentary pause before he speaks the House assumes an attentive stillness, in which can be heard the rustling of the trees without, a horn from an early coach, and the voice of the watch crying the hour.

The Dynasts

Grace is alone in the wood after Fitzpiers has visited the dying Giles:

No sign of any other comer greeted her ear, the only perceptible sounds being the tiny cracklings of the dead leaves which, like a feather bed, had not yet done rising to their normal level where indented by the pressure of her husband's receding footsteps.

The Woodlanders

Clym, hoping for Eustacia's return to him, measures her possible approach by the sounds of the heath:

When a leaf floated to the earth he turned his head, thinking it might be her footfall. A bird searching for worms in the mould of the flower-beds sounded like her hand on the latch of the gate; and at dusk, when soft, strange ventriloquisms came from holes in the ground, hollow stalks, curled dead leaves, and other crannies wherein breezes, worms, and insects can work their will, he fancied that they were Eustacia, standing without and breathing wishes of reconciliation.

The Return of the Native

When Nicholas Long returns to his farm it is simply described as:

. . . an ordinary farm-stead, from the back of which rose indistinct breathings, belchings, and snortings, the rattle of halters, and other familiar features of an agriculturist's home.

The Waiting Supper

At the old Roman arena where Henchard elects to meet Susan again:

. . . the whole was grown over with grass, which now, at the end of summer, was bearded with withered bents that formed waves under the brush of the wind, returning to the attentive ear Aeolian modulations, and detaining for moments the flying globes of thistledown.

The Mayor of Casterbridge

'I know the happenings from their sound . . .'[108]
The well-known passage above about the voices of the trees, and many others in this book, show that Hardy could not help but differentiate in detail. His sounds are precise: he knows that moment with church bells when 'the tenor after tolling stops its hum', and how 'the flag-rope gibbers hoarse.'[109] *Many of his descriptions bear the mark of personal experience.*

102

It was about the middle of the early apple-harvest, and the laden trees were shaken at intervals by the gatherers; the soft pattering of the falling crop upon the grassy ground being diversified by the loud rattle of vagrant ones upon a rail, hencoop, basket, or lean-to roof, or upon the rounded and stooping backs of the collectors – mostly children, who would have cried bitterly at receiving such a smart blow from any other quarter, but smilingly assumed it to be but fun in apples.

Desperate Remedies

The rain now came down heavily, but they pursued their path with alacrity, the produce of the several fields between which the lane wound its way being indicated by the peculiar character of the sound emitted by the falling drops. Sometimes a soaking hiss proclaimed that they were passing by a pasture, then a patter would show that the rain fell upon some large-leafed root crop, then a paddling plash announced the naked arable, the low sound of the wind in their ears rising and falling with each pace they took.

Desperate Remedies

Wildeve and Eustacia commiserate about the hateful heath:

'How mournfully the wind blows round us now!'

She did not answer. Its tone was indeed solemn and pervasive. Compound utterances addressed themselves to their senses, and it was possible to view by ear the features of the neighbourhood. Acoustic pictures were returned by the darkened scenery; they could hear where the tracts of heather began and ended; where the furze was growing stalky and tall; where it had been recently cut; in what direction the fir-clump lay, and how near was the pit in which the hollies grew; for these differing features had their voices no less than their shapes and colours.[110]

The Return of the Native

The water at the back of the house could be heard, idly spinning whirlpools in its creep between the rows of dry feather-headed reeds which formed a stockade along each bank. Their presence was denoted by sounds as of a congregation praying humbly, produced by their rubbing against each other in the slow wind.

The Return of the Native

The Voice of Things

Forty Augusts – aye, and several more – ago,
　　When I paced the headlands loosed from dull employ,
The waves huzza'd like a multitude below,
　　In the sway of an all-including joy
　　　　Without cloy.

103

Blankly I walked there a double decade after,
  When thwarts had flung their toils in front of me,
And I heard the waters wagging in a long ironic laughter
  At the lot of men, and all the vapoury
    Things that be.

Wheeling change has set me again standing where
  Once I heard the waves huzza at Lammas-tide;
But they supplicate now – like a congregation there
  Who murmur the Confession – I outside,
    Prayer denied.

As the darkness thickened the wind increased, and each blast raked the iron railings before the houses till they hummed as if in a song of derision.

The Hand of Ethelberta

Twenty years after Hardy published this passage there was an amusing sequel:

It was this year that Hardy met Dr Grieg, the composer, and his wife, and when, discussing Wagner music, he said to Grieg that the wind and rain through trees, iron railings, and keyholes fairly suggested Wagner music; to which the rival composer responded severely that he himself would sooner have the wind and rain.

The Life of Thomas Hardy

Just as Hardy, in a poem written after a visit to the Vatican's Hall of the Muses, found himself 'inconstant' to any one Art, being to each in turn 'swayed like a river-weed as the ripples run',[111] *so sound and scent and colour and form all spoke to him. Tess, in the rank, fecund, uncultivated garden is fascinated by the sound of Angel Clare's harp:*

Tess was conscious of neither time nor space. The exaltation which she had described as being producible at will by gazing at a star came now without any determination of hers; she undulated upon the thin notes of the second-hand harp, and their harmonies passed like breezes through her, bringing tears into her eyes. The floating pollen seemed to be his notes made visible, and the dampness of the garden the weeping of the garden's sensibility. Though near night-fall, the rank-smelling weed-flowers glowed as if they would not close for intentness, and the waves of colour mixed with the waves of sound.

Tess of the d'Urbervilles

Perhaps the finest and most typical of Hardy's writing about sounds is as Eustacia stands waiting on the heath at night:

It might reasonably have been supposed that she was listening to the wind, which rose somewhat as the night advanced, and laid hold of the attention. The wind, indeed, seemed made for the scene, as the scene seemed made for the hour. Part of its tone was quite special; what was heard there could be heard nowhere else. Gusts in innumerable series followed each other from the north-west, and when each one of them raced past the sound of its progress resolved into three. Treble, tenor, and bass notes were to be found therein. The general ricochet of the whole over pits and prominences had the gravest pitch of the chime. Next there could be heard the baritone buzz of a holly tree. Below these in force, above them in pitch, a dwindled voice strove hard at a husky tune, which was the peculiar local sound alluded to. Thinner and less immediately traceable than the other two, it was far more impressive than either. In it lay what may be called the linguistic peculiarity of the heath; and being audible nowhere on earth off a heath, it afforded a shadow of reason for the woman's tenseness, which continued as unbroken as ever.

Throughout the blowing of these plaintive November winds that note bore a great resemblance to the ruins of human song which remain to the throat of fourscore and ten. It was a worn whisper, dry and papery, and it brushed so distinctly across the ear that, by the accustomed, the material minutiae in which it originated could be realized as by touch. It was the united products of infinitesimal vegetable causes, and these were neither stems, leaves, fruit, blades, prickles, lichen, nor moss.

They were the mummied heath-bells of the past summer, originally tender and purple, now washed colourless by Michaelmas rains, and dried to dead skins by October suns. So low was an individual sound from these that a combination of hundreds only just emerged from silence, and the myriads of the whole declivity reached the woman's ear but as a shrivelled and intermittent recitative. Yet scarcely a single accent among the many afloat tonight could have such power to impress a listener with thoughts of its origin. One inwardly saw the infinity of those combined multitudes; and perceived that each of the tiny trumpets was seized on, entered, scoured, and emerged from by the wind as thoroughly as if it were as vast as a crater.

'The spirit moved them.' A meaning of the phrase forced itself upon the attention; and an emotional listener's fetichistic mood might have ended in one of more advanced quality. It was not, after all, that the left-hand expanse of old blooms spoke, or the right-hand, or those of the slope in front; but it was the single person of something else speaking through each at once.

The Return of the Native

When the Hardys' dog, Wessex, died (to the relief of house staff, visitors, and postmen[112]), the poem Hardy wrote was mostly about sounds.

Dead 'Wessex' the Dog to the Household

Do you think of me at all,
    Wistful ones?
Do you think of me at all
    As if nigh?
Do you think of me at all

At the creep of evenfall,
Or when the sky-birds call
　　As they fly?

Do you look for me at times,
　　Wistful ones?
Do you look for me at times
　　Strained and still?
Do you look for me at times,
When that hour for walking
　　chimes,
On that grassy path that climbs
　　Up the hill?

You may hear a jump or trot,
　　Wistful ones?
You may hear a jump or trot –
　　Mine, as 'twere –
You may hear a jump or trot
On the stair or path or plot;
But I shall cause it not,
　　Be not there.

Should I call as when I knew you,
　　Wistful ones?
Should I call as when I knew you,
　　Shared your home;
Should I call as when I knew you,
I shall not turn to view you,
I shall not listen to you,
　　Shall not come.

SCENTS

On an early page of one of his notebooks, Hardy thought it worth copying from some Notes
to Aeschylus:

Scent. A preternatural scent was suppsd to attend the pres^{ce} of a deity. See Aeschylus,
Virgil etc.

Literary Notes I

There are fewer evocations of scent than of sound and colour in Hardy's writings. He may have taken it for granted in the way he characterised the country boy's differing attitude to wild flowers from the town boy's – 'it is part of the country boy's life. It grows in his soul – he does not want it in his buttonhole.' Clym Yeobright, possibly like the young Tommy, had grown up on the heath 'permeated with . . . its odours.'[113] Hardy also knew how elusive scents are – as elusive as human emotions:

So volatile and intangible was the story that to convey it in words would have been as hard as to cage a perfume.

The Well-Beloved

But he always noticed scents – the 'sweet breath' of the wet ferns as they dried in the sun, and the 'salt-edged air' that drew him back to the magic land of Lyonnesse where he had courted Emma; the cider-making which meant that Giles Winterborne 'looked and smelt like Autumn's very brother', when 'the blue stagnant air of autumn which hung over everything was heavy with a sweet cidery smell.'[114]

This autumn [1873] Hardy assisted at his father's cider-making – a proceeding he had always enjoyed from childhood – the apples being from old trees that have now long perished. It was the last time he ever took part in a work whose sweet smells and oozings in the crisp autumn air can never be forgotten by those who have had a hand in it.

The Life of Thomas Hardy

The woodland barking season also had its smells:

It was a pleasant time. The smoke from the little fire of peeled sticks rose between the sitters and the sunlight, and behind its blue films stretched the naked arms of the prostrate trees. The smell of the uncovered sap mingled with the smell of the burning wood, and the sticky inner surface of the scattered bark glistened as it revealed its pale madder hues to the eye.

The Woodlanders

– and on Egdon Heath:

It was a stagnant, warm, and misty night, full of all the heavy perfumes of new vegetation not yet dried by hot sun, and among these particularly the scent of the fern.

The Return of the Native

Angel Clare returns to Talbothays, and from a knoll above it:

. . . he again looked into that green trough of sappiness and humidity, the valley of the Var or Froom. Immediately he began to descend from the upland to the fat alluvial soil below, the atmosphere grew heavier; the languid perfume of the summer fruits, the mists,

107

the hay, the flowers, formed therein a vast pool of odour which at this hour seemed
to make the animals, the very bees and butterflies, drowsy.

Tess of the d'Urbervilles

*Scents for Hardy (as for Proust) were linked with memories, potent agents of recall — as in the
poem "Shut Out That Moon" on page 215.*

*While the troopers, so soon to go to war and death, dally on their horses in the summer evening
by the mill-stream, miller Loveday throws them cherries which they catch in their caps:*

It was a cheerful, careless, unpremeditated half-hour, which returned like the scent of
a flower to the memories of some of those who enjoyed it, even at a distance of many
years after, when they lay wounded and weak in foreign lands.

The Trumpet-Major

The History of an Hour

Vain is the wish to try rhyming it, writing it;
Pen cannot weld into words what it was;
Time will be squandered in toil at inditing it;
Clear is the cause!

Yea, 'twas too satiate with soul, too ethereal;
June-morning scents of a rose-bush in flower
Catch in a clap-net of hempen material;
So catch that hour!

COLOURS

At seven [the young Clym Yeobright] painted the Battle of Waterloo with tiger-lily
pollen and blackcurrant juice, in the absence of water-colours.

The Return of the Native

*Whether this is an echo of Hardy's childhood experience or pure invention, it is a hint of his love
of colour. His first prize-winning architectural essay in 1863 had been 'On the Application of
Coloured Bricks and Terra Cotta to Modern Architecture'. During 1863 he even contemplated
becoming an art critic; probably his* Schools of Painting *notebook was compiled to further this.
But, as he tells us, the love of poetry won first place in his affections, and by 1865 his art appreciation
had taken other forms, which he later recommended as a more valuable approach: concentrating
his attention on one master only at each of the daily lunch-time visits he made to the National
Gallery.*[115] *Some of his own later watercolours are in the Dorset County Museum.*

*Colour plays a large part in his writing, as many passages have already shown. In his mind
different colours symbolised joy and grief, life and death, or the weary daily imprisonment in the*

shuttle of time — the subject of later pages here. He uses colour rather like sound, to present a quick sketch — like that of a haymaking scene:

The white shirt-sleeves of the mowers glistened in the sun, the scythes flashed, voices echoed, snatches of song floated about, and there were glimpses of red waggon-wheels, purple gowns, and many-coloured handkerchiefs.

The Romantic Adventures of a Milkmaid

. . . or the vital backdrop against which things happen:

The scene was the corner of Mary Street in Budmouth-Regis, near the King's statue, at which point the white angle of the last house in the row cut perpendicularly an embayed and nearly motionless expanse of salt water projected from the outer ocean — to-day lit in bright tones of green and opal. Dick and Smart had just emerged from the street, and there on the right, against the brilliant sheet of liquid colour, stood Fancy Day; and she turned and recognized him.

Under the Greenwood Tree

At Bob Loveday's wedding feast Hardy meticulously notices 'the most beautiful colour that the eye of an artist in beer could desire'; that Tom-Putts apples must be used for colour in cider; and that Miss Matilda's eyes were 'really eel-colour, like many other nice brown eyes.'[116]

But it is his descriptions of colour in land, sea and sky which show his subtle awareness of it, his characteristic way of thinking, and often the special knowledge of a painter.

Above Lulwind Cove Cytherea scans the landward view:

Nothing was visible save the strikingly brilliant, still landscape. The wide concave which lay at the back of the hill in this direction was blazing with the western light, adding an orange tint to the vivid purple of the heather, now at the very climax of bloom, and free from the slightest touch of the invidious brown that so soon creeps into its shades. The light so intensified the colours that they seemed to stand above the surface of the earth and float in mid-air like an exhalation of red. In the minor valleys, between the hillocks and ridges which diversified the contour of the basin, but did not disturb its general sweep, she marked brakes of tall, heavy-stemmed ferns, five or six feet high, in a brilliant light-green dress — a broad riband of them with the path in their midst winding like a stream along the little ravine that reached to the foot of the hill, and delivered up the path to its grassy area. Among the ferns grew holly bushes deeper in tint than any shadow about them, whilst the whole surface of the scene was dimpled with small conical pits, and here and there were round ponds, now dry, and half overgrown with rushes.

Desperate Remedies

The rain had quite ceased, and the sun was shining through the green, brown, and yellow leaves, now sparkling and varnished by the raindrops to the brightness of similar effects in the landscapes of Ruysdael and Hobbema, and full of those infinite beauties that arise from the union of colour with high lights. The air was rendered so transparent by the heavy fall of rain that the autumn hues of the middle distance were as rich as those near at hand, and the remote fields intercepted by the angle of the tower appeared in the same plane as the tower itself.

Far from the Madding Crowd

Paula's party takes a drive while staying at Baden:

The sun streamed yellow behind their backs as they wound up the long inclines, lighting the red trunks, and even the blue-black foliage itself. The summer had already made impression upon that mass of uniform colour by tipping every twig with a tiny sprout of virescent yellow; while the minute sounds which issued from the forest revealed that the apparently still place was becoming a perfect reservoir of insect life.

A Laodicean

. . . and the Swancourts drive, as Hardy did, from St Juliot to Barwith Strand:

The journey was along a road by neutral green hills, upon which hedgerows lay trailing like ropes on a quay. Gaps in these uplands revealed the blue sea, flecked with a few dashes of white and a solitary white sail, the whole brimming up to a keen horizon which lay like a line ruled from hillside to hillside. Then they rolled down a pass, the chocolate-toned rocks forming a wall on both sides, from one of which fell a heavy jagged shade over half the roadway. A spout of fresh water burst from an occasional crevice, and pattering down upon broad green leaves, ran along as a rivulet at the bottom. Unkempt locks of heather overhung the brow of each steep, whence at divers points a bramble swung forth into mid-air, snatching at their head-dresses like a claw.

They mounted the last crest, and the bay which was to be the end of their pilgimage burst upon them. The ocean blueness deepened its colour as it stretched to the foot of the crags, where it terminated in a fringe of white – silent at this distance, though moving and heaving like a counterpane upon a restless sleeper. The shadowed hollows of the purple and brown rocks would have been called blue had not that tint been so entirely appropriated by the water beside them.

A Pair of Blue Eyes

The seasons are of course defined also by colour – the drab greys and whites of winter (page 87f.), the cider country in spring:

There the air was blue as sapphire – such a blue as outside that apple-region was never seen. Under the blue the orchards were in a blaze of pink bloom, some of the richly flowered trees running almost up to where they drove along.

The Woodlanders

110

– while nearby, in autumn,

. . . were to be seen gardens and orchards now bossed, nay encrusted, with scarlet and gold fruit, stretching to infinite distance under a luminous lavender mist.

The Woodlanders

In the evening [Clym] set out on the journey. Although the heat of summer was yet intense the days had considerably shortened, and before he had advanced a mile on his way all the heath purples, browns, and greens had merged in a uniform dress without airiness or gradation, and broken only by touches of white where the little heaps of clean quartz sand showed the entrance to a rabbit-burrow, or where the white flints of a footpath lay like a thread over the slopes.

The Return of the Native

On that same ill-fated day Mrs Yeobright, making what was to be her last journey across the heath, had seen 'the sapphirine hue of the zenith in spring and early summer. . .replaced by a metallic violet.' Ethelberta had watched where 'a zinc sky met a leaden sea', when the wind whined and 'no bird sang.'[117] A score or more of metallic descriptions by Hardy are usually sad or sinister images at some threatening moment in his story – as in the rivalry between the two architects expressed at Stancy Castle garden-party:

A lavender haze hung in the air, the trees were as still as those of a submarine forest; while the sun, in colour like a brass plaque, had a hairy outline in the livid sky.

A Laodicean

Two prospective brothers-in-law travel together to try to stop Ethelberta's marriage to Mountclere:

Some unforeseen incident delayed the boat, and they walked up and down the pier to wait. The prospect was gloomy enough. The wind was north-east; the sea along shore was a chalky green, though comparatively calm, this part of the coast forming a shelter from wind in its present quarter. The clouds had different velocities, and some of them shone with a coppery glare, produced by rays from the west which did not enter the inferior atmosphere at all. It was reflected on the distant waves in patches, with an effect as if the waters were at those particular spots stained with blood. This departed, and what daylight was left to the earth came from strange and unusual quarters of the heavens. The zenith would be bright, as if that were the place of the sun; then all overhead would close, and a whiteness in the east would give the appearance of morning; while a bank as thick as a wall barricaded the west, which looked as if it had no acquaintance with sunsets, and would blush red no more.

The Hand of Ethelberta

111

A Thought in Two Moods

I saw it – pink and white – revealed
    Upon the white and green;
The white and green was a daisied field,
    The pink and white Ethleen.

And as I looked it seemed in kind
    That difference they had none;
The two fair bodiments combined
    As varied miens of one.

A sense that, in some mouldering year,
    As one they both would lie,
Made me move quickly on to her
    To pass the pale thought by.

She laughed and said: 'Out there, to me,
    You looked so weather-browned,
And brown in clothes, you seemed to be
    Made of the dusty ground!'

If in this poem Hardy is using colours to say something about the essential oneness of nature and humanity, in the following he is also speaking on a favourite theme – that the landscape seen is different for everyone who sees it:

Alike and Unlike
(Great-Orme's Head)

We watched the selfsame scene on that long drive,
Saw the magnificent purples, as one eye,
Of those near mountains; saw the storm arrive;
Laid up the sight in memory, you and I,
As if for joint recallings by and by.

But our eye-records, like in hue and line,
Had superimposed on them, that very day,
Gravings on your side deep, but slight on mine! –
Tending to sever us thenceforth alway;
Mine commonplace; yours tragic, gruesome, gray.

ANIMALS

HORSES

The young Henchard, having just, in an alcoholic daze, sold his wife, goes out into the twilight:

The difference between the peacefulness of inferior nature and the wilful hostilities of mankind was very apparent in this place. In contrast with the harshness of the act just ended within the tent was the sight of several horses crossing their necks and rubbing each other lovingly as they waited in patience to be harnessed for the homeward journey.

The Mayor of Casterbridge

Bathsheba could just discern in the wan light of daybreak a team of her own horses. They stopped to drink at a pond on the other side of the way. She watched them flouncing into the pool, drinking, tossing up their heads, drinking again, the water dribbling from their lips in silver threads. There was another flounce, and they came out of the pond, and turned back again towards the farm.

Far from the Madding Crowd

Thomas Hardy had grown up with the heathcroppers; and he knew how mutually interdependent were country people (like Farmer Boldwood) and their horses:

His house stood recessed from the road, and the stables, which are to a farm what a fireplace is to a room, were behind, their lower portions being lost amid bushes of laurel. Inside the blue door, open half-way down, were to be seen at this time the backs and tails of half-a-dozen warm and contented horses standing in their stalls; and as thus viewed, they presented alternations of roan and bay, in shapes like a Moorish arch, the tail being a streak down the midst of each. Over these, and lost to the eye gazing in from the outer light, the mouths of the same animals could be heard busily sustaining the above-named warmth and plumpness by quantities of oats and hay. The restless and shadowy figure of a colt wandered about a loose-box at the end, whilst the steady grind of all the eaters was occasionally diversified by the rattle of a rope or the stamp of a foot.

Pacing up and down at the heels of the animals was Farmer Boldwood himself. This place was his almonry and cloister in one;[118] here, after looking to the feeding of his four-footed dependants, the celibate would walk and meditate of an evening till the moon's rays streamed in through the cobwebbed windows, or total darkness enveloped the scene.

Far from the Madding Crowd

But one of the passions of Hardy's life was his concern for ill-treated creatures:

[1888] *July 13*. After being in the street: What was it on the faces of those horses? – Resignation. Their eyes looked at me, haunted me. The absoluteness of their resignation

113

was terrible. When afterwards I heard their tramp as I lay in bed, the ghosts of their eyes came in to me, saying, "Where is your justice, O man and ruler?"

The Life of Thomas Hardy

I think more cruelties are perpetrated on animals by butchers, drovers, and cab-people, than by vivisectors. I wish you and I could work together some day for the prevention of such barbarities.

Letter to Mrs Florence Henniker, 15 Jan., 1894

Hardy often commends his wife Emma's 'admirable courage' in challenging cruelty when she met it in the street, and himself championed, through his writings, the cause of animal welfare. One of his least attractive characters, Alfred Neigh, is responsible for a shocking situation on his estate:

In the enclosure, and on the site of the imaginary house, was an extraordinary group. It consisted of numerous horses in the last stage of decrepitude, the animals being such mere skeletons that at first Ethelberta hardly recognized them to be horses at all; they seemed rather to be specimens of some attenuated heraldic animal, scarcely thick enough through the body to throw a shadow; or enlarged castings of the fire-dog of past times. These poor creatures were endeavouring to make a meal from herbage so trodden and thin that scarcely a wholesome blade remained; the little that there was consisted of the sourer sorts common on such sandy soils, mingled with tufts of heather and sprouting ferns. . . . Adjoining this enclosure was another and smaller one, formed of high boarding . . . Ethelberta looked through the crevices, and saw that in the midst of the yard stood trunks of trees as if they were growing, with branches also extending, but these were sawn off at the points where they began to be flexible, no twigs or boughs remaining. Each torso was not unlike a hat-stand, and suspended to the pegs and prongs were lumps of some substance which at first she did not recognize; they proved to be a chronological sequence to the previous scene. Horses' skulls, ribs, quarters, legs, and other joints were hung thereon, the whole forming a huge open-air larder emitting not too sweet a smell.

(– *Hearing hounds baying in a shed nearby, the sisters understood:*)
"These poor horses are waiting to be killed for their food."

The Hand of Ethelberta

And at Christminster:

There drove up at this moment with a belated Doctor, robed and panting, a cab whose horse failed to stop at the exact point required for setting down the hirer, who jumped out and entered the door. The driver, alighting, began to kick the animal in the belly.

"If that can be done," said Jude, "at college gates in the most religious and educational city in the world, what shall we say as to how far we've got?"

Jude the Obscure

Hardy was a realist however, knowing life is imperfect. He uses the following description as a metaphor for the 'breaking-in' of George Somerset as an architect:

114

The operation called lunging, in which a haltered colt is made to trot round and round a horsebreaker who holds the rope, till the beholder grows dizzy in looking at them, is a very unhappy one for the animal concerned. During its progress the colt springs upwards, across the circle, stops, flies over the turf with the velocity of a bird, and indulges in all sorts of graceful antics; but he always ends in one way – thanks to the knotted whipcord – in a level trot round the lunger with the regularity of a horizontal wheel, and in the loss for ever to his character of the bold contours which the fine hand of Nature gave it. Yet the process is considered to be the making of him.

A Laodicean

In his pity, Hardy knew too that the poor, who could depend on a horse for their livelihood, could not always care for him adequately:

[Tess] led out the horse Prince, only a degree less rickety than the vehicle.

The poor creature looked wonderingly round at the night, at the lantern, at their two figures, as if he could not believe that at that hour, when every living thing was intended to be in shelter and at rest, he was called upon to go out and labour . . .

Tess of the d'Urbervilles

In his eighty-fourth year Hardy wrote the fine ode ''Compassion'', to celebrate the RSPCA's centenary. It was only one of many poems about the creatures who, as his reading of Darwin confirmed, were one with humankind.

Horses Aboard

Horses in horsecloths stand in a row
On board the huge ship that at last lets go:
Whither are they sailing? They do not know,
Nor what for, nor how, –
         They are horses of war,
And are going to where there is fighting afar;
But they gaze through their eye-holes unwitting they are,
And that in some wilderness, gaunt and ghast,
Their bones will bleach ere a year has passed,
And the item be as 'war-waste' classed, –
And when the band booms, and the folk say 'Good-bye!'
And the shore slides astern, they appear wrenched awry
From the scheme Nature planned for them, – wondering why.

When Hardy lived, war was probably the chief horror for horses. Asked, in 1899, to express his opinion on 'A Crusade for Peace', Hardy included a plea that horses should not be used in battle, except for transport.[119] *A few years later, in* The Dynasts, *he frequently described their sufferings in Napoleon's war, being unusual in the very fact of his awareness of their part in the carnage. During the bitter winter retreat from Moscow:*

We are struck by the mournful taciturnity that prevails. Nature is mute. Save for the incessant flogging of the wind-broken and lacerated horses there are no sounds.

Stage directions

CHORUS

> . . . Dusk draws around;
> The marching remnants drowse amid their talk,
> And worn and harrowed horses slumber as they walk.

The Dynasts

DOGS, CATS, AND OTHER QUADRUPEDS

Hardy was always conscious of animals. He notes the treatment of sheep in the market ring, of cattle going for slaughter (and left money to two societies to try to lessen their suffering in transit). He writes with affectionate familiarity of how 'little furred and feathered heads' behave on the river bank; or of the fox and its bark, 'its three hollow notes being rendered at intervals of a minute with the precision of a funeral bell' — the fox who knows that — but not why — 'the hand of all men is against him'. He describes the detail of a rabbit's torment in a gin, and the agonies of pig-killing;[120] and the following poem, written when he was eighty-five, also shows his awareness of many human social issues still live today:

The Lady in the Furs

'I'm a lofty lovely woman',
    Says the lady in the furs,
In the glance she throws around her
    On the poorer dames and sirs:
'This robe, that cost three figures,
    Yes, is mine,' her nod avers.

'True, my money did not buy it,
    But my husband's, from the trade;
And they, they only got it
    From things feeble and afraid
By murdering them in ambush
    With a cunning engine's aid.

116

'True, my hands, too, did not shape it
    To the pretty cut you see,
But the hands of midnight workers
    Who are strangers quite to me:
It was fitted, too, by dressers
    Ranged around me toilsomely.

'But I am a lovely lady,
    Though sneerers say I shine
By robbing Nature's children
    Of apparel not mine,
And that I am but a broom-stick,
    Like a scarecrow's wooden spine.'

                        1925

At Max Gate a sad little graveyard bears witness to the fond Hardys' succession of pets, some of whom were killed straying on the nearby railway line. Hardy wrote several poems about his cats: the mourning "Last Words to a Dumb Friend" too long to quote here; "The Death of Regret", originally written about a cat 'strangled in a rabbit wire on the barrow in sight of this house, and she is buried by a sycamore in our garden here,' wrote Florence Hardy to a friend. But, she continues, 'my husband thought the poem too good for a cat and so made it apply to a person.'[121] *It was probably of this same cat that Hardy wrote to Mrs Henniker in December 1910:*

Yes; the poor cat was such a loss. She was 'the study cat', and used to sleep on my writing table on any clean sheets of paper, and be much with me. I might possibly have saved her life if I had known where to look for her.

Gabriel Oak's dog is intriguingly described in detail, with his faded coat:

In substance it had originally been hair, but long contact with sheep seemed to be turning it by degrees into wool of a poor quality and staple.

— and his wisdom:

Long experience had so precisely taught the animal the difference between such exclamations as 'Come in!' and 'D - ye, come in!' that he knew to a hair's breadth the rate of trotting back from the ewes' tails that each call involved, if a staggerer with the sheep-crook was to be escaped.

                                    Far from the Madding Crowd

— and Hardy even excuses the puppy's fatal chasing of the sheep as a logicality. As Henchard leaves the fairground in the early morning, while the showmen sleep, it is, typically, a little dog who is the only observer:

But the Seven Sleepers had a dog;[122] and dogs of the mysterious breeds that vagrants own, that are as much like cats as dogs and as much like foxes as cats, also lay about here. A little one started up under one of the carts, barked as a matter of principle, and quickly lay down again. He was the only positive spectator of the hay-trusser's exit from the Weydon Fair-field.

The Mayor of Casterbridge

The Mongrel

In Havenpool Harbour the ebb was strong,
And a man with a dog drew near and hung,
And taxpaying day was coming along,
    So the mongrel had to be drowned.
The man threw a stick from the paved wharf-side
Into the midst of the ebbing tide,
And the dog jumped after with ardent pride
    To bring the stick aground.

But no; the steady suck of the flood
To seaward needed, to be withstood,
More than the strength of mongrelhood
    To fight its treacherous trend.
So, swimming for life with desperate will,
The struggler with all his natant skill
Kept buoyant in front of his master, still
    There standing to wait the end.

The loving eyes of the dog inclined
To the man he held as a god enshrined,
With no suspicion in his mind
    That this had all been meant.
Till the effort not to drift from shore
Of his little legs grew slower and slower,
And, the tide still outing with brookless power,
    Outward the dog, too, went.

Just ere his sinking what does one see
Break on the face of that devotee?
A wakening to the treachery
    He had loved with love so blind?
The faith that shone in that mongrel's eye
That his owner would save him by and by
Turned to much like a curse as he sank to die,
    And a loathing of mankind.

In the following poem he leaves us ' "tiptoe" between man and nature'.[123]

The Fallow Deer at the Lonely House

One without looks in to-night
    Through the curtain-chink
From the sheet of glistening white;
One without looks in to-night
    As we sit and think
    By the fender-brink.

We do not discern those eyes
    Watching in the snow;
Lit by lamps of rosy dyes
We do not discern those eyes
    Wondering, aglow,
    Fourfooted, tiptoe.

INSECTS, REPTILES, WORMS

In the shimmering heat of the heath:

The intermittent husky notes of the male grasshoppers from every tuft of furze were enough to show that amid the prostration of the larger animal species an unseen insect world was busy in all the fullness of life.

The Return of the Native

Everywhere they reveal themselves. As Loveday sits in the dark by the mill-pond:

The light shone out upon the broad and deep mill-head, illuminating to a distinct individuality every moth and gnat that entered the quivering chain of radiance stretching across the water towards him . . .

The Trumpet-Major

It was a stagnant, warm, and misty night . . . The lantern, dangling from Christian's hand, brushed the feathery fronds in passing by, disturbing moths and other winged insects, which flew out and alighted upon its horny panes.

The Return of the Native

The milkmaids, in Sunday best, cling to the bank to avoid the flooded lane:

119

Their gauzy skirts had brushed up from the grass innumerable flies and butterflies which, unable to escape, remained caged in the transparent tissue as in an aviary.

Tess of the d'Urbervilles

All dark objects on the earth that lay towards the sun were overspread by a purple haze, against which a swarm of wailing gnats shone forth luminously, rising upward and floating away like sparks of fire.

Desperate Remedies; The Return of the Native[124]

Tess and Angel idle in the meads:

Looking over the damp sod in the direction of the sun, a glistening ripple of gossamer webs was visible to their eyes under the luminary, like the track of moonlight on the sea. Gnats, knowing nothing of their brief glorification, wandered across the shimmer of this pathway, irradiated as if they bore fire within them, then passed out of its line, and were quite extinct.

Tess of the d'Urbervilles

[Clym's] familiars were creeping and winged things, and they seemed to enrol him in their band. Bees hummed around his ears with an intimate air, and tugged at the heath and furze-flowers at his side in such numbers as to weigh them down to the sod. The strange amber-coloured butterflies which Egdon produced, and which were never seen elsewhere, quivered in the breath of his lips, alighted upon his bowed back, and sported with the glittering point of his hook as he flourished it up and down. Tribes of emerald-green grasshoppers leaped over his feet, falling awkwardly on their backs, heads, or hips, like unskilful acrobats, as chance might rule; or engaged themselves in noisy flirtations under the fern-fronds with silent ones of homely hue. Huge flies, ignorant of larders and wire-netting, and quite in a savage state, buzzed about him without knowing that he was a man. In and out of the fern-dells snakes glided in their most brilliant blue and yellow guise, it being the season immediately following the shedding of their old skins, when their colours are brightest. Litters of young rabbits came out from their forms to sun themselves upon hillocks, the hot beams blazing through the delicate tissue of each thin-fleshed ear, and firing it to a blood-red transparency in which the veins could be seen. None of them feared him.

The Return of the Native

After Mrs Yeobright is stung by an adder, Sam finds more adders to attempt a folk-cure:

'I have only been able to get one alive and fresh as he ought to be,' said Sam. 'These limp ones are two I killed to-day at work; but as they don't die till the sun goes down they can't be very stale meat.'

The live adder regarded the assembled group with a sinister look in its small black eye, and the beautiful brown and jet pattern on its back seemed to intensify with indignation.

120

Mrs Yeobright saw the creature, and the creature saw her; she quivered throughout, and averted her eyes.

'Look at that,' murmured Christian Cantle. 'Neighbours, how do we know but that something of the old serpent in God's garden, that gied the apple to the young woman with no clothes, lives on in adders and snakes still? Look at his eye – for all the world like a villainous sort of black currant. 'Tis to be hoped he can't ill-wish us! There's folks in heath who've been overlooked already. I will never kill another adder as long as I live.'

The Return of the Native

A caterpillar who had found its way on to Bathsheba's dress unwittingly took part in Sgt Troy's dazzling swordplay. Hardy was sometimes obsessively conscious of worms (particularly in their graveyard connection).

At Stancy Castle:

The arrow-slit and the electric wire that entered it, like a worm uneasy at being unearthed, were distinctly visible now . . .

A Laodicean

[Margery] went on her way across the fields. . . The dampness was such that innumerable earthworms lay in couples across the path till, startled even by her light tread, they withdrew suddenly into their holes.

The Romantic Adventures of a Milkmaid

(Jude also had great difficulty in avoiding the worms underfoot.) More than once Hardy referred to an earthworm silently drawing a leaf into its hole; and they were not to be left out of The Dynasts.

The Eve of Waterloo
(Chorus of Phantoms)

The eyelids of eve fall together at last,
And the forms so foreign to field and tree
Lie down as though native, and slumber fast!

Sore are the thrills of misgiving we see
In the artless champaign at this harlequinade,
Distracting a vigil where calm should be!

The green seems opprest, and the Plain afraid
Of a Something to come, whereof these are the proofs, –
Neither earthquake, nor storm, nor eclipse's shade!

Yea, the coneys are scared by the thud of hoofs,
And their white scuts flash at their vanishing heels,
And swallows abandon the hamlet-roofs.

The mole's tunnelled chambers are crushed by wheels,
The lark's eggs scattered, their owners fled;
And the hedgehog's household the sapper unseals.

The snail draws in at the terrible tread,
But in vain; he is crushed by the felloe-rim;
The worm asks what can be overhead,

And wriggles deep from a scene so grim,
And guesses him safe; for he does not know
What a foul red flood will be soaking him!

Beaten about by the heel and toe
Are butterflies, sick of the day's long rheum,
To die of a worse than the weather-foe.

Trodden and bruised to a miry tomb
Are ears that have greened but will never be gold,
And flowers in the bud that will never bloom.

So the season's intent, ere its fruit unfold,
Is frustrate, and mangled, and made succumb,
Like a youth of promise struck stark and cold! . . .
The Dynasts

Max Gate,
20:2:1908

My dear Clodd,
    I must send a line or two in answer to your letter. What you remind me of — the lyrical account of the fauna of Waterloo field on the eve of the battle is, curiously enough, the page . . . that struck me, in looking back over the book, as being the most original in it. Though, of course, a thing may be original without being good. However, it does happen that (so far as I know) in the many treatments of Waterloo in literature, those particular personages who were present have never been alluded to before. . . .
                Always yours sincerely,
                    Thomas Hardy.

Curiously absent from the field of Waterloo are the spiders who left so many fields and windows sheeted with webs in his novels and poems:

It was a foggy morning, and the trees shed in noisy water-drops the moisture they had collected from the thick air, an acorn occasionally falling from its cup to the ground in company with the drippings. In the meads sheets of spiders'-web, almost opaque with wet, hung in folds over the fences, and the falling leaves appeared in every variety of brown, green, and yellow hue.

Under the Greenwood Tree

Somerset, stranded in a disused tower at Stancy Castle, looks around him:

Spiders'-webs in plenty were there, and one in particular just before him was in full use as a snare, stretching across the arch of the window, with radiating threads as its ribs. Somerset had plenty of time, and he counted their number – fifteen. He remained so silent that the owner of this elaborate structure soon forgot the disturbance which had resulted in the breaking of his diagonal ties, and crept out from the corner to mend them.

A Laodicean

Hardy knew how cobwebs changed in light and wind. In Lisieux the figures carved on the mediaeval houses 'were cloaked with little cobwebs which waved in the breeze, so that each figure seemed alive',[125] *and Melbury:*

. . . watched Winterborne out of sight under the boughs, where cobwebs glistened in the now clearing air, lengthening and shortening their shine like elastic needles.

The Woodlanders

More often than a natural observation, these webs are recurrent images, as will be shortly considered. A note of March 1886 about The Dynasts *reads:*

The human race to be shown as one great network or tissue which quivers in every part when one point is shaken, like a spider's web if touched. . .

The human race is also shown to have connections with another insect, the honey-bee. Granfer Cantle sang, unforgettably, 'in the voice of a bee up a flue'[126]; *Captain de Stancy, after an early disaster, had learnt to suppress his sexual instincts so that:*

. . . a chamber of his nature had been preserved intact during many later years, like the one solitary sealed-up cell occasionally retained by bees in a lobe of drained honey-comb.

A Laodicean

In the observatory tower,

All was warm, sunny, and silent, except that a solitary bee, which had somehow got

123

within the hollow of the abacus, was singing round inquiringly, unable to discern that ascent was the only mode of escape.

Two on a Tower

Dick Dewy's bees swarmed, propitiously, on his wedding-day; and at the Weatherbury farm Hardy knew what had to be done:

The Weatherbury bees were late in their swarming this year. It was in the latter part of June, and . . . Bathsheba was standing in her garden, watching a swarm in the air and guessing their probable settling place. Not only were they late this year, but unruly. Sometimes throughout a whole season all the swarms would alight on the lowest attainable bough – such as part of a currant-bush or espalier apple-tree; next year they would, with just the same unanimity, make straight off to the uppermost member of some tall, gaunt costard, or quarrenden,[127] and there defy all invaders who did not come armed with ladders and staves to take them.

This was the case at present. Bathsheba's eyes, shaded by one hand, were following the ascending multitude against the unexplorable stretch of blue till they ultimately halted by one of the unwieldy trees spoken of. A process somewhat analogous to that of alleged formations of the universe, time and times ago, was observable. The bustling swarm had swept the sky in a scattered and uniform haze, which now thickened to a nebulous centre:[128] this glided on to a bough and grew still denser, till it formed a solid black spot upon the light.

. . . Bathsheba resolved to hive the bees herself, if possible. She had dressed the hive with herbs and honey, fetched a ladder, brush, and crook, made herself impregnable with armour of leather gloves, straw hat, and large gauze veil – once green but now faded to snuff colour – and ascended a dozen rungs of the ladder.

But Sgt Troy arrives, bent on helping her. He dons her armour, and mounts:

. . . Bathsheba looked on from the ground whilst he was busy sweeping and shaking the bees from the tree, holding up the hive with the other hand for them to fall into . . . He came down holding the hive at arm's length, behind which trailed a cloud of bees.

"Upon my life," said Troy, through the veil, "holding up this hive makes one's arm ache worse than a week of sword-exercise."

Far from the Madding Crowd

At Yalbury Wood they are taking the honey, Geoffrey Day having dug two holes beside the hives:

The preliminaries of execution were arranged, the matches fixed, the stake kindled, the two hives placed over the two holes, and the earth stopped round the edges. Geoffrey then stood erect, and rather more, to straighten his backbone after the digging.

"They were a peculiar family," said Mr Shiner, regarding the hives reflectively. Geoffrey nodded.

124

"Those holes will be the grave of thousands!" said Fancy. "I think 'tis rather a cruel thing to do."

Her father shook his head. "No," he said, tapping the hives to shake the dead bees from their cells, "if you suffocate 'em this way, they only die once: if you fumigate 'em in the new way, they come to life again, and die o' starvation; so the pangs o' death be twice upon 'em."

"I incline to Fancy's notion," said Mr Shiner, laughing lightly.

"The proper way to take honey, so that the bees be neither starved nor murdered, is a puzzling matter," said the keeper steadily.

. . .The lantern-light had disturbed many bees that had escaped from hives destroyed some days earlier, and, demoralized by affliction, were now getting a living as marauders about the doors of other hives. Several flew round the head and neck of Geoffrey; then darted upon him with an irritated bizz.

Under the Greenwood Tree

Summer-time,
With the hay, and bees a-chime.

BIRDS

Thomas Hardy's earliest memory (being given a toy concertina) dates back to when he was four.

Also he remembered, perhaps a little later than this, being in the garden at Bockhampton with his father on a bitterly cold winter day. They noticed a fieldfare, half-frozen, and the father took up a stone idly and threw it at the bird, possibly not meaning to hit it. The fieldfare fell dead, and the child Thomas picked it up and it was as light as a feather, all skin and bone, practically starved. He said he had never forgotten how the body of the fieldfare felt in his hand: the memory had always haunted him.

The Life of Thomas Hardy

It seems that this memory was recounted to Florence Hardy in the last month of two of the poet's life. The idea of birds came so naturally to him (as did music — there is probably a connection through birdsong) that they figure constantly as the most natural of similes or participants in a scene. They also developed into one of his most significant symbols. Hardy himself — 'smallish, fragile, and bright-eyed' — had an affinity with birds, as others noted. Charles Morgan, an Oxford undergraduate, in a fascinating description, saw him as 'sprightly, alert, bird-like. . .a small bird with a great head.' Two years later, Hardy being eighty-three, Godfrey Elton at Oxford wrote: 'Had it not been for my constant consciousness that I was sitting before a Classic, I should not have guessed that I was with a man who wrote; rather an elderly country gentleman with a bird-like alertness and a rare and charming youthfulness . . .'[129] Llewellyn Powys, after visiting him, queried: 'What was it that he reminded me of? A night-hawk? A falcon owl?' And Auden, going far beyond his physical presence, wrote of Hardy's 'hawk's-eye view'.[130]

He had watched birds from his earliest days, and knew their habits:

I Watched a Blackbird

I watched a blackbird on a budding sycamore
One Easter Day, when sap was stirring twigs to the core;
 I saw his tongue, and crocus-coloured bill
 Parting and closing as he turned his trill;
 Then he flew down, seized on a stem of hay,
And upped to where his building scheme was under way,
As if so sure a nest were never shaped on spray.

On the morning of his departure [Swithin] had sat on the edge of his bed, the sunlight streaming through the early mist, the house-martins scratching the back of the ceiling over his head as they scrambled out from the roof for their day's gnat-chasing, the thrushes cracking snails on the garden stones outside with the noisiness of little smiths at work on little anvils.

          Two on a Tower

It was one of those hostile days of the year when . . . ducks and drakes play with hilarious delight at their own family game or spread out one wing after another in the slower enjoyment of letting the delicious moisture penetrate to their innermost down.

        The Hand of Ethelberta

It was that particular half-hour of the day in which the birds of the forest prefer walking to flying; and there being no wind, the hopping of the smallest songster over the dead leaves reached [Somerset's] ear from behind the undergrowth.

          A Laodicean

[1882] *August* . . . This month blackbirds and thrushes creep about under fruit-bushes and in other shady places in gardens rather like four-legged animals than birds. . . . I notice that a blackbird has eaten nearly a whole pear lying in the garden-path during the course of the day.

        The Life of Thomas Hardy

Over all rose abruptly a square solid tower. . .darkened with ivy on one side, wherein wings could be heard flapping uncertainly, as if they belonged to a bird unable to find a proper perch. Hissing noises supervened, and then a hoot, proclaiming that a brood of young owls were residing there in the company of older ones . . .

          A Laodicean

Hardy could sketch other bird sounds with great sensitivity: the man in the beautiful poem "Copying Architecture in an Old Minster", falling deeper and deeper into reverie about the past characters in tombs around him, muses:

126

I catch their cheepings, though thinner than
The overhead creak of a passager's pinion
When leaving land behind.

— Or in "The Revisitation", where the soldier tries to follow the old route to find his lost lover
of the past:

Maybe flustered by my presence
Rose the peewits, just as all those years back, wailing soft and loud,
And revealing their pale pinions like a fitful phosphorescence
Up against the cope of cloud,

Where their dolesome exclamations
Seemed the voicings of the self-same throats I had heard when life was green,
Though since that day uncounted frail forgotten generations
Of their kind had flecked the scene . . .

The young Hardys lived for a time at Riverside Villa, Sturminster Newton.

Overlooking the River Stour

The swallows flew in the curves of an eight
Above the river-gleam
In the wet June's last beam:
Like little cross-bows animate
The swallows flew in the curves of an eight
Above the river-gleam.

Planing up shavings of crystal spray
A moor-hen darted out
From the bank thereabout,
And through the stream-shine ripped his way;
Planing up shavings of crystal spray
A moor-hen darted out.

Closed were the kingcups; and the mead
Dripped in monotonous green,
Though the day's morning sheen
Had shown it golden and honeybee'd;
Closed were the kingcups; and the mead
Dripped in monotonous green.

127

And never I turned my head, alack,
    While these things met my gaze
    Through the pane's drop-drenched glaze,
To see the more behind my back. . . .
O never I turned, but let, alack,
    These less things hold my gaze!

Beside watching birds, Hardy knew their history locally in the heathland:

Though these shaggy hills were apparently so solitary, several keen round eyes were always ready on such a wintry morning as this to converge upon a passer-by. Feathered species sojourned here in hiding which would have created wonder if found elsewhere. A bustard haunted the spot, and not many years before this five and twenty might have been seen in Egdon at one time. Marsh-harriers looked up from the valley by Wildeve's. A cream-coloured courser had used to visit this hill, a bird so rare that not more than a dozen have ever been seen in England; but a barbarian rested neither night or day till he had shot the African truant, and after that event cream-coloured coursers thought fit to enter Egdon no more.[131]

The Return of the Native

Other barbarities (beside the scourge of frost[132]) were practised on birds – like the shoots which left wounded birds dying around Tess all night, which served to symbolise her own suffering as an innocent creature ignobly treated. Hardy measured such cruelties by the strong to the weak against St Paul's letter on love (I Corinthians XIII):

The Blinded Bird

So zestfully canst thou sing?
And all this indignity,
With God's consent, on thee!
Blinded ere yet a-wing
With the red-hot needle thou,
I stand and wonder how
So zestfully thou canst sing!

Resenting not such wrong,
Thy grievous pain forgot,
Eternal dark thy lot,
Groping thy whole life long,
After that stab of fire;
Enjailed in pitiless wire;
Resenting not such wrong!

Who hath charity? This bird,
Who suffereth long and is kind,
Is not provoked, though blind
And alive ensepulchred?
Who hopeth, endureth all things?
Who thinketh no evil, but sings?
Who is divine? This bird.

In an echo of this, Nelson laments the public censure of his private life:

He who is with himself dissatisfied,
Though all the world find satisfaction in him,
Is like a rainbow-coloured bird gone blind,
That gives delight it shares not.
The Dynasts

The Dynasts shows well how Hardy thought of birds even in unlikely situations. Napoleon, on the Kremlin tower, broods over the deserted city of Moscow whose capture has cost so dear:

CHORUS OF RUMOURS (aerial music)

Mark you thereon a small lone figure gazing
Upon his hard-gained goal? It is He!
The startled crows, their broad black pinions raising,
Forsake their haunts, and wheel disquietedly.
The scene slowly darkens.

Hardy then describes how the 'scorched-earth' city goes up in flames. The stage directions end:

. . . The blaze gains the Kremlin, and licks its walls, but does not kindle it. Explosions and hissings are constantly audible, amid which can be fancied cries and yells of people caught in the combustion. Large pieces of canvas aflare sail away on the gale like balloons. Cocks crow, thinking it sunrise, ere they are burnt to death.

The day of the great battle dawns over the Spanish village of Albuera:

. . . Behind the stream some of the French forces are visible. Away behind these stretches a great wood several miles in area, out of which the Albuera stream emerges, and behind the furthest verge of the wood the morning sky lightens momently. The birds in the wood, unaware that this day is to be different from every other day they have known there, are heard singing their overtures with their usual serenity.

The Dynasts

Birdsong was important to Hardy.

In a Museum

I

Here's the mould of a musical bird long passed from light,
Which over the earth before man came was winging;
There's a contralto voice I heard last night,
That lodges in me still with its sweet singing.

II

Such a dream is Time that the coo of this ancient bird
Has perished not, but is blent, or will be blending
Mid visionless wilds of space with the voice that I heard,
In the full-fugued song of the universe unending.
Exeter

[1878] *March 5.* Concert at Sturminster. A Miss Marsh of Sutton [Keinton?] Mandeville sang "Should he upbraid", to Bishop's old tune. She is the sweetest of singers – thrush-like in the descending scale, and lark-like in the ascending – drawing out the soul of listeners in a gradual thread of excruciating attenuation like silk from a cocoon.

The Life of Thomas Hardy

[1877] *May 30.* Walking to Marnhull. The prime of bird-singing. The thrushes and blackbirds are the most prominent, – pleading earnestly rather than singing, and with such modulation that you seem to see their little tongues curl inside their bills in their emphasis. A bullfinch sings from a tree with a metallic sweetness piercing as a fife . . .

The Life of Thomas Hardy

The cuckoo's note was at its best, between April tentativeness and midsummer decrepitude . . .

Interlopers at the Knap

[1893] *April.* I note that a clever thrush, and a stupid nightingale, sing very much alike.

The Life of Thomas Hardy

The Peace Peal
(After Four Years of Silence)

Said a wistful daw in Saint Peter's tower,
High above Casterbridge slates and tiles,
'Why do the walls of my Gothic bower
Shiver, and shrill out sounds for miles?

This gray old rubble
Has scorned such din
Since I knew trouble
And joy herein
How still did abide them
These bells now swung,
While our nest beside them
Securely clung! . . .
It means some snare
For our feet or wings;
But I'll be ware
Of such baleful things!'
And forth he flew from his louvred niche
To take up life in a damp dark ditch.
  – So mortal motives are misread,
And false designs attributed,
In upper spheres of straws and sticks,
Or lower, of pens and politics.
At the end of the War

Of all the hundred and more Hardy poems in which birds figure, the following is as characteristic and significant as any. He greatly admired his fellow-poet, Shelley, whose "Ode to a Skylark" must be one of his most well-known poems. Hardy's poem, written after he had passed through 'the neighbourhood of Leghorn' in the train, has something important to say about poetry, and the part birds played in his own artistic immortality:

Shelley's Skylark
(The neighbourhood of Leghorn: March 1887)

Somewhere afield here something lies
In Earth's oblivious eyeless trust
That moved a poet to prophecies –
A pinch of unseen, unguarded dust:

The dust of the lark that Shelley heard,
And made immortal through times to be; –
Though it only lived like another bird,
And knew not its immortality:

Lived its meek life; then, one day, fell –
A little ball of feather and bone;
And how it perished, when piped farewell,
And where it wastes, are alike unknown.

131

Maybe it rests in the loam I view,
Maybe it throbs in a myrtle's green,
Maybe it sleeps in the coming hue
Of a grape on the slopes of yon inland scene.

Go find it, faeries, go and find
That tiny pinch of priceless dust,
And bring a casket silver-lined,
And framed of gold that gems encrust;

And we will lay it safe therein,
And consecrate it to endless time;
For it inspired a bard to win
Ecstatic heights in thought and rhyme.

TREES, LEAVES AND FLOWERS

In a review of some of William Barnes's poems Hardy writes of Barnes's epithets and descriptions as being 'singularly precise, and often beautiful, definitions of the thing signified.' He then goes on to be precise himself:

When "the rustlèn copse" is spoken of in connection with early winter, it should be known that the particular copse signified is an oak copse, and that the dead oak leaves of young underwood linger on their branches far into the winter weather, giving out to the wind the distinctive sound of which the writer has taken note.

Unsigned Review of Poems of Rural Life in the Dorset Dialect *by William Barnes, 1879*

No wonder they were friends. The nearby heath, the plantation by the Bockhampton garden, and the daily walks to school had combined with his particular mind and ear to give Hardy the kind of knowledge of trees about which J.M. Barrie teased him:[133]

It was far too dark to distinguish firs from other trees by the eye alone, but the peculiar dialect of sylvan language which the piny multitude used would have been enough to proclaim their class at any time . . .

Two on a Tower

These firs stood at the base of Swithin's observatory tower on a small hill:

The gloom and solitude which prevailed round the base were remarkable. The sob of the environing trees was here expressly manifest; and moved by the light breeze their thin straight stems rocked in seconds, like inverted pendulums; while some boughs and twigs rubbed the pillar's sides, or occasionally clicked in catching each other. Below the level of their summits the masonry was lichen-stained and mildewed, for the sun never pierced that moaning cloud of blue-black vegetation. Pads of moss grew in the joints of the stonework, and here and there shade-loving insects had engraved on the mortar patterns of no human style or meaning; but curious and suggestive. Above the trees the case was different: the pillar rose into the sky a bright and cheerful thing, unimpeded, clean and flushed with the sunlight.

Two on a Tower

There was no wind, in a human sense; but a steady stertorous breathing from the fir-trees showed that, now as always, there was movement in apparent stagnation. Nothing but an absolute vacuum would paralyze their utterance.

Two on a Tower

Sobs and moans, however, were not always part of the scene. Trees often form a happier background – as for Dick and Fancy's wedding procession, and for life 'under the greenwood tree':

Now among dark perpendicular firs, like the shafted columns of a cathedral; now through a hazel copse, matted with primroses and wild hyacinths; now under broad beeches in bright young leaves they threaded their way into the high road over Yalbury Hill . . . and in the space of a quarter of an hour Fancy found herself to be Mrs Richard Dewy, though, much to her surprise, feeling no other than Fancy Day still . . .

Under the Greenwood Tree

The point in Yalbury Wood which abutted on the end of Geoffrey Day's premises was closed with an ancient tree, horizontally of enormous extent, though having no great pretensions to height. Many hundreds of birds had been born amidst the boughs of this single tree; tribes of rabbits and hares had nibbled at its bark from year to year; quaint tufts of fungi had sprung from the cavities of its forks; and countless families of moles and earthworms had crept about its roots. Beneath and beyond its shade spread a carefully-tended grass-plot, its purpose being to supply a healthy exercise-ground for young chickens and pheasants: the hens, their mothers, being enclosed in coops placed upon the same green flooring.

Under the Greenwood Tree

Sometimes the woodlands could be sheltering. Grace walked

. . . [a] track under the bare trees and over the cracking sticks, screened and roofed in from the outer world of wind by a network of boughs. . .

The Woodlanders

– sometimes they were themselves in need of protection:

133

At length Clym reached the margin of a fir and beech plantation that had been enclosed from heath land in the year of his birth. Here the trees, laden heavily with their new and humid leaves, were now suffering more damage than during the hightest winds of winter, when the boughs are specially disencumbered to do battle with the storm. The wet young beeches were undergoing amputations, bruises, cripplings, and harsh lacerations, from which the wasting sap would bleed for many a day to come, and which would leave scars visible till the day of their burning. Each stem was wrenched at the root, where it moved like a bone in its socket, and at every onset of the gale convulsive sounds came from the branches, as if pain were felt. In a neighbouring brake a finch was trying to sing; but the wind blew under his feathers till they stood on end, twisted round his little tail, and made him give up his song.

Yet a few yards to Yeobright's left, on the open heath, how ineffectively gnashed the storm! Those gusts which tore the trees merely waved the furze and heather in a light caress. Egdon was made for such times as these.

The Return of the Native

The Woodlanders *tells of professional copsework, where the woods included 'the spectral arms of the peeled trees as they lay' as well as the unbarked trees still growing for another year; and of the changes the seasons brought:*

Although the time of bare boughs had now set in there were sheltered hollows amid the Hintock plantations and copses in which a more tardy leave-taking than on windy summits was the rule with the foliage. This caused here and there an apparent mixture of the seasons; so that in some of the dells they passed by holly-berries in full red growing beside oak and brambles whose verdure was rich and deep as in the month of August. To Grace these well-known peculiarities were as an old painting restored.

Now could be beheld that change from the handsome to the curious which the features of a wood undergo at the ingress of the winter months. Angles were taking the place of curves, and reticulations of surfaces – a change constituting a sudden lapse from the ornate to the primitive on Nature's canvas, and comparable to a retrogressive step from the art of an advanced school of painting to that of the Pacific Islander.

The Woodlanders

On Midsummer eve:

The leaves over Hintock unrolled their creased tissues, and the woodland seemed to change from an open filigree to a solid opaque body of infinitely larger shape and importance. The boughs cast green shades, which disagreed with the complexion of the girls who walked there; and a fringe of the same boughs which overhung Mr Melbury's garden dripped on his seed-plots when it rained, pitting their surface all over as with pock-marks, till Melbury declared that gardens in such a place were no good at all. The two trees that had creaked all the winter left off creaking, the whirr of the night-hawk, however, forming a very satisfactory continuation of uncanny music from that quarter. Except at midday the sun was not seen complete by the Hintock people, but rather in the form of numerous little stars staring through the leaves.

Such an appearance it had on Midsummer eve of this year, and as the hour grew later, and nine o'clock drew on, the irradiation of the day-time became broken up by the weird shadows and ghostly nooks of indistinctness. Imagination could trace amid the trunks and boughs swarthy faces and funereal figures.[134]

The Woodlanders

It was an exceptionally soft, balmy evening for the time of year, which was just that transient period in the May month when beech trees have suddenly unfolded large limp young leaves of the softness of butterflies' wings. Boughs bearing such leaves hung low around and completely inclosed them, so that it was as if they were in a great green vase, which had moss for its bottom and leaf sides.

The Woodlanders

It was a lovely May sunset, and the birch trees which grew on this margin of the vast Egdon wilderness had put on their new leaves, delicate as butterflies' wings, and diaphanous as amber.

The Return of the Native

How Hardy loved those diaphanous leaves, when

> . . . the May month flaps its glad green leaves like wings,
> Delicate-filmed as new-spun silk . . .[135]

or later, when:

[1884] *June 3*. The leaves are approaching their finished summer shape, the evergreens wear new pale suits over the old deep attire. I watered the thirsty earth at Max Gate, which drank in the liquid with a swallowing noise.

The Life of Thomas Hardy

Leaves, like trees, were part of his symbol and imagery network, but he also noted their appearance and behaviour and the order in which they fell.[136] When they weren't glad and green they were inevitably part of the natural cycle of death and decay:

The rains had imparted a phosphorescence to the pieces of touchwood and rotting leaves that lay about [Grace's] path, which, as scattered by her feet, spread abroad like luminous milk.

The Woodlanders

With the departure of the sun the calm mood of the winter day changed. Out of doors there began noises as of silk smartly rubbed; the restful dead leaves of the preceding autumn were stirred to irritated resurrection, and whirled about unwillingly, and tapped against the shutters. It soon began to rain.

Tess of the d'Urbervilles

A Night in November

I marked when the weather changed,
And the panes began to quake,
And the winds rose up and ranged,
That night, lying half-awake.

Dead leaves blew into my room,
And alighted upon my bed,
And a tree declared to the gloom
Its sorrow that they were shed.

One leaf of them touched my hand,
And I thought that it was you
There stood as you used to stand,
And saying at last you knew!
(?) 1913

This poem reflects the early months after Hardy's bereavement in November 1912. The following poem, also published in 1922, seems to look back to his courtship at St Juliot, his marriage and early married life in London, and (inevitably) to the time of burial. As in many poems, Emma is associated with a pattern of branches.

Epeisodia

I

Past the hills that peep
Where the leaze is smiling,
On and on beguiling
Crisply-cropping sheep;
Under boughs of brushwood
Linking tree and tree
In a shade of lushwood,
        There caressed we!

II

Hemmed by city walls
That outshut the sunlight,
In a foggy dun light,

Where the footstep falls
With a pit-pat wearisome
In its cadency
On the flagstones drearisome,
  There pressed we!

III

Where in wild-winged crowds
Blown birds show their whiteness
Up against the lightness
Of the clammy clouds;
By the random river
Pushing to the sea,
Under bents that quiver,
  There shall rest we.

FLOWERS

Beneath all that was charming and simple in this young woman there lurked a real firmness, unperceived at first, as the speck of colour lurks unperceived in the heart of the palest parsley flower.

          The Trumpet-Major

[1884] *February*. When trees and underwood are cut down, and the ground bared, three crops of flowers follow. First a sheet of yellow, they are primroses. Then a sheet of blue; they are wild hyacinths, or as we call them, graegles. Then a sheet of red; they are ragged robins, or as they are called here, robin-hoods. What have these plants been doing through the scores of years before the trees were felled, and how did they come there?

          The Life of Thomas Hardy

In his novels Hardy seldom alludes to garden flowers (when he does, sometimes taking poetic licence as to the exact period of their flowering). In both novels and poems wild flowers often appear,[137] *and the images of bloom and blossom and rose are frequent. Emma is often associated with daisies and roses, particularly in the* Poems of 1912-13. *The following poem may well be linked with her:*

The Background and the Figure
(Lover's Ditty)

I think of the slope where the rabbits fed,
 Of the periwinks' rockwork lair,
Of the fuchsias ringing their bells of red –
 And the something else seen there.

Between the blooms where the sod basked bright,
   By the bobbing fuchsia trees,
Was another and yet more eyesome sight –
   The sight that richened these.

I shall seek those beauties in the spring,
   When the days are fit and fair,
But only as foils to the one more thing
   That also will flower there!

In "Molly Gone",[138] *flower-gardening with his sister Mary is one of his chief regrets after her death:*

No more planting by Molly and me
   Where the beds used to be
Of sweet-william; no training the clambering rose
   By the framework of fir
Now bowering the pathway, whereon it swings gaily and blows
   As if calling commendment from her.

In A Pair of Blue Eyes, *Mrs Smith and Mrs Worm hold a lengthy and amusingly idiosyncratic conversation about garden flowers, in which Mrs Smith castigates Jacob's ladders as being obnoxiously prolific and, 'in the secret souls of 'em . . . weeds, and not flowers at all, if the truth was known.' (Their fault seems to lie in their rankness – an example of Nature run riot, out of control, and as a consequence of this, and of 'The Unfulfilled Intention', prone to blights, cramps, and horrid growths, like fungi and cankers. Hardy loads his descriptions, setting them not as simply natural pictures, but as an accompaniment and an image of human misery and the blighted life. This aspect of Hardy's attitude to Nature will be considered in more detail later in this book.)*

   Though flowers appear in about a hundred of Hardy's poems, only five have a specific flower in their title. This is one of the most poignant:

The Lodging-House Fuchsias

Mrs Masters's fuchsias hung
Higher and broader, and brightly swung,
   Bell-like, more and more
Over the narrow garden-path,
Giving the passer a sprinkle-bath
   In the morning.

She put up with their pushful ways,
And made us tenderly lift their sprays,
   Going to her door:
But when her funeral had to pass
They cut back all the flowery mass
   In the morning.

To the east of Casterbridge lay moors and meadows through which much water flowed. The wanderer in this direction who should stand still for a few moments on a quiet night, might hear singular symphonies from these waters, as from a lampless orchestra, all playing in their sundry tones from near and far parts of the moor. At a hole in a rotten weir they executed a recitative; where a tributary brook fell over a stone breastwork they trilled cheerily; under an arch they performed a metallic cymballing; and at Durnover Hole they hissed. The spot at which their instrumentation rose loudest was a place called Ten Hatches, whence during high springs there proceeded a very fugue of sounds.

The river here was deep and strong at all times, and the hatches on this account were raised and lowered by cogs and a winch. A path led from the second bridge over the highway . . . to these Hatches, crossing the stream at their head by a narrow plank bridge. But after nightfall human beings were seldom found going that way, the path leading only to a deep reach of the stream called Blackwater, and the passage being dangerous.

Henchard, however . . . struck into this path of solitude, following its course beside the stream till the dark shapes of the Ten Hatches cut the sheen thrown upon the river by the weak lustre that still lingered in the west. In a second or two he stood beside the weir-hole where the water was at its deepest.

The Mayor of Casterbridge

Mr Maybold leant over the parapet of the bridge and looked into the river. He saw — without heeding — how the water came rapidly from beneath the arches, glided down a little steep, then spread itself over a pool in which dace, trout, and minnows sported at ease among the long green locks of weed that lay heaving and sinking with their roots towards the current.

Under the Greenwood Tree

Returning from one of these dark walks [Tess and Angel] reached a great gravel-cliff immediately over the levels, where they stood still and listened. The water was now high in the streams, squirting through the weirs, and tinkling under culverts; the smallest gullies were all full; there was no taking short cuts anywhere, and foot-passengers were compelled to follow the permanent ways. From the whole extent of the invisible vale came a multitudinous intonation; it forced upon their fancy that a great city lay below them, and that the murmur was the vociferation of its populace.

"It seems like tens of thousands of them," said Tess; "holding public-meetings in their market-places, arguing, preaching, quarrelling, sobbing, groaning, praying, and cursing."

Tess of the d'Urbervilles

139

Clare, sleep-walking, carries Tess to the brink of the river:

Its waters, in creeping down these miles of meadow-land, frequently divided, serpentining in purposeless curves, looping themselves around little islands that had no name, returning and embodying themselves as a broad main stream further on. Opposite the spot to which he had brought her was such a general confluence, and the river was proportionately voluminous and deep. Across it was a narrow foot-bridge; but now the autumn flood had washed the handrail away, leaving the bare plank only, which, lying a few inches above the speeding current, formed a giddy pathway for even steady heads. . . . He now mounted the plank, and, sliding one foot forward, advanced along it. . . . The swift stream raced and gyrated under them, tossing, distorting, and splitting the moon's reflected face. Spots of froth travelled past, and intercepted weeds waved behind the piles.

Tess of the d'Urbervilles

Hardy knew the Frome and its tributaries as only a boy who had grown up near them could.[139]
He was always conscious of rivers: in Desperate Remedies *there is an intriguing meeting between Cytherea and Edward after they have first seen only each other's reflections in the river. In 1876, travelling in Germany, Hardy enjoyed a view from a Heidelberg tower:*

. . . a singular optical effect that was almost tragic. Owing to mist the wide landscape itself was not visible, but [*quoting his own note*] 'the Rhine glared like a riband of blood, as if it serpentined through the atmosphere above the earth's surface'.

The Life of Thomas Hardy

That same year the Hardys moved to Sturminster Newton – 'their happiest days'.

[*July* 1876] Rowed on the Stour in the evening, the sun setting up the river. Just afterwards a faint exhalation visible on the surface of water as we stirred it with the oars. A fishy smell from the numerous eels and other fish beneath. Mowers salute us. Rowed among the water-lilies to gather them. Their long ropy stems.

Passing the island drove out a flock of swallows from the bushes and sedge, which had gone there to roost. Gathered meadow-sweet. Rowed with difficulty through the weeds, the rushes on the border standing like palisades against the bright sky. . . . A cloud in the sky like a huge quill-pen.

The Life of Thomas Hardy

[1877] *November* 12. A flooded river after the incessant rains of yesterday. Lumps of froth float down like swans in front of our house. At the arches of the large stone bridge the froth has accumulated and lies like hillocks of salt against the bridge; then the arch chokes, and after a silence coughs out air and froth, and gurgles on.

The Life of Thomas Hardy

On Sturminster Foot-Bridge
(Onomatopoeic)

Reticulations creep upon the slack stream's face
   When the wind skims irritably past,
The current clucks smartly into each hollow place
That years of flood have scrabbled in the pier's sodden base;
   The floating-lily leaves rot fast.

On a roof stand the swallows ranged in wistful waiting rows,
   Till they arrow off and drop like stones
Among the eyot-withies at whose foot the river flows:
And beneath the roof is she who in the dark world shows
   As a lattice-gleam when midnight moans.

Mr Barnes does not merely use the beauties of nature as a background. . . . He gives us whole poems of still life. . . . In these the slow green river Stour, with its deep pools whence the trout leaps to the May-fly undisturbed by anglers, is found to be the dearest river of his memories, and the inspirer of some of his happiest effusions. Its multitudinous patches of water-lilies yellow and white, its pollard willows, its heavy-headed bulrushes, are for ever haunting him; and such is the loving fidelity with which the stream is depicted, that one might almost construct a bird's-eye view of its upper course by joining together the vignettes which are given of this and that point in its length.

   An Unsigned Review of Poems of Rural Life in the Dorset Dialect *by William Barnes, 1879*

'THE NEVER SPEECHLESS SEA'

[Anne] passed along by the houses facing the sea, and scanned the shore, the footway, and the open road close to her, which illuminated by the slanting moon to a great brightness, sparkled with minute facets of crystallized salts from the water sprinkled there during the day. The promenaders at the further edge appeared in dark profiles; and beyond them was the grey sea, parted into two masses by the tapering braid of moonlight across the waves.

   The Trumpet-Major

[1879 *August*] At Weymouth. *Plaits* visible on the comparatively smooth sea.

   Memoranda I

It was one of those very still nights when, if you stand on the high hills anywhere within two or three miles of the sea, you can hear the rise and fall of the tide along the shore, coming and going every few moments like a sort of great snore of the sleeping world.

A Tradition of Eighteen Hundred and Four

[1875] Evening. Just after sunset. Sitting with E. on a stone under the wall before the Refreshment cottage. The sounds are two, and only two. On the left Durlstone Head roaring high and low, like a giant asleep. On the right a thrush. Above the bird hangs the new moon, and a steady planet.

The Life of Thomas Hardy

Once at Swanage

The spray sprang up across the cusps of the moon,
   And all its light loomed green
   As a witch-flame's weirdsome sheen
At the minute of an incantation scene;
And it greened our gaze — that night at demilune.

Roaring high and roaring low was the sea
   Behind the headland shores:
   It symboled the slamming of doors,
Or a regiment hurrying over hollow floors. . . .
And there we two stood, hands clasped; I and she!

At the top [Pierston and Avice] turned and stood still. To the left of them the sky was streaked like a fan with the lighthouse rays, and under their front, at periods of a quarter of a minute, there arose a deep, hollow stroke like the single beat of a drum, the intervals being filled with a long-drawn rattling, as of bones between huge canine jaws. It came from the vast concave of Deadman's Bay, rising and falling against the pebble dyke.

The Well-Beloved

[Ethelberta and Picotee] went further, and stood on the foreshore, listening to the din. Seaward appeared nothing distinct save a black horizontal band embodying itself out of the grey water, strengthening its blackness, and enlarging till it looked like a nearing wall. It was the concave face of a coming wave. On its summit a white edging arose with the aspect of a lace frill; it broadened, and fell over the front with a terrible concussion. Then all before them was a sheet of whiteness, which spread with amazing rapidity, till they found themselves standing in the midst of it, as in a field of snow. Both felt an insidious chill encircling their ankles, and they rapidly ran up the beach.
. . . They retreated further up the beach, when the hissing fleece of froth slid again down the shingle, dragging the pebbles under it with a rattle as of a beast gnawing bones.

The Hand of Ethelberta

The precipice was still in view, and before it several huge columns of rock appeared, detached from the mass behind. Two of these were particularly noticeable in the grey air — one vertical, stout and square; the other slender and tapering. They were individualized as husband and wife by the coast men. The waves leapt up their sides like a pack of hounds; this, however, though fearful in its boisterousness, was nothing to the terrible games that sometimes went on round the knees of those giants in stone.

The Hand of Ethelberta

It was half-past eleven before the *Spruce*. . .had steamed back again to Sandbourne. The direction and increase of the wind had made it necessary to keep the vessel still further to sea on their return than in going, that they might clear without risk the windy, sousing, thwacking, basting, scourging Jack Ketch[140] of a corner called Old-Harry Point, which lay about halfway along their track and stood, with its detached stumps of white rock, like a skeleton's lower jaw, grinning at British navigation. Here strong currents and cross currents were beginning to interweave their scrolls and meshes, the water rising behind them in tumultuous heaps, and slamming against the fronts and angles of cliff, whence it flew into the air like clouds of flour. Who could now believe that this roaring abode of chaos smiled in the sun as gently as an infant during the summer days not long gone by, every pinnacle, crag, and cave returning a doubled image across the glassy sea?

The Hand of Ethelberta

[Cytherea and Edward] were opposite Ringsworth Shore. The cliffs here were formed of strata completely contrasting with those of the further side of the Bay, whilst in and beneath the water hard boulders had taken the place of sand and shingle, between which, however, the sea glided noiselessly, without breaking the crest of a single wave, so strikingly calm was the air. The breeze had entirely died away, leaving the water of that rare glassy smoothness which is unmarked even by the small dimples of the least aerial movement. Purples and blues of divers shades were reflected from this mirror accordingly as each undulation sloped east or west. They could see the rocky bottom some twenty feet beneath them, luxuriant with weeds of various growths, and dotted with pulpy creatures reflecting a silvery and spangled radiance upwards to their eyes.

Desperate Remedies

The Singing Lovers

I rowed: the dimpled tide was at the turn,
And mirth and moonlight spread upon the bay:
There were two singing lovers in the stern;
But mine had gone away, –
Whither, I shunned to say!

The houses stood confronting us afar,
A livid line against the evening glare;

The small lamps livened; then out-stole a star;
  But my Love was not there, –
  Vanished, I sorrowed where!

His arm was round her, both full facing me
With no reserve. Theirs was not love to hide;
He held one tiller-rope, the other she;
  I pulled – the merest glide, –
  Looked on at them, and sighed.

The moon's glassed glory heaved as we lay swinging
Upon the undulations. Shoreward, slow,
The plash of pebbles joined the lovers' singing,
  But she of a bygone vow
  Joined in the song not now!
 Weymouth

The sea at Bonchurch, I.O.W., where in 1910 Hardy had visited Swinburne's grave, was the significant setting for his poem about one of his most-admired poets, "A Singer Asleep". Too long to quote here, it ends memorably:

So here, beneath the waking constellations,
Where the waves peal their everlasting strains,
And their dull subterrene reverberations
Shake him when storms make mountains of their plains –
Him once their peer in sad improvisations,
And deft as wind to cleave their frothy manes –
I leave him, while the daylight gleam declines
  Upon the capes and chines.

As his 1895 Preface to A Pair of Blue Eyes *showed, Hardy's most profound experience of the sea came from his Cornish wooing of Emma.*

There lonely I found her,
The sea-birds around her,
And other than nigh things uncaring to know.[141]

[1872] *August.* At Beeny. The Cliff: green towards the land, blue-black towards the sea. . . . Every ledge has a little starved green grass upon it; all vertical parts bare. Seaward, a dark grey ocean beneath a pale green sky, upon which lie branches of red cloud. A lather of foam round the base of each rock. The sea is full of motion internally, but still as a whole. Quiet & silent in the distance, noisy & restless close at hand.

                Memoranda I

Beeny Cliff
March 1870 – March 1913

I

O the opal and the sapphire of that wandering western sea,
And the woman riding high above with bright hair flapping free –
The woman whom I loved so, and who loyally loved me.

II

The pale mews plained below us, and the waves seemed far away
In a nether sky, engrossed in saying their ceaseless babbling say,
As we laughed light-heartedly aloft on that clear-sunned March day.

III

A little cloud then cloaked us, and there flew an irised rain,
And the Atlantic dyed its levels with a dull misfeatured stain,
And then the sun burst out again, and purples prinked the main.

IV

 – Still in all its chasmal beauty bulks old Beeny to the sky,
And shall she and I not go there once again now March is nigh,
And the sweet things said in that March say anew there by and by?

V

What if still in chasmal beauty looms that wild weird western shore,
The woman now is – elsewhere – whom the ambling pony bore,
And nor knows nor cares for Beeny, and will laugh there nevermore.

HARDY'S REALISM

All his life Hardy pondered the art of writing. He set out to record 'impressions, not convictions'; and impressions, but not 'a mere photograph'.[142] *So in art he did not care for simple reproductions:*

[1890] *August 5* . . . Art is a disproportioning – (i.e. distorting, throwing out of proportion) – of realities, to show more clearly the features that matter in those realities, which, if merely copied or reported inventorially, might possibly be observed, but would more probably be overlooked. Hence ''realism'' is not Art.

He explained further what kind of 'realism' he sought in his natural descriptions:

January 1881. Style – Consider the Wordsworthian dictum (the more perfectly the natural

145

object is reproduced, the more truly poetic the picture). This reproduction is achieved by seeing into the *heart of a thing* (as rain, wind, for instance), and is realism, in fact, though through being pursued by means of the imagination it is confounded with invention, which is pursued by the same means. It is, in short, reached by what M. Arnold calls 'the imaginative reason'.

The Life of Thomas Hardy

On the one hand, Hardy knew that the natural world could be very beautiful.

Stephen walked back to the rectory through the meadows, as he had come, surrounded by the soft musical purl of the water through little weirs, the modest light of the moon, the freshening smell of the dews outspread around. It was a time when mere seeing is meditation, and meditation peace. Stephen was hardly philosopher enough to avail himself of Nature's offer.

A Pair of Blue Eyes

Hardy's own philosophy about Nature is the subject of a later part of this book. But at the end of so many observations and descriptions here of the natural world in all its aspects, it needs to be noted too that Hardy was, in a commonly accepted sense, a realist. He had no illusions about Nature, – or townsfolk who sentimentalised about the country:

As Nature was hardly invented at this early part of the century, Bob's Matilda could not say much about the glamour of the hills, or the shimmering of the foliage, or the wealth of glory in the distant sea, as she would doubtless have done had she lived later on; but she did her best to be interesting, asking Bob about matters of social interest in the neighbourhood, to which she seemed quite a stranger.

. . . "What a lovely place you've got here!" said Miss Johnson, when the miller had received her from the captain. "A real stream of water, a real mill-wheel, and real fowls, and everything!"

"Yes, 'tis real enough," said Loveday, looking at the river with balanced sentiments; "and so you will say when you've lived here a bit as mis'ess, and had the trouble of claning the furniture."

The Trumpet-Major

In the following poem he mocks not only those who think the bucolic life a life apart – but also himself (or the speaker) who expects Phyllis's 'inner poetries' to be more high-flown, more in tune with the Great Mother, than they are:

The Milkmaid

Under a daisied bank
There stands a rich red ruminating cow,
And hard against her flank
A cotton-hooded milkmaid bends her brow.

146

Captions in order of sequence of photographs

Sunlit sheep at Corfe
River Frome: Winter floods
'Raiment of gold . . .'
'A firmament of snow . . .'
Spiderweb
Atlantic storm brewing
Furrows at Came, Dorset
Woodland track on a frosty morning

The flowery river-ooze
Upheaves and falls; the milk purrs in the pail;
    Few pilgrims but would choose
The peace of such a life in such a vale.

    The maid breathes words — to vent,
It seems, her sense of Nature's scenery,
    Of whose life, sentiment,
And essence, very part itself is she.

    She bends a glance of pain,
And, at a moment, lets escape a tear;
    Is it that passing train,
Whose alien whirr offends her country ear? —

    Nay! Phyllis does not dwell
On visual and familiar things like these;
    What moves her is the spell
Of inner themes and inner poetries:

    Could but by Sunday morn
Her gay new gown come, meads might dry to dun,
    Trains shriek till ears were torn,
If Fred would not prefer that Other One.

Hardy knew about life in the country — that, for example, 'the tenant-farmers [were] the natural enemies of tree, bush, and brake', and that often the view could be unremittingly dreary. At Flintcomb Ash, Tess first

. . . reached the farmhouse, which was almost sublime in its dreariness. There was not a tree within sight; there was not, at this season, a green pasture — nothing but fallow and turnips everywhere; in large fields divided by hedges plashed to unrelieved levels.

Beyond the farmhouse, when work began, she found:

. . . the whole field was in colour a desolate drab; it was a complexion without features, as if a face, from chin to brow, should be only an expanse of skin. The sky wore, in another colour, the same likeness; a white vacuity of countenance with the lineaments gone. So these two upper and nether visages confronted each other all day long, the white face looking down on the brown face, without anything standing between them but the two girls crawling over the surface of the former like flies.

Tess of the d'Urbervilles

He knew that the natural scene could often be contrary or uninspiring:

The air was disturbed by stiff summer blasts, productive of windfalls and premature descents of leafage. It was an hour when unripe apples shower down in orchards, and unbrowned chestnuts descend in their husks upon the park glades.

Two on a Tower

Christmas had passed. Dreary winter with dark evenings had given place to more dreary winter with light evenings. Rapid thaws had ended in rain, rain in wind, wind in dust. Showery days had come – the season of pink dawns and white sunsets; and people hoped that the March weather was over.

The Trumpet-Major

When the evening sun faded, the 'previously gilded' hills became 'dreary';[143] *and in London,*

It was one of those ripe and mellow afternoons that sometimes colour London with their golden light at this time of the year, and produce those marvellous sunset effects which, if they were not known to be made up of kitchen coal-smoke and animal exhalations, would be rapturously applauded.

The Well-Beloved

Hardy could be perfectly detached in considering the natural world. Despite his love of birds and his hatred of their suffering through frost or human cruelty, he describes with apparently uncaring matter-of-factness how Swithin St Cleeve catches birds to allay his and Lady Constantine's hunger while camping out at the observatory:[144]

When he reappeared, he produced, not a rabbit, but four sparrows and a thrush.

"I could do nothing in the way of a rabbit without setting a wire," he said. "But I have managed to get these by knowing where they roost."

He showed her how to prepare the birds, and, having set her to roast them by the fire, departed with the pitcher, to replenish it at the brook which flowed near the homestead in the neighbouring Bottom. . . .

. . . The birds were now ready, and the table was spread.

Two on a Tower

The eternal stars, says Swithin, are not what they seem:

"And to add a new weirdness to what the sky possesses in its size and formlessness, there is involved the quality of decay. For all the wonder of these everlasting stars, eternal spheres, and what not, they are not everlasting, they are not eternal; they burn out like candles. You see that dying one in the body of the Greater Bear? Two centuries ago it was as bright as the others. The senses may become terrified by plunging among them as they are, but there is a pitifulness even in their glory . . ."

Two on a Tower

Hardy was, because of the same realism, unable to go as far as his wife in, for example, her wish totally to abolish vivisection. The money he left in his will was

to be applied *so far as is practicable* to the investigation of the means by which animals are conveyed from their houses to the slaughter-houses with a view to the *lessening* of their sufferings in such transit. [*My italics*].

The Life of Thomas Hardy

Like most human beings, Hardy's attitudes to many things, including Nature, were self-contradictory. With his heart (and eyes) he often felt passionately, and with his mind he often controlled or modified that feeling.

He Never Expected Much
[*or*]
[*A reflection*] *on My Eighty-Sixth Birthday*

Well, World, you have kept faith with me,
    Kept faith with me;
Upon the whole you have proved to be
    Much as you said you were.
Since as a child I used to lie
Upon the leaze and watch the sky,
Never, I own, expected I
    That life would all be fair.

'Twas then you said, and since have said,
    Times since have said,
In that mysterious voice you shed
    From clouds and hills around:
'Many have loved me desperately,
Many with smooth serenity,
While some have shown contempt of me
    Till they dropped underground.

'I do not promise overmuch,
    Child; overmuch;
Just neutral-tinted haps and such,'
    You said to minds like mine.
Wise warning for your credit's sake!
Which I for one failed not to take,
And hence could stem such strain and ache
    As each year might assign.

II

HARDY'S NATURE IMAGERY

Hardy's nature imagery goes so deep that here we can only lift the lid and peer inside at the most important shapes and outlines, which can lead a reader to further intriguing discoveries.

The connections Hardy made between the world of nature and the world of his human experience were manifold. His formative years, spent like Clym 'permeated with the heath' and other natural features, made him instinctively express things in terms of nature, turn instinctively and inevitably to nature for his comparisons or points of reference:

Love's dewy freshness could not live under a vertical sun.
Distress came over him like cold air from a cave.
A tenderness spread over Grace like a dew.
The next noteworthy move in Jude's life was that in which he appeared gliding steadily onward through a dusky landscape of some three years' later leafage . . .[145]

So, knitting them inextricably together, he connects and compares humans with the rest of the natural world:

He was a round-faced, good-humoured fellow to look at, having two little pieces of moustache on his upper lip, like a pair of minnows rampant . . .

The Well-Beloved

"I don't want you to come to me all of a sudden," said Henchard in jerks, and moving like a great tree in a wind.

The Mayor of Casterbridge

On the edge of the table adjoining Mr Power a shining nozzle of metal was quietly resting, like a dog's nose. It was directed point-blank at the young man.
Dare started. "Ah – a revolver?" he said.

A Laodicean

Mrs Garland had 'that ploughed-ground appearance near the corner of her once handsome eyes';[146] and Elfride's eyes ('a sublimation of all of her. . .there she lived') were blue:

. . . blue as autumn distance – blue as the blue we see between the retreating mouldings of hills and woody slopes on a sunny September morning. A misty and shady blue, that had no beginning or surface, and was looked *into* rather than *at*.

As to her presence, it was not powerful; it was weak. Some women can make their personality pervade the atmosphere of a whole banqueting hall; Elfride's was no more pervasive than that of a kitten.

A Pair of Blue Eyes

As the dairymaids try to escape the flooded lane:

The rosy-cheeked, bright-eyed quartet looked so charming in their light summer attire, clinging to the roadside bank like pigeons on a roof-slope, that [Angel] stopped to regard them before coming close.

Tess of the d'Urbervilles

Tess in love ' – unlike anything else in nature – ' was yet marked by

. . . the buoyancy of her tread, like the skim of a bird which has not quite alighted.

Tess of the d'Urbervilles

When the reaping-machine was brought up:

Presently there arose from within a ticking like the love-making of the grasshopper;

Tess of the d'Urbervilles

– and the English, on fine days watching Buonaparte's invasion preparations on the French coast, saw:

. . . a huge army moving and twinkling like a school of mackerel under the rays of the sun.

The Trumpet-Major

Egbert Mayne was moved by the music of Messiah:

The varying strains shook and bent him to themselves as a rippling brook shakes and bends a shadow.

An Indiscretion in the Life of an Heiress

Lucy Savile had changed with the years:

A pervasive grayness overspread her once dark brown hair, like morning rime on heather. The parting down the middle was wide and jagged; once it had been a thin white line, a narrow crevice between two high banks of shade.

Fellow-Townsmen

Queen Iseult sings sadly of her absent love Tristram (in a play written when Hardy was in his eighty-third year):

> Could he but come to me
> Amid these murks that lour,
> My hollow life would be
> So brimmed with ecstasy
> As heart-dry honeysuck by summer shower:

> Could he but come, could he
> But come to me!
>
> *The Famous Tragedy of the Queen of Cornwall*

The warring upheaval of Europe that is the setting for The Dynasts *is, perhaps unexpectedly – but characteristically of Hardy – full of natural imagery as well as natural allusions:*[147]

The soldiery are like a thicket of reeds in which every reed should be a man. A gloomy-eyed figure [*Napoleon*] stalks. . .with the restlessness of a wild animal.

The armies on the move are

. . . a silent insect-creep. . .this movement as of molluscs on a leaf . . .

As they build a defensive breastwork at Torres Vedras:

. . . innumerable human figures are busying themselves like cheese-mites all along the northernmost frontage;

– and before the Battle of Waterloo:

As the curtain of mist is falling . . . from all parts of Europe long and sinister black files are crawling hitherward in serpentine black lines, like slowworms through grass.

– (There is of course a good reason for these images which show the ordinary man as a pawn at his superiors' command,[148] *and also as no better than an insect, in both the Darwinian universe and the inscrutable mind of The Will – aspects of Hardy's impressions which will be illustrated later.)*

The transport ships supporting the Peninsular War:

. . . convoyed by battleships, float on before the wind almost imperceptibly, like preened duck feathers across a pond;

– and in Dorset a scurrying refugee from Napoleon's supposed landing says:

> All yesterday the firing at Boulogne
> Was like the seven thunders heard in Heaven
> When the fierce angel spoke. So did he draw
> Men's eyes that way, the while his thousand boats
> Full-manned, flat-bottomed for the shallowest shore,
> Dropped down to west, and crossed our frontage here.
> Seen from above they specked the water-shine
> As will a flight of swallows towards dim eve,

Descending on a smooth and loitering stream
To seek some eyot's sedge.

The Dynasts[149]

*   *   *

In reverse, Hardy often likens the world of nature to his own human world:

Open-air cucumber leaves have collapsed like green umbrellas with all the stays broken.

Memoranda I

The rain fell upon the keel of the old lerret[150] like corn thrown in handfuls by some colossal sower.

The Well-Beloved

(The rain also makes a 'banner of gauze'; and the sun's rays 'stream though the atmosphere like straying hair'.[151])

At Stonehenge as dawn broke:

The uniform concavity of black cloud was lifting bodily like the lid of a pot, letting in at the earth's edge the coming day.

Tess of the d'Urbervilles

Herons came, with a great bold noise as of opening doors and shutters, out of the boughs of a plantation which they frequented at the side of the mead; or, if already on the spot, hardily maintained their standing in the water as the pair walked by, watching them by moving their heads round in a slow, horizontal, passionless wheel, like the turn of puppets by clockwork.

Tess of the d'Urbervilles

Wildeve walked a pace or two among the heather without replying. The pause was filled up by the intonation of a pollard thorn a little way to windward, the breezes filtering through its unyielding twigs as through a strainer. It was as if the night sang dirges with clenched teeth.

The Return of the Native

The scene without grew darker; mud-coloured clouds bellied downwards from the sky like vast hammocks slung across it . . .

The Return of the Native

While overtaking and conversing with her [Jocelyn] had not observed that the rising wind, which had proceeded from puffing to growling, and from growling to screeching,

156

with the accustomed suddenness of its changes here, had at length brought what it promised by these vagaries – rain. The drops, which had at first hit their left cheeks like the pellets of a popgun, soon assumed the character of a raking fusillade from the bank adjoining, one shot of which was sufficiently smart to go through Jocelyn's sleeve.

The Well-Beloved

[Eustacia] went on, and as the path was an infinitely small parting in the shaggy locks of the heath, the reddleman followed exactly in her trail.

The Return of the Native

Particularly notable, as in the last quotations, is Hardy's likening of nature to the human body: 'On a day which had a summer face and a winter constitution' ... (In his '1867' notebook, he had copied three instances of a similar body imagery in Gray: 'The cheek of Sorrow', 'the toiling hand of Care', and 'Contemplation's sober eye'; and in his own copies of, for example, Shakespeare, he marked phrases like 'toothed briars' and 'liberty plucks justice by the nose'.[152])

We have already seen many examples of this – Old Harry Point looking 'like a skeleton's lower jaw'; the sea 'like a sort of great snore of the sleeping world', 'the earthquake's lifting arm'; how 'the sun grows passionate-eyed' and 'the waves 'huzza'd like a multitude below'.[153]

They were passing under a huge oak-tree whose limbs, irregular with shoulders, knuckles, and elbows, stretched horizontally over the lane in a manner recalling Absalom's death.[154]

Two on a Tower

The wind continued to rise till at length something from the lungs of the gale alighted like a feather upon the pane, and remained there sticking.

The Hand of Ethelberta

Lady Constantine and Swithin climb the ancient earthwork through the firs:

Thus they reached the foot of the column, ten thousand spirits in prison seeming to gasp their griefs from the funereal boughs overhead, and a few twigs scratching the pillar with the drag of impish claws as tenacious as those figuring in St Anthony's temptation.[155]

Two on a Tower

In poem after poem one reads expressions like 'Time's finger', or 'the foam-fingered sea'; 'the hot-faced sun' and 'its sneering glare'; 'the night's pinch', 'the tempest's wanton breath' and 'the barrows, bulging as they bosoms were'; how 'the stars wag as though they were / Panting for joy' or 'the hills ... Spoke, as they grayly gazed'; or

> Yes; trees were turning in their sleep
> Upon their windy pillows of gray . . .[156]

A January Night
(1879)

The rain smites more and more,
The east wind snarls and sneezes;
Through the joints of the quivering door
    The water wheezes.

The tip of each ivy-shoot
Writhes on its neighbour's face;
There is some hid dread afoot
    That we cannot trace.

Is it the spirit astray
Of the man at the house below
Whose coffin they took in to-day?
    We do not know.[157]

The Wound

I climbed to the crest,
    And, fog-festooned,
The sun lay west
    Like a crimson wound.

Like that wound of mine
    Of which none knew,
For I'd given no sign
    That it pierced me through.[158]

Sunset was also described as an image of death when young George Somerset was sketching in its glow, and after the shearing supper (page 48); or as an empty platform when the show is over. It is part of both the glory and the sadness of the universe. (In his copy of Richard II *Hardy marked Salisbury's sorrowful lines: 'Thy sun sets weeping in the lowly west, / Witnessing storms to come, woe, and unrest'.) In Hardy's world of images the reader comes to recognise the signals, or the signature: the frosted white or the gray ashen pallor, the dark, clouded, shadowed, leafless world of misery; and the warmly sunned richness of green leaves, the gleam and glow of light, the star in the heaven as emblem of bliss or wisdom, in the world of joy and laughter.*

    These and many others are the concrete images Hardy uses as part of his total vision of the pattern of life: a life in which the human mind is not (as with Wordsworth) necessarily in harmony with Nature, its setting – but locked into a relationship with it which is constantly fraught with tragedy. All Hardy's writing is ultimately informed by his unending search to understand reality, and its relation to the human mind. He sees that in the course of living the mind perceives reality in limited ways, incompletely, idiosyncratically – and often diverges from reality as it becomes more prejudiced, rigid, and fixed in its own world. For example, Hardy apologises for a trifling error in his own recollection by saying that it

. . . affords an instance of how our imperfect memories insensibly formalize the fresh originality of living fact – from whose shape they slowly depart, as machine-made castings depart by degrees from the sharp hand-work of the mould.

Preface to Wessex Tales

PATTERNS

Much of Hardy's grappling with the realities of the mind in its setting is expressed in his imagery, and particularly in the patterns which form the weave of his writing. Patterns are everywhere – dapples and flecks, light and shadows; lines of all kinds (gates, tracks, cracks, webs, boughs, lattices, veins, engravings); silhouettes and outlines. They carry a great weight of meaning.

[1882] *June 3* . . . As, in looking at a carpet, by following one colour a certain pattern is suggested, by following another colour, another; so in life the seer should watch that pattern among general things which his idiosyncrasy moves him to observe, and describe that alone. This is, quite accurately, a going to Nature; yet the result is no mere photograph, but purely the product of the writer's own mind.

The Life of Thomas Hardy

So the poet looks at Nature, the human setting, but draws the pattern he himself sees there. The pattern comes to represent how the thinking, or the impressions, of a human mind grow and develop in the real world.

That world is always in flux; we change too, but not always in time with our world, and often the changes are imperceptible to us. Often we only realize the pattern of life as it is fading forever from our sight; we only understand something when it's over.

'We live forward, we understand backward,' *copied Hardy into a notebook*[159]. Tess of the d'Urbervilles *was in an early version called* Too Late, Beloved! – *and 'too late' is a constant Hardy theme.*

The tones around me that I hear,
The aspects, meanings, shapes I see,
Are those removed ones missed when near,
And now perceived too late by me!

From The Rambler[160]

Before and after Summer

I

Looking forward to the spring
One puts up with anything,
On this February day
Though the winds leap down the street
Wintry scourgings seem but play,
And these later shafts of sleet
  – Sharper pointed than the first –
And these later snows – the worst –
Are as a half-transparent blind
Riddled by rays from sun behind.

II

Shadows of the October pine
Reach into this room of mine:
On the pine there swings a bird;
He is shadowed with the tree.
Mutely perched he bills no word;
Black as I am even is he.
For those happy suns are past,
Fore-discerned in winter last.
When went by their pleasure, then?
I, alas, perceived not when.

*Here is a most characteristic Hardy pattern – the riddled rays and shafts of sleet, the blocks of
light and shadow, which image outer reality, or through which it is perceived. A pattern symbolises
this intricate connection between mind and reality as an experience progresses – its beginning,
its developing moments and its final outcome. Hardy brings to his patterns his widely-read and
complex mind, and his appreciation of the visual arts and their techniques – including the Gothic
patterns of light and shadow and scrolls, tendrils, and curves deriving from Nature, with which
his early reading and his architect's training had made him familiar. He actually links Nature
with architecture – whose shape and form are more important than the ever-decaying materials used:*

This is, indeed, the actual process of organic nature herself, which is one continuous
substitution. She is always discarding the matter, while retaining the form.

Memories of Church Restoration[161]

*He also brings his feeling for the natural world into the choice of concrete images – such as the
tracery of tree branches, the dapple of light through them, the veins in hands and leaves.*

One of Hardy's most important images is the leaf and the tree.

A fresh love-leaf crumpled soon may die.[162]

Even half-god power
In spinning dooms
Had I, this frozen scene should flower,
And sand-swept plains and Arctic glooms
Should green them gay with waving leaves,
Mid which old friends and I would walk
With weightless feet and magic talk
　　　　Uncounted eves.

From *Could I but Will*

In a very early poem, written while he was an apprentice architect in London, he echoes the bitterness of his unmoneyed background, having no 'nest-egg' with which to further his wooing:

Postponement

Snow-bound in woodland, a mournful word,
Dropt now and then from the bill of a bird,
Reached me on wind-wafts; and thus I heard,
　　　　Wearily waiting: −

'I planned her a nest in a leafless tree,
But the passers eyed and twitted me,
And said: "How reckless a bird is he,
　　　　Cheerily mating!"

'Fear-filled, I stayed me till summer-tide,
In lewth of leaves to throne her bride;
But alas! her love for me waned and died,
　　　　Wearily waiting.

'Ah, had I been like some I see,
Born to an evergreen nesting-tree,
None had eyed and twitted me,
　　　　Cheerily mating!'
1866

[*Lewth:* warmth or shelter]

Vere Collins reported a conversation he had with Hardy in December 1920 on the last stanza of this poem. Hardy explained that

161

H: . . . earlier in the poem the young man is described as not being able to marry for want of money; and the woman as not waiting, but marrying someone else.

C: I understand that. The 'being born to an evergreen tree' means, then, simply and solely having money?

H: Yes.

Talks with Thomas Hardy at Max Gate

Although in this poem Hardy virtually cast himself as a bird, it was with trees that he came to identify more closely.

> I travel as a phantom now,
> For people do not wish to see
> In flesh and blood so bare a bough
>   As Nature makes of me.[163]

In "The Voice", a great key poem in the group written after his wife Emma's death, the voice he thinks he hears on the wind is gradually borne further away and dissolved to a mere whisper of sibilants, leaving him bare and comfortless:

The Voice

> Woman much missed, how you call to me, call to me,
> Saying that now you are not as you were
> When you had changed from the one who was all to me,
> But as at first, when our day was fair.
>
> Can it be you that I hear? Let me view you, then,
> Standing as when I drew near to the town
> Where you would wait for me; yes, as I knew you then,
> Even to the original air-blue gown!
>
> Or is it only the breeze, in its listlessness
> Travelling across the wet mead to me here,
> You being ever dissolved to wan wistlessness,
> Heard no more again far or near?
>
> Thus I; faltering forward,
> Leaves around me falling,
> Wind oozing thin through the thorn from norward
> And the woman calling.

December 1912

And in a later poem:

The Tree and the Lady

     I have done all I could
For that lady I knew! Through the heats I have shaded her,
Drawn to her songsters when summer has jaded her,
     Home from the heath or the wood.

     At the mirth-time of May,
When my shadow first lured her, I'd donned my new bravery
Of greenth: 'twas my all. Now I shiver in slavery,
     Icicles grieving me gray.

     Plumed to every twig's end
I could tempt her chair under me. Much did I treasure her
During those days she had nothing to pleasure her;
     Mutely she used me as friend.

     I'm a skeleton now,
And she's gone, craving warmth. The rime sticks like a skin to me;
Through me Arcturus peers; Nor'lights shoot into me;
     Gone is she, scorning my bough!

The skeleton, and the star and Aurora lights glinting through the branches (as Oak saw Vega 'suspended amid the leafless trees, and Cassiopeia's chair. . .daintily poised on the uppermost boughs'[164]) are fundamental elements in the pattern image. In another poem where he links himself with a tree, the pattern is also clear:

The Prospect

     The twigs of the birch imprint the December sky
        Like branching veins upon a thin old hand;
     I think of summer-time, yes, of last July,
        When she was beneath them, greeting a gathered band
           Of the urban and bland.

     Iced airs wheeze through the skeletoned hedge from the north,
        With steady snores, and a numbing that threatens snow,
     And skaters pass; and merry boys go forth
        To look for slides. But well, well do I know
           Whither I would go!
December 1912

This poem is one of many which show Emma also connected with trees and their pattern — if Thomas's tree is usually leafless with the death of love or in his old age, Emma is seen first in her prime, or in the first flush of their love, under rich foliage, ('Under boughs of brushwood. . .In a shade of lush-wood,'[165]) — here delightedly welcoming her garden-party guests. The pattern of leaf growth to fall is like the pattern of life and human consciousness, steadily working through the years, the world of nature sharing — or contrasting with — the developing pattern of the human mind from birth to death. When the poet sees the 'twigs . . . imprint the December sky' and the same branching veins on his hand, he becomes aware of the relation between his own inner world and the outer world of his setting — of how changes have happened in both, and time has passed.

When he looks back on his courtship of Emma and their first parting in March 1870, there again are the branches, and the pattern is specifically shown as the pattern of Fate, the 'foreshadowing' of 'what fortune might weave'.

At the Word 'Farewell'

She looked like a bird from a cloud
    On the clammy lawn,
Moving alone, bare-browed
    In the dim of dawn.
The candles alight in the room
    For my parting meal
Made all things withoutdoors loom
    Strange, ghostly, unreal.

The hour itself was a ghost,
    And it seemed to me then
As of chances the furthermost
    I should see her again.
I beheld not where all was so fleet
    That a Plan of the past
Which had ruled us from birthtime to meet
    Was in working at last:

No prelude did I there perceive
    To a drama at all,
Or foreshadow what fortune might weave
    From beginnings so small:
But I rose as if quicked by a spur
    I was bound to obey,
And stepped through the casement to her
    Still alone in the gray.
'I am leaving you. . . .Farewell!' I said,
    As I followed her on

By an alley bare boughs overspread;
    'I soon must be gone!'
Even then the scale might have been turned
    Against love by a feather,
But crimson one cheek of hers burned
    When we came in together.[166]

After Emma's death he again associates her with the alley of boughs:

The saddest moments of all are when I go into the garden and to that long straight walk at the top that you know, where she used to walk every evening just before dusk, the cat trotting faithfully behind her; and at times when I almost expect to see her as usual coming in from the flower-beds with a little trowel in her hand.

                  Letter to Mrs Henniker, 17 December 1912

The Going

Why did you give no hint that night
That quickly after the morrow's dawn,
And calmly, as if indifferent quite,
You would close your term here, up and be gone
    Where I could not follow
    With wing of swallow
To gain one glimpse of you ever anon!

    Never to bid good-bye,
    Or lip me the softest call,
Or utter a wish for a word, while I
Saw morning harden upon the wall,
    Unmoved, unknowing
    That your great going
Had place that moment, and altered all.

Why do you make me leave the house
And think for a breath it is you I see
At the end of the alley of bending boughs
Where so often at dusk you used to be;
    Till in darkening dankness
    The yawning blankness
Of the perspective sickens me!

    You were she who abode
    By those red-veined rocks far West,

You were the swan-necked one who rode
Along the beetling Beeny Crest,
   And, reining nigh me,
   Would muse and eye me,
While Life unrolled us its very best.

Why, then, latterly did we not speak,
Did we not think of those days long dead,
And ere your vanishing strive to seek
That time's renewal? We might have said,
   'In this bright spring weather
   We'll visit together
Those places that once we visited.'

   Well, well! All's past amend,
   Unchangeable. It must go.
I seem but a dead man held on end
To sink down soon. . . .O you could not know
   That such swift fleeing
   No soul foreseeing –
Not even I – would undo me so!
December 1912

In the March following Emma's death (November 1912) Hardy made a pilgrimage to Cornwall and revisited St Juliot Rectory, where they had met in March 1870. The 'lushwood' and the 'arched fane of leafage' have diminished to a tracery of bare branches which finally underlines that all is over:[167]

Where They Lived

   Dishevelled leaves creep down
   Upon that bank to-day,
Some green, some yellow, and some pale brown;
   The wet bents bob and sway;
The once warm slippery turf is sodden
Where we laughingly sat or lay.

   The summerhouse is gone,
   Leaving a weedy space;
The bushes that veiled it once have grown
   Gaunt trees that interlace,
Through whose lank limbs I see too clearly
   The nakedness of the place.

And where were hills of blue,
Blind drifts of vapour blow,
And the names of former dwellers few,
If any, people know,
And instead of a voice that called, 'Come in, Dears,'
Time calls, 'Pass below!'

Patterns of this kind in Hardy's writings (often repeated in the poem's pattern on the page) seem to signify, then, an experience, or a growth of consciousness, at all stages of a long and perhaps unseen development. The summer trees change to an engraving of twigs on the skies or a skeletal outline as the experience dies. The pattern often shows the ever-widening gap between the human mind and external reality; it grows up around us without our noticing, encloses us in its stiffening bonds, as we lose touch with reality, lose our flexible response to life and get caught in rigidities of our own making.[168]

Ten Years Since

'Tis ten years since
I saw her on the stairs,
Heard her in house-affairs,
And listened to her cares;
And the trees are ten feet taller,
And the sunny spaces smaller
Whose bloomage would enthrall her;
And the piano wires are rustier,
And smell of bindings mustier,
And lofts and lumber dustier
Than when, with casual look
And ear, light note I took
Of what shut like a book
Those ten years since!
November 1922[169]

It is not until something (like a death) awakens us that we realise how fixed in our attitudes, how blindly unaware of change, we have become — and the patterns have changed. Newman Flower recalled how when (in August 1922) Hardy showed him the house in Sturminster Newton where he and Emma once lived, the poet gazed at a particular tree in the garden:

Presently he exclaimed as if to himself:

"How it's grown! I planted that tree when I came here. It was then a small thing not so high as my shoulder."

He waited a moment as if thinking. Then:

"I suppose that was a long time ago. I brought my first wife here after our

167

honeymoon[170]. . . . She had long golden hair. . . . How that tree has grown! But that was in 1876. . . . How it has changed . . .'' He paused, still staring at the tree − then remarked: "Time changes everything except something within us which is always surprised by change.''

*   *   *

LINES

If the body imagery says something about the oneness of all created things, it also shows, like the lines of nature which tell us about ourselves and sometimes screen and edit what we see, the importance of the natural setting as the world which men and women inhabit: a world, a universe, whose laws seem often at variance with the sensibilities, and the minds, of human beings. These paradoxes at the heart of Hardy's impressions will be more fully illustrated later; but his patterns reflect and symbolise them.

The skeletal forms of nature are part of the line patterns which are so often seen by Hardy − the red-veined rocks, the 'tangled bine-stems. . .like strings of broken lyres', the gated crossroads, the 'silken strings' of rain, the sun's rays which 'riddled the ribs of the sunshade', the floors 'criss-crossed by their feet', the hieroglyphs of lineage and all the engravings and scrawls of experience on human minds and faces.[171]

[1886] *December* 7. Winter. The landscape has turned from a painting to an engraving. . .
The Life of Thomas Hardy

On an early winter afternoon, clear but not cold, when the vegetable world was a weird multitude of skeletons through whose ribs the sun shone freely, a gleaming landau came to a pause on the crest of a hill in Wessex . . .

A Laodicean

When Stephen watches Knight and Elfride (with her 'plenteous twines of beautiful hair') in the dark summer-house after all the dots, sparkles and threads of light made by the struck match:

Their two foreheads were close together, almost touching, and both were looking down. Elfride was holding her watch, Knight was holding the light with one hand, his left arm being round her waist. Part of the scene reached Stephen's eyes through the horizontal bars of woodwork, which crossed their forms like the ribs of a skeleton.

As he walks away in despair, now pierced and illuminated by new knowledge of the state of affairs, sometimes pausing 'under the low-hanging arms of the trees', he hears the church bell toll the first strokes of a death-knell:

168

The young man saw from amid the trees a bright light shining, the rays from which radiated like needles through the sad plumy foliage of the yews. Its direction was from the centre of the churchyard.

A Pair of Blue Eyes

Elfride, puzzled by 'strange conjunctions of phenomena', linked with Fate, in her love-affair with Stephen, sits thinking at her window − and sees other conjunctions in nature which match her inner landscape:

She looked out, but to no purpose. The dark rim of the upland drew a keen sad line against the pale glow of the sky, unbroken except where a young cedar on the lawn, that had outgrown its fellow trees, shot its pointed head across the horizon, piercing the firmamental lustre like a sting.

A Pair of Blue Eyes

The lines of nature mirror the lines of human life: the mazes of the woodland paths image the complexities of the mind and its problems.

Thus these people with converging destinies went along the road together, till the track of the carriage and that of Winterborne parted . . .

The Woodlanders

[Grace] traced the remainder of the woodland track, dazed by the complications of her position.

− Later, waiting for her father's return from his interview with Mrs Charmond:

In an indefinite dread . . . she left the house. . .and took a loitering walk in the woodland track by which she imagined he would come home. This track under the bare trees and over the cracking sticks, screened and roofed in from the outer world of wind by a network of boughs, led her slowly on . . .

The Woodlanders

The labyrinth is a metaphor which occurs more than once. Elfride in A Pair of Blue Eyes *seems to be in a maze of relationships which she is too inexperienced to handle − a labyrinth of class, equality and the female/male spectrum, and her virtual imprisonment in Cornwall. In* Desperate Remedies *the labyrinth is explicit − and not just because it is a novel of detection and mystery. Both Cytherea and Edward are faced with it: Cytherea in the problems of her life after her father is accidentally killed:*

She unknowingly stood, as it were, upon the extreme posterior edge of a tract in her life, in which the real meaning of Taking Thought had never been known. It was the last hour of experience she ever enjoyed with a mind entirely free from a knowledge of that labyrinth into which she stepped immediately afterwards − to continue a perplexed course along its mazes for the greater portion of twenty-nine subsequent months.

Desperate Remedies

– while Edward was:

. . . fully conscious of the labyrinth into which he had wandered between his wish to behave honourably in the dilemma of his engagement to his cousin Adelaide and the intensity of his love for Cytherea.

Desperate Remedies

Another inexperienced young woman for whom Hardy felt great tenderness (Eustacia) had a dream as she was entering the labyrinth of her relationship with Clym Yeobright – a dream full of characteristic images:

She dreamt a dream; and few human beings, from Nebuchadnezzar to the Swaffham tinker,[172] ever dreamt a more remarkable one. Such an elaborately developed, perplexing, exciting dream was certainly never dreamed by a girl in Eustacia's situation before. It had as many ramifications as the Cretan labyrinth, as many fluctuations as the Northern Lights, as much colour as a parterre in June, and was as crowded with figures as a coronation. . . .

There was, however, gradually evolved from its transformation scenes a less extravagant episode, in which the heath dimly appeared behind the general brilliancy of the action. She was dancing to wondrous music, and her partner was the man in silver armour who had accompanied her through the previous fantastic changes, the visor of his helmet being closed. The mazes of the dance were ecstatic. Soft whispering came into her ear from under the radiant helmet, and she felt like a woman in Paradise. Suddenly these two wheeled out from the mass of dancers, dived into one of the pools of the heath, and came out somewhere beneath into an iridescent hollow, arched with rainbows. 'It must be here,' said the voice by her side, and blushingly looking up she saw him removing his casque to kiss her. At that moment there was a cracking noise, and his figure fell into fragments like a pack of cards.

The Return of the Native

Often the complexity of life is shown in the way we see patterns not directly, but reflected on to some other place or surface. In the bell-tower at Cytherea and Edward's so-long-deferred wedding, after so much tragedy, the ringers are seen, as

Their ever-changing shadows mingle on the wall in an endless variety of kaleidoscopic forms . . .

– while in contrast with their candle-light (it is ten o'clock at night):

. . . is the scene discernible through the screen beneath the tower archway. At the extremity of the long mysterious avenue of the nave and chancel can be seen shafts of moonlight streaming in at the east window of the church – blue, phosphoric, and ghostly.

Desperate Remedies

When Farfrae's sensationally new horse-drill appears in the road outside:

The sun fell so flat on the houses and pavement opposite Lucetta's residence that they poured their brightness into her rooms. Suddenly, after a rumbling of wheels, there were added to this steady light a fantastic series of circling irradiations upon the ceiling, and the companions turned to the window. Immediately opposite a vehicle of strange description had come to a standstill, as if it had been placed there for exhibition.

And at another time of ominous uncertainty, when a weather change put the harvest disastrously in doubt:

The fact was, that no sooner had the sickles begun to play than the atmosphere suddenly felt as if cress would grow in it without other nourishment. It rubbed people's cheeks like damp flannel when they walked abroad. There was a gusty, high, warm wind; isolated raindrops starred the window-panes at remote distances: the sunlight would flap out like a quickly opened fan, throw the pattern of the window upon the floor of the room in a milky, colourless shine, and withdraw as suddenly as it had appeared.

The Mayor of Casterbridge

At a critical moment of death and discovery, Knight enters the dead Mrs Jethway's cottage:

The fire was out, but the moonlight entered the quarried window, and made patterns upon the floor. The rays enabled them to see . . .

A Pair of Blue Eyes

She Who Saw Not

'Did you see something within the house
That made me call you before the red sunsetting?
Something that all this common scene endows
With a richened impress there can be no forgetting?'

' – I have found nothing to see therein,
O Sage, that should have made you urge me to enter,
Nothing to fire the soul, or the sense to win;
I rate you as a rare misrepresenter!'

' – Go anew, Lady, – in by the right. . .
Well: why does your face not shine like the face of Moses?'

' – I found no moving thing there save the light
And shadow flung on the wall by the outside roses.'

' – Go yet once more, pray. Look on a seat.'
' – I go. . . .O Sage, it's only a man that sits there
With eyes on the sun. Mute, – average head to feet.'
' – No more?' – 'No more. Just one the place befits there,

'As the rays reach in through the open door,
And he looks at his hand, and the sun glows through his fingers,
While he's thinking thoughts whose tenour is no more
To me than the swaying rose-tree shade that lingers.'

No more. And years drew on and on
Till no sun came, dank fogs the house enfolding;
And she saw inside, when the form in the flesh had gone,
As a vision what she had missed when the real beholding.

WEBS

With the dank fogs in the ageing house Hardy might well have added another favourite pattern image: cobwebs. They had a particular fascination for him. (One of his housemaids told how he always pointed them out even when dust or other housekeeping imperfections went unnoticed.)[173]
He easily saw webs as images:

Swithin points out the stars:

"Look, for instance, at those pieces of darkness in the Milky Way," he went on, pointing with his finger to where the galaxy stretched across over their heads with the luminousness of a frosted web.

Two on a Tower

Anne and the crowd watch Nelson's Victory *disappear over the horizon:*

The courses[174] of the *Victory* were absorbed into the main, then her topsails went, and then her top-gallants. She was now no more than a dead fly's wing on a sheet of spider's web; and even this fragment diminished. Anne could hardly bear to see the end, and yet she resolved not to flinch . . .

The Trumpet-Major

Mrs Pearston the elder was evidently sinking. The hand she gave him, which had formerly been as thin as a leaf, was now but a cobweb.

The Well-Beloved, 1892 version

Webs, though − or perhaps because − often beautiful, represent the transient and the insubstantial.

The vows of man and maid are frail as filmy gossamere.[175]

When Lady Constantine discovered, after her secret marriage, that she was pregnant:

In her terror she said she had sown the wind to reap the whirlwind.[176] Then the instinct of self-preservation flamed up in her like a fire. Her altruism in subjecting her self-love to benevolence, and letting Swithin go away from her, was demolished by the new necessity, as if it had been a gossamer web.

Two on a Tower

The poem "Aquae Sulis", about the shadowy goddess who had inhabited the temple near the Roman Baths, is full of 'the flutter of a filmy shape' and 'a gossamery noise fading off in the air'; and when Somerset looks for his friends among the gaming tables at Monte Carlo:

He beheld a hundred diametrically opposed wishes issuing from the murky intelligences around a table, and spreading down across each other upon the figured diagram in their midst, each to its own number. It was a network of hopes; which at the announcement, 'Sept, Rouge, Impair, et Manque', disappeared like magic gossamer, to be replaced in a moment by new. That all the people there, including himself, could be interested in what to the eye of perfect reason was a somewhat monotonous thing − the property of numbers to recur at certain longer or shorter intervals in a machine containing them − in other words, the blind groping after fractions of a result the whole of which was well known − was one testimony among many of the powerlessness of logic when confronted with imagination.

A Laodicean

Hardy links these webs with human experiences and realisations, and with the workings of the imagination. In a letter to the Daily Chronicle *written on Christmas Day, 1899, he wrote of the ghosts and phantoms of literature:*

In short, and speaking generally, these creatures of the imagination are uncertain, fleeting, and quivering, like winds, mists, gossamer-webs and fallen autumn leaves.[177]

A cobweb, unnoticed until marked by frost or rain, can represent the pattern of our life working unnoticed over the years (page 88). Probably after re-reading Tess *for a new edition, Hardy added the cobweb verse in the following poem: it emphasises the theme of when and how human understanding of an experience occurs.*

On the flat road a man at last appears:
　　How much his whitening hairs
Owe to the settling snow's mute anchorage,
And how much to a life's rough pilgrimage,
　　One cannot certify.

　　The frost is on the wane,
And cobwebs hanging close outside the pane
Pose as festoons of thick white worsted there,
Of their pale presence no eye being aware
　　Till the rime made them plain.

　　A second man comes by;
His ruddy beard brings fire to the pallid scene:
　　His coat is faded green;
　　Hence seems it that his mien
　　Wears something of the dye
Of the berried holm-trees that he passes nigh.

The snow-feathers so gently swoop that though
　　But half an hour ago
The road was brown, and now is starkly white,
A watcher would have failed defining quite
　　When it transformed it so.
Near Surbiton

The web — woven, knitted, or spun — is a symbol of 'the closely-knit interdependence' of humankind.[178]

December, 1886. To Lady Carnarvon's "small and early" . . . Her drawing-room was differently arranged from its method during her summer crushes. . . . Lady Carnarvon went about the room weaving little webs of sympathy between her guests.

　　　　　　　　　　　　　　　　　　　　　The Life of Thomas Hardy

Hardly anything could be more isolated or more self-contained than the life of these two [Marty and Winterborne] walking here in the lonely hour before day, when grey shades, material and mental, are so very grey. And yet their lonely courses formed no detached design at all, but were part of the pattern in the great web of human doings then weaving in both hemispheres from the White Sea to Cape Horn.

　　　　　　　　　　　　　　　　　　　　　　　　　The Woodlanders

It is also a metaphor for entanglement – physically, like the leaf which hangs like a suspended criminal;[179] and mentally, 'the subtle intertwining of nature and mind in a common death-bound motion.'[180] It suggests the unpleasant, the stifling, and decay, both personal and natural. Lady Constantine's unattractive brother, trying to engineer a marriage for her against her will, suspects her relationship with Swithin:

Throughout the meal Louis sat like a spider in the corner of his web, observing them narrowly, and at moments flinging out an artful thread here and there, with a view to their entanglement.

Two on a Tower

'The Will' or 'First Cause' (of which more later) is often imaged as the 'World-Weaver' or 'Spinner of the Years'. In the following poem (dating from the Boer War) webs are associated with fog, death, and a sad revelation by firelight; and contrasted with summer green, streams, and home.

A Wife in London
(December 1899)

I

She sits in the tawny vapour
    That the Thames-side lanes have uprolled,
    Behind whose webby fold on fold
Like a waning taper
    The street-lamp glimmers cold.

A messenger's knock cracks smartly,
    Flashed news is in her hand
    Of meaning it dazes to understand
Though shaped so shortly:
    He – has fallen – in the far South Land. . . .

II

'Tis the morrow; the fog hangs thicker,
    The postman nears and goes:
    A letter is brought whose lines disclose
By the firelight flicker
    His hand, whom the worm now knows:

Fresh – firm – penned in highest feather –
    Page-full of his hoped return,
    And of home-planned jaunts by brake and burn
In the summer weather,
    And of new love that they would learn.

And in a poem whose personal reflection of his own lengthy illness in 1880-1881 he tried to disguise, the delirium and distress and imprisonment of sickness are horridly imaged:

A Wasted Illness
(Overheard)

Through vaults of pain,
Enribbed and wrought with groins of ghastliness,
I passed, and garish spectres moved my brain
    To dire distress.

And hammerings,
And quakes, and shoots, and stifling hotness, blent
With webby waxing things and waning things
    As on I went.

'Where lies the end
To this foul way?' I asked with weakening breath.
Thereon ahead I saw a door extend –
    The door to Death.

It loomed more clear:
'At last!' I cried. 'The all-delivering door!'
And then, I knew not how, it grew less near
    Than theretofore.

And back slid I
Along the galleries by which I came,
And tediously the day returned, and sky,
    And life – the same.

And all was well:
Old circumstance resumed its former show,
And on my head the dews of comfort fell
    As ere my woe.

I roam anew,
Scarce conscious of my late distress. . . . And yet
Those backward steps to strength I cannot view
    Without regret.

For that dire train
Of waxing shapes and waning, passed before,
And those grim chambers, must be ranged again
    To reach that door.

In the following poem death and the entanglement of the mind is most poignantly imaged:

Bereft, She Thinks She Dreams

I dream that the dearest I ever knew
    Has died and been entombed.
I am sure it's a dream that cannot be true,
    But I am so overgloomed
By its persistence, that I would gladly
    Have quick death take me,
Rather than longer think thus sadly;
    So wake me, wake me!

It has lasted days, but minute and hour
    I expect to get aroused
And find him as usual in the bower
    Where we so happily housed.
Yet stays this nightmare too appalling,
    And like a web shakes me,
And piteously I keep on calling,
    And no one wakes me!

Between two lovers comes, at a certain time of year which he will always associate with it, though he doesn't know why it happened,

The Rift
(Song: Minor Mode)

'Twas just at gnat and cobweb-time,
When yellow begins to show in the leaf,
That your old gamut changed its chime
From those true tones – of span so brief! –
That met my beats of joy, of grief,
      As rhyme meets rhyme.

So sank I from my high sublime!
We faced but chancewise after that,
And never I knew or guessed my crime. . . .
Yes; 'twas the date – or nigh thereat –
Of the yellowing leaf; at moth and gnat
      And cobweb-time.

And in more than one poem[181] the cobwebs, like the cracks of decay, signify the damage of passing time which is an inescapable part of the tissue of the universe:

177

Now no Christmas brings in neighbours,
And the New Year comes unlit;
Where we sang the mole now labours,
And spiders knit.

FromThe House of Hospitalities[182]

*   *   *

FROST

If Christmas used to be a time of fellowship, nevertheless 'the bond and slavery of frost' and cold are frequent images of fear, death and misery, of Time's action, and of the cruelty of the universe.

Frost has always a curious effect upon my mind, for which I can never account fully – that something is imminent of a tragic nature.

Letter to Florence Henniker, 30 January, 1899

But fear fell upon me like frost. . . .

From *Family Portraits*

Above the poet's bed:

. . . the half-obliterated pencillings on the wall-paper. . .were, no doubt, the thoughts and spirit-strivings which had come to him in the dead of night, when he could let himself go and have no fear of the frost of criticism.

An Imaginative Woman

It iced me, and I perished . . .

'Your eye-light wanes with an ail of care,
Frets freeze gray your face and hair.'

Sir John's widow puts up a brass to him in church:

As a memory Time's fierce frost should never kill.[183]

Modern psychology might point to Hardy's childhood experiences of the lethal potential of frost – like the frozen field-fare (page 125), or the extraordinary sight which he saw as a boy when returning at three in the morning with his father, after playing their fiddles 'at a gentleman-farmer's house':

178

It was bitterly cold, and the moon glistened bright upon the encrusted snow, amid which they saw motionless in the hedge what appeared to be a white human figure without a head. . . . [It] proved to be a very tall thin man in a long white smock-frock, leaning against the bank in a drunken stupor, his head hanging forward so low that at a distance he had seemed to have no head at all. . . .

The Life of Thomas Hardy

(Aware that he might freeze to death, the Hardys got him to his cottage nearby, where his wife's abuse caused them to wonder if it 'might have been as well to leave him where he was'. . .)

When the returning emigrant – 'bosom all day burning' to come back to his ancestral village – is met by the local inhabitants with chilling indifference,

The casement closed again,
And I was left in the frosty lane.[184]

Jude, shunned at Christminster,

. . . was still haunted by his dream. Even now he did not distinctly hear the freezing negative that those scholared walls had echoed to his desire.

Jude the Obscure

Tess, after the glacial terror of the Arctic birds (page 88), walks from Flintcomb-Ash to Emminster to meet and win help from her parents-in-law – and everything goes wrong:

Tess hoped for some accident that might favour her, but nothing favoured her. The shrubs on the Vicarage lawn rustled uncomfortably in the frosty breeze; she could not feel by any stretch of imagination, dressed to her highest as she was, that the house was the residence of near relations; and yet nothing essential, in nature or emotion, divided her from them: in pains, pleasures, thoughts, birth, death, and after-death, they were the same. . . .

Nobody answered to her ringing. . . . The wind was so nipping that the ivy-leaves had become wizened and gray, each tapping incessantly upon its neighbour with a disquieting stir of her nerves. . . . Still nobody came.

Tess of the d'Urbervilles

The night before Cytherea's planned, but dreaded, marriage to Aeneas Manston, she is kept awake by sinister noises:

She thought, 'Is it the intention of Fate that something connected with these noises shall influence my future as in the last case of the kind?' . . .

She pulled the blind aside and looked out. All was plain. The evening previous had closed in with a grey drizzle, borne upon a piercing air from the north, and now its

179

effects were visible. The hoary drizzle still continued; but the trees and shrubs were laden with icicles to an extent such as she had never before witnessed. A shoot of the diameter of a pin's head was iced as thick as her finger; all the boughs in the park were bent almost to the earth with the immense weight of the glistening incumbrance; the walks were like a looking-glass. Many boughs had snapped beneath their burden, and lay in heaps upon the icy grass. Opposite her eye, on the nearest tree, was a fresh yellow scar, showing where the branch that had terrified her had been splintered from the trunk.

'I never could have believed it possible,' she thought, surveying the bowed-down branches, 'that trees would bend so far out of their true positions without breaking.' By watching a twig she could see a drop collect upon it from the hoary fog, sink to the lowest point, and there become coagulated as the others had done.

'Or that I could so exactly have imitated them,' she continued. 'On this morning I am to be married – unless this is a scheme of the great Mother to hinder a union of which she does not approve. Is it possible for my wedding to take place in the face of such weather as this?'

Desperate Remedies

Discouragement
(Natura Naturans)

To see the Mother, naturing Nature, stand
All racked and wrung by her unfaithful lord,
Her hopes dismayed by his defiling hand,
Her passioned plans for bloom and beauty marred.

Where she would mint a perfect mould, an ill;
Where she would don divinest hues, a stain,
Over her purposed genial hour a chill,
Upon her charm of flawless flesh a blain:

Her loves dependent on a feature's trim,
A whole life's circumstance on hap of birth,
A soul's direction on a body's whim,
Eternal Heaven upon a day of Earth,
Is frost to flower of heroism and worth,
And fosterer of visions ghast and grim.
Westbourne Park Villas, 1863-7. *(From old MS.)*

In Tenebris I
Percussus sum sicut foenum, et aruit cor meum,' – Ps ci.[185]

Wintertime nighs;
But my bereavement-pain

It cannot bring again!
　　Twice no one dies.

　　Flower-petals flee;
But, since it once hath been,
No more that severing scene
　　Can harrow me.

　　Birds faint in dread:
I shall not lose old strength
In the lone frost's black length:
　　Strength long since fled!

　　Leaves freeze to dun;
But friends can not turn cold
This season as of old
　　For him with none.

　　Tempests may scath;
But love can not make smart
Again this year his heart
　　Who no heart hath.

　　Black is night's cope;
But death will not appal
One who, past doubtings all,
　　Waits in unhope.

BIRDS

In her movements, in her gaze, [Thomasin] reminded the beholder of the feathered creatures who lived around her home. All similes and allegories concerning her began and ended with birds. There was as much variety in her motions as in their flight. When she was musing she was a kestrel, which hangs in the air by an invisible motion of its wings. When she was in a high wind her light body was blown against trees and banks like a heron's. When she was frightened she darted noiselessly like a kingfisher. When she was serene she skimmed like a swallow, and that is how she was moving now.

The Return of the Native

Sue, in her new summer clothes, flexible and light as a bird, her little thumb stuck up by the stem of her white cotton sunshade, went along as if she hardly touched ground, and as if a moderately strong puff of wind would float her over the hedge into the next field.

Jude the Obscure

When Bathsheba, riding through the wood, 'dexterously dropped backwards flat upon the pony's back' to avoid the branches,

– the rapidity of her glide into this position was that of a kingfisher – its noiselessness that of a hawk.

Far from the Madding Crowd

The poem To Shakespeare *takes as theme how this 'bright baffling soul . . . display'd[st] a life of commonplace' among his fellows, many of whom did not know him. It ends:*

> So, like a strange bright bird we sometimes find
> To mingle with the barn-door brood awhile,
> Then vanish from their homely domicile –
> Into man's poesy, we wot not whence,
>   Flew thy strange mind,
> Lodged there a radiant guest, and sped for ever thence.
> 1916

Birds came naturally to Hardy as images. Emma 'looked like a bird from a cloud', and he describes himself in his first days at school as

> Pink, tiny, crisp-curled,
> My pinions yet furled
> From the winds of the world.[186]

For him 'snow-feathers' both 'swoop' and 'sail'; 'a tale . . . is born full-winged', and 'a kiss . . . took wing' and 'pursues its flight'; and for poor Eustacia 'the wings of her soul were broken by the cruel obstructiveness of all about her.'[187] Sometimes the introduction of a bird-image may seem eccentric, like the 'murky bird' of "A Confession to a Friend in Trouble", or when Elfride waits in vexation for Stephen to wave to her from the church-tower:

It was not till the end of half an hour that two figures were seen above the parapet of the dreary old pile, motionless as bitterns on a ruined mosque.[188]

A Pair of Blue Eyes

Certainly birds were strongly symbolic for Hardy. They often represent those made helpless and captive, both by humankind and by the laws of the universe.

[1885] *May 28.* Waiting at the Marble Arch while Em called a little way further on. . . . This hum of the wheel – the roar of London! What is it composed of? Hurry, speech, aughters, moans, cries of little children. The people in this tragedy laugh, sing, smoke, toss off wines, etc., make love to girls in drawing-rooms and areas; and yet are playing their parts in the tragedy just the same. Some wear jewels and feathers, some wear rags. All are caged birds, the only difference lies in the size of the cage. This too is part of the tragedy.

The Life of Thomas Hardy

Poems like "The Blinded Bird" and many other passages show how deeply he felt this:

> O, doth a bird beshorn of wings
> Go earth-bound wilfully!

From The Impercipient

[Eustacia] leant against the door-post, and gave him her hand. Charley took it in both his own with a tenderness beyond description, unless it was like that of a child holding a captured sparrow.

The Return of the Native

George III suffers violent paroxysms: yet, reports his attendant:

> He has quite often named
> The late Princess, as gently as a child
> A little bird found starved.

The Dynasts

Unable to escape from Oak's measured denunciation of Sergeant Troy,

No Christmas robin detained by a window-pane ever pulsed as did Bathsheba now.

Far from the Madding Crowd

Hardy's heroines are often imaged as trapped birds:

[Springrove] took [Cytherea's] hand as before, and found it as cold as the water about them. It was not relinquished till he reached her door. His assurance had not removed the constraint of her manner: he saw that she blamed him mutely and with her eyes, like a captured sparrow.

Desperate Remedies

Cytherea is (metaphorically) trapped into marrying Manston by his offer to pay for better medical treatment for her brother:

Thus terrified, driven into a corner, panting and fluttering about for some loophole of escape, yet still shrinking from the idea of being Manston's wife, the poor little bird

183

endeavoured to find out from Miss Aldclyffe whether it was likely that Owen would be well treated in the hospital.

'County Hospital!' said Miss Aldclyffe; 'why, it is only another name for slaughter-house.'

Desperate Remedies

— and (physically) trapped later as he chases her round the room:

'At last! my Cytherea!' he cried, overturning the table, springing over it, seizing one of the long brown tresses, pulling her towards him, and clasping her round. She writhed downwards between his arms and breast, and fell fainting on the floor. For the first time his action was leisurely. He lifted her upon the sofa, exclaiming, 'Rest there for a little while, my frightened little bird!'

Desperate Remedies

Sue agrees at last to marry Jude:

. . . letting Jude kiss her freely, and returning his kisses in a way she had never done before. Times had decidedly changed. 'The little bird is caught at last!' she said, a sadness showing in her smile.

'No — only nested,' he assured her.

Jude the Obscure

— while a crucial difference between him and Gillingham shows in the latter's advice to Phillotson.

'Well — if you've got any sound reason for marrying her again, do it now in God's name! I was always against your opening the cage-door and letting the bird go in such an obviously suicidal way.'

Jude the Obscure

Locked in a disastrous mutual misunderstanding when they met in a German hotel, Miss Power and Somerset

. . . parted amid the flowering shrubs and caged birds in the hall, and he saw her no more.

A Laodicean

Hardy's tenderness towards his heroines extends to children. The boys at West Poley, who have meddled with damming the millstream at its source, find themselves caught in the Mendip cave with rising water and no apparent way of escape. They say their prayers and are resigned to death, when the young narrator idly throws a stone out through the small hole in the cave roof high above them. A miracle happens:

Something greeted my ears at that moment . . . that caused me well-nigh to leap out of my shoes. Even now I cannot think of it without experiencing a thrill. It came from the gaping hole.

If my readers can imagine for themselves the sensations of a timid bird, who, while watching the approach of his captors to strangle him, feels his wings loosening from the tenacious snare, and flight again possible, they may conceive my emotions when I realized that what greeted my ears from above were the words of a human tongue, direct from the cavity.

'Where, in the name of fortune, did that stone come from?'
The voice was the voice of the miller.

Our Exploits at West Poley

Michael Henchard seems to be the only male character who is closely associated with a caged bird – in his case a poignant symbol of his life's apparent failure, a song that never reached its full resonance:

Mrs Donald Farfrae had discovered in a screened corner a new bird-cage, shrouded in newspaper, and at the bottom of the cage a little ball of feathers – the dead body of a goldfinch. Nobody could tell her how the bird and cage had come there; though that the poor little songster had been starved to death was evident. The sadness of the incident had made an impression on her. She had not been able to forget it for days, despite Farfrae's tender banter; and now when the matter had been nearly forgotten it was again revived.

'Oh, please ma'am, we know how that bird-cage came there. That farmer's man who called on the evening of the wedding – he was seen wi' it in his hand as he came up the street; and 'tis thoughted that he put it down while he came in with his message, and then went away forgetting where he had left it.'

This was enough to set Elizabeth thinking, and in thinking she seized hold of the idea, at one feminine bound, that the caged bird had been brought by Henchard for her as a wedding gift and token of repentance. He had not expressed to her any regrets or excuses for what he had done in the past; but it was part of his nature to extenuate nothing, and live on as one of his own worst accusers. She went out, looked at the cage, buried the starved little singer, and from that hour her heart softened towards the self-alienated man.[189]

The Mayor of Casterbridge

Above all Tess, probably Hardy's favourite heroine,

. . . who had been caught during her days of immaturity like a bird in a springe,

and at Flintcomb-Ash was

. . . between the Amazons and the farmer like a bird caught in a clap-net,

185

There seemed only one escape for her hunted soul. She suddenly took to her heels with the speed of the wind, and, without looking behind her, ran along the road till she came to a gate which opened directly into a plantation. Into this she plunged, and did not pause till she was deep enough in its shade to be safe against any possibility of discovery.

Under foot the leaves were dry, and the foliage of some holly bushes which grew among the deciduous trees was dense enough to keep off draughts. She scraped together the dead leaves till she had formed them into a large heap, making a sort of nest in the middle. Into this Tess crept.

Such sleep as she got was naturally fitful; she fancied she heard strange noises, but persuaded herself that they were caused by the breeze. She thought of her husband in some vague warm clime on the other side of the globe, while she was here in the cold. Was there another such a wretched being as she in the world?. . . .

. . . She heard a new strange sound among the leaves. It might be the wind; yet there was scarcely any wind. Sometimes it was a palpitation, sometimes a flutter; sometimes it was a sort of gasp or gurgle. Soon she was certain that the noises came from wild creatures of some kind, the more so when, originating in the boughs overhead, they were followed by the fall of a heavy body upon the ground. . . .

Directly the assuring and prosaic light of the world's active hours had grown strong she crept from under her hillock of leaves, and looked around boldly. Then she perceived what had been going on to disturb her. . . . Under the trees several pheasants lay about, their rich plumage dabbled with blood; some were already dead, some feebly twitching a wing, some staring up at the sky, some pulsating quickly, some contorted, some stretched out – all of them writhing in agony, except the fortunate ones whose tortures had ended during the night by the inability of nature to bear more.

Tess guessed at once the meaning of this. The birds had been driven down into this corner the day before by some shooting-party; and while those that had dropped dead under the shot, or had died before nightfall had been searched for and carried off, many badly wounded birds had escaped and hidden themselves away, or risen among the thick boughs, where they had maintained their position till they grew weaker with loss of blood in the night-time, when they had fallen one by one as she had heard them.

She had occasionally caught glimpses of these men in girlhood, looking over hedges, or peering through bushes, and pointing their guns, strangely accoutred, a bloodthirsty light in their eyes. She had been told that, rough and brutal as they seemed just then, they were not like this all the year round, but were, in fact, quite civil persons save during certain weeks of autumn and winter, when, like the inhabitants of the Malay Peninsula, they ran amuck, and made it their purpose to destroy life – in this case harmless feathered creatures, brought into being by artificial means solely to gratify these propensities – at once so unmannerly and so unchivalrous towards their weaker fellows in Nature's teeming family.

With the impulse of a soul who could feel for kindred sufferers as much as herself,

Tess's first thought was to put the still living birds out of their torture. . . .

'Poor darlings — to suppose myself the most miserable being on earth in the sight o' such misery as yours!' she exclaimed, her tears running down as she killed the birds tenderly. 'And not a twinge of bodily pain about me! I be not mangled, and I be not bleeding, and I have two hands to feed and clothe me.' She was ashamed of herself for her gloom of the night, based on nothing more tangible than a sense of condemnation under an arbitrary law of society which had no foundation in Nature.[190]

Tess of the d'Urbervilles

The Caged Thrush Freed and Home Again
(Villanelle)

'Men know but little more than we,
Who count us least of things terrene,
How happy days are made to be!

'Of such strange tidings what think ye,
O birds in brown that peck and preen?
Men know but little more than we!

'When I was borne from yonder tree
In bonds to them, I hoped to glean
How happy days are made to be,

'And want and wailing turned to glee;
Alas, despite their mighty mien
Men know but little more than we!

'They cannot change the Frost's decree,
They cannot keep the skies serene;
How happy days are made to be

'Eludes great Man's sagacity
No less than ours, O tribes in treen!
Men know but little more than we
How happy days are made to be.'

In their physical vulnerability birds symbolise other sufferings beside captivity — the laws of the universe, of power by the strong over the weak, and the hostility of the natural setting.

When Ethelberta's plan to leave her husband is foiled by him:

Ethelberta might have fallen dead with the shock, so terrible and hideous was it. Yet

she did not. She neither shrieked nor fainted; but no poor January fieldfare was ever colder
no ice-house more dank with perspiration, than she was then.

The Hand of Ethelberta

*The archduchess Maria Louisa, coming in from the garden, exclaims to Metternich (who has just
spoken of her powerlessness):*

> Those five poor little birds
> That haunt out there beneath the pediment,
> Snugly defended from the north-east wind,
> Have lately disappeared. I sought a trace
> Of scattered feathers, which I dread to find!

> METTERNICH
> They are gone, I ween, the way of tender flesh
> At the assaults of winter, want, and foes.

The Dynasts

The Faithful Swallow

> When summer shone
> Its sweetest on
> An August day,
> 'Here evermore,'
> I said, 'I'll stay;
> Not go away
> To another shore
> As fickle they!'

> December came:
> 'Twas not the same!
> I did not know
> Fidelity
> Would serve me so.
> Frost, hunger, snow;
> And now, ah me,
> Too late to go!

*Birds, with their fidelity and fortitude – a kind of spiritual strength even in powerlessness –
their joyous song, their soaring flight, symbolise all that is lovely and desirable: beauty (and its
inspiration for art), freedom and happiness.*

*Bathsheba's heart lifts as she plans to get away for a few days from any chance encounter with
Boldwood. The thunder-shower is passed:*

Freshness was exhaled in an essence from the varied contours of bank and hollow, as if the earth breathed maiden breath; and the pleased birds were hymning to the scene.

Far from the Madding Crowd

As Mrs Yeobright looked longingly at the beautiful heron flying up in the sunlight in freedom, so when the fuddled Henchard at the fair seeks freedom from his marriage-bond:

. . . a swallow, one among the last of the season, which had by chance found its way through an opening into the upper part of the tent, flew to and fro in quick curves above their heads, causing all eyes to follow it absently. In watching the bird till it made its escape the assembled company neglected to respond to the workman's offer, and the subject dropped.

The Mayor of Casterbridge

The sculptor Pierston searches all his life for the Well-Beloved, who flits from one human form to another:

'To see the creature who has hitherto been perfect, divine, lose under your very gaze the divinity which has informed her, grow commonplace, turn from flame to ashes, from a radiant vitality to a relic, is anything but a pleasure for any man, and has been nothing less than a racking spectacle to my sight. Each mournful emptied shape stands for ever after like the nest of some beautiful bird from which the inhabitant has departed and left it to fill with snow.'

The Well-Beloved

In "Song of Hope" the joys of that 'sweet To-morrow' included 'Larks, of a glory'; the tree who had 'done all I could' for the sheltering Lady had 'drawn to her songsters' (page 163); the sorrow of 'gaunt age' is that 'sunshine bird and bloom frequent no more.'[191]
As the milkmaid Margery sets off for the joy of the ball with her adored Baron,

She walked to the music of innumerable birds, which increased as she drew away from the open meads towards the groves. She had overcome all difficulties.

The Romantic Adventures of a Milkmaid

*   *   *

Yet, with that constant awareness of the paradoxes and complexities of life, birds for Hardy can also be sinister – 'an ominous bird a-wing'.[192] The nightingale that sang at the end of Under the Greenwood Tree was an ironic twist away from its usual love-symbolism; "The Prophetess" is about the Mocking-Bird; in "On a Heath" where all is ominous and unknown, dark and unseen, the picture is completed when

The herons flapped to norward
In the firs upon my right.

Above all the night-jar presages or accompanies doom.

The first time the boy Jude climbs the hill to see the night lights of the beloved Christminster which is to betray him in later life, a carter tells him of its exclusivity:

'O, they never look at anything that folks like we can understand,' the carter continued, by way of passing the time. 'On'y foreign tongues used in the days of the Tower of Babel, when no two families spoke alike. They read that sort of thing as fast as a night-hawk will whir.'

Jude the Obscure

Stephen waits 'with a beating heart' — but in vain — for Elfride:

The faint sounds heard only accentuated the silence. The rising and falling of the sea, far away along the coast, was the most important. A minor sound was the scurr of a distant night-hawk . . .

With all these soft sounds there came not the only soft sound he cared to hear — the footfall of Elfride.

A Pair of Blue Eyes

After Fitzpiers, on Midsummer Eve, 'captured [Grace] as if she had been a bird', he went on to chase Suke Damson into the hayfield, where they subsequently spent the night.

In the moonlight Suke looked very beautiful, the scratches and blemishes incidental to her outdoor occupation being invisible under these pale rays. While they remained silent on the hay the coarse whirr of the eternal night-hawk burst sarcastically from the top of a tree at the nearest corner of the wood.

The Woodlanders

Margery, with some illusions as to its outcome, and in a sense alone in a world she does not know, is excited about her impending meeting with the Baron:

She dressed herself with care, went to the top of the garden, and looked over the stile. The view was eastward, and a great moon hung before her in a sky which had not a cloud. Nothing was moving except on the minutest scale, and she remained leaning over, the night-hawk sounding his croud from the bough of an isolated tree on the open hill-side.

The Romantic Adventures of a Milkmaid

Clym Yeobright sets out across the heath, hoping to be reconciled with his mother, and unaware that she lies dying in the heat only a mile or two away:

In almost every one of the isolated and stunted thorns which grew here and there a night-hawk revealed its presence by whirring like the clack of a mill as long as he could

190

hold his breath, then stopping, flapping his wings, wheeling round the bush, alighting, and after a silent interval of listening beginning to whirr again. At each brushing of Clym's feet white miller-moths[193] flew into the air just high enough to catch upon their dusty wings the mellowed light from the west, which now shone across the depressions and levels of the ground without falling thereon to light them up.

Yeobright walked on amid this quiet scene with a hope that all would soon be well. *(He finds his mother; and begins to carry her to her home.)* At the beginning of his undertaking he had thought but little of the distance which yet would have to be traversed before Blooms-End could be reached; but though he had slept that afternoon he soon began to feel the weight of his burden. Thus he proceeded, like Aeneas with his father; the bats circling round his head, nightjars flapping their wings within a yard of his face, and not a human being within call.

The Return of the Native

A Hurried Meeting

It is August moonlight in the tall plantation,
Whose elms, by aged squirrels' footsteps worn,
   Outscreen the noon, and eve, and morn.
On the facing slope a faint irradiation
  From a mansion's marble front is borne,
    Mute in its woodland wreathing,
  Up here the night-jar whirrs forlorn,
And the trees seem to withhold their softest breathing.

To the moonshade slips a woman in muslin vesture:
Her naked neck the gossamer-web besmears,
   And she sweeps it away with a hasty gesture.
Again it touches her forehead, her neck, her ears,
    Her fingers, the backs of her hands.
    She sweeps it away again,
    Impatiently, and then
She takes no notice; and listens, and sighs, and stands.

The night-hawk stops. A man shows in the obscure:
    They meet, and passively kiss,
And he says: 'Well, I've come quickly. About this –
    Is it really so? You are sure?'
   'I am sure. In February it will be.
   That such a thing should come to me!
We should have known. We should have left off meeting.
Love is a terrible thing: a sweet allure
    That ends in heart-outeating!'

'But what shall we do, my Love, and how?'
'You need not call me by that name now.'
Then he more coldly: 'What is your suggestion?'
'I've told my mother, and she sees a way,
Since of our marriage there can be no question.
We are crossing South – near about New Year's Day
    The event will happen there.
It is the only thing that we can dare
    To keep them unaware!'
    'Well, you can marry me.'
She shook her head. 'No: that can never be.

''Twill be brought home as hers. She's forty-one,
When many a woman's bearing is not done,
    And well might have a son. –
We should have left off specious self-deceiving:
    I feared that such might come,
    And knowledge struck me numb.
Love is a terrible thing: witching when first begun,
    To end in grieving, grieving!'

And with one kiss again the couple parted:
Inferior clearly he; she haughty-hearted.
He watched her down the slope to return to her place,
The marble mansion of her ancient race,
And saw her brush the gossamers from her face
As she emerged from shade to the moonlight ray.
    And when she had gone away
  The night-jar seemed to imp, and say,
    'You should have taken warning:
Love is a terrible thing: sweet for a space,
    And then all mourning, mourning!'

*   *   *

INSECTS

Napoleon's Grand Army, in desperate retreat from Moscow:

An object like a dun-piled caterpillar,
Shuffling its length in painful heaves along . . .

The Dynasts

192

Granfer Cantle, in The Return of the Native, *singing*

. . . in the voice of a bee up a flue;

Elfride, in the procession along the path from rectory to church to show it to the young architect, running along:

. . . nowhere in particular, yet everywhere; sometimes in front, sometimes behind, sometimes at the sides, hovering about the procession like a butterfly; not definitely engaged in travelling, yet somehow chiming in at points with the general progress.

A Pair of Blue Eyes

The birch trees . . . had put on their new leaves, delicate as butterflies' wings, and diaphanous as amber.

The Return of the Native

During his inspection of Stancy Castle, Somerset finds Miss Power's private apartments, and notices the foreign novels, the latest reviews, and the telegraph apparatus which she has installed:

These things, ensconced amid so much of the old and hoary, were as if a stray hour from the nineteenth century had wandered like a butterfly into the thirteenth, and lost itself there.

A Laodicean

In his notebooks, Hardy had once made notes on the tiger-beetle:[194] *they surfaced in his picture of Eustacia:*

There was a certain obscurity in Eustacia's beauty. . . . In her winter-dress, as now, she was like the tiger-beetle, which, when observed in dull situations, seems to be of the quietest neutral colour, but under a full illumination blazes with dazzling splendour.

The Return of the Native

Earlier pages showed Hardy's painting of insects; but often they are more than just descriptions. Clym's familiars (page 120) serve as an image of his oneness with his natural setting, something which was to separate him from Eustacia. Later a single page brings two important images, shortly before Mrs Yeobright's death, of insects as examples of the fleeting lives and happiness of humanity, and its insignificance on the face of the universe.

On that same fateful, scorching walk across the heath:

Occasionally she came to a spot where independent worlds of ephemerons were passing their time in mad carousal, some in the air, some on the hot ground and vegetation, some in the tepid and stringy water of a nearly dried pool. All the shallower ponds had decreased to a vaporous mud amid which the maggoty shapes of innumerable small creatures

193

could be indistinctly seen, heaving and wallowing with enjoyment. Being a woman not disinclined to philosophize she sometimes sat down under her umbrella to rest and to watch their happiness . . .

The Return of the Native

Asking the way of a labourer, she is told to follow a distant furze-cutter:

She followed the figure indicated. He appeared of a russet hue, not more distinguishable from the scene around him than the green caterpillar from the leaf it feeds on. . .

The silent being who thus occupied himself seemed to be of no more account in life than an insect. He appeared as a mere parasite of the heath, fretting its surface in his daily labour as a moth frets a garment, entirely engrossed with its products, having no knowledge of anything in the world but fern, furze, heath, lichens, and moss.

The Return of the Native

Something Tapped

Something tapped on the pane of my room
When there was never a trace
Of wind or rain, and I saw in the gloom
My weary Beloved's face.

'O I am tired of waiting,' she said,
'Night, morn, noon, afternoon;
So cold it is in my lonely bed,
And I thought you would join me soon!'

I rose and neared the window-glass,
But vanished thence had she:
Only a pallid moth, alas,
Tapped at the pane for me.

August 1913

*   *   *

NIGHT AND DARKNESS

. . .night numbed the air,
And dark the mournful moorland lay.[195]

The Dorset heathland where Hardy grew up often looks very dark: his poetic description of Egdon

194

(page 35) actually gives a good impression of how the remaining undeveloped heathland is. It's not surprising therefore that he was much aware of darkness in the natural setting, and that it figures in his imagery. For Eustacia:

Egdon was her Hades, and since coming there she had imbibed much of what was dark in its tone, though inwardly and eternally unreconciled thereto. Her appearance accorded well with this smouldering rebelliousness, and the shady splendour of her beauty was the real surface of the sad and stifled warmth within her. A true Tartarean dignity sat upon her brow, and not factitiously or with marks of constraint, for it had grown in her with years.

The Return of the Native

But the heath was

at all seasons a familiar surrounding to Olly and Mrs Yeobright; and the addition of darkness lends no frightfulness to the face of a friend.

The Return of the Native

Thus the usual Hardy paradox. For everything in life that is not 'the face of a friend', dark is for him, as throughout Western history, an image of pain, evil, death and misery:

. . . all that is terrible and dark in history and legend — the last plague of Egypt, the destruction of Sennacherib's host, the agony in Gethsemane.

The Return of the Native

In his Bible (Authorised Version), Hardy marked many passages in the Book of Job, including the last two verses of Chapter X. He quoted them when describing Manston's unhappiness:

Manston found himself alone a few minutes later. He buried his face in his hands, and murmured, 'O my lost one! O my Cytherea! That it should come to this is hard for me! 'Tis now all darkness, — "A land of darkness, as darkness itself; and of the shadow of death, without any order, and where the light is as darkness." '

Desperate Remedies

The wood as Under the Greenwood Tree *begins is 'dark as the grave'; and the opening lines of "In Tenebris III" are:*

> There have been times when I well might have passed and the ending
> have come —
> Points in my path when the dark might have stolen on me, artless,
> unrueing —

Darkness and death are linked as Sue looks out of her Christminster window:

At some distance opposite, the outer walls of Sarcophagus College – silent, black and windowless – threw their four centuries of gloom, bigotry, and decay into the little room she occupied, shutting out the moonlight by night and the sun by day.

Jude the Obscure

Darkness often represents ignorance and the unknown.

The thing is dark, Dear. I do not know.

Or when 'the Lord Most High' is reminded of humanity's existence on Earth, he replies:

'Dark, then, its life! For not a cry
Of aught it bears do I now hear.'[196]

Hardy dramatises this in a poem some of whose lines remain obscure:

Just the Same

I sat. It all was past;
Hope never would hail again;
Fair days had ceased at a blast,
The world was a darkened den.

The beauty and dream were gone,
And the halo in which I had hied
So gaily gallantly on
Had suffered blot and died!

I went forth, heedless whither,
In a a cloud too black for name:
– People frisked hither and thither;
The world was just the same.[197]

But pain can be worse than ignorance. "Had You Wept" ends memorably:

Why did you not make war on me with those who weep like rain?
You felt too much, so gained no balm for all your torrid sorrow,
And hence our deep division, and our dark undying pain.

"The Trampwoman's Tragedy" comes because she did not care about her 'lover's dark distress';
and the spectre of sin rises when the spurned lover of "The Flirt's Tragedy" suffers endlessly,
like Cain, from his

> vengeance too dark on the woman
> Whose lover he slew.

For Hardy had a very strong sense of evil as darkness. Biblical influence was profound: he must have absorbed much of the imagery of the Psalms, and, for example, lines like St John's account of how Judas, having betrayed Jesus, 'went immediately out: and it was night.' In "The Unborn", he pities those who have still to come to life on an uncaring planet, but think it a place:

> 'Where all is gentle, true, and just,
> And darkness is unknown'.

Above all at the moment of Alec d'Urberville's assault on Tess:

Darkness and silence ruled everywhere around. Above them rose the primeval yews and oaks of The Chase, in which were poised gentle roosting birds in their last nap; and about them stole the hopping rabbits and hares. But, might some say, where was Tess's guardian angel? Where was the providence of her simple faith? Perhaps, like that other god of whom the ironical Tishbite[198] spoke, he was talking, or he was pursuing, or he was in a journey, or he was sleeping and not to be awaked.

Why was it that upon this beautiful feminine tissue, sensitive as gossamer, and practically blank as snow as yet, there should have been traced such a coarse pattern as it was doomed to receive; why so often the coarse appropriates the finer thus, the wrong man the woman, the wrong woman the man, many thousands of years of analytical philosophy have failed to explain to our sense of order.

Tess of the d'Urbervilles

Night has many of the same connotations, and contrasts, as darkness — though perhaps without quite its depth of evil. Night can be beautiful: as was 'the great and particular glory of the Egdon waste' (page 36), and Eustacia herself, 'Queen of Night.'

Eustacia Vye was the raw material of a divinity. . . . To see her hair was to fancy that a whole winter did not contain darkness enough to form its shadow: it closed over her forehead like nightfall extinguishing the western glow. . . .

She had pagan eyes, full of nocturnal mysteries. . . . So fine were the lines of her lips that, though full, each corner of her mouth was as clearly cut as the point of a spear. This keenness of corner was only blunted when she was given over to sudden fits of gloom, one of the phases of the night-side of sentiment which she knew too well for her years.

Her presence brought memories of such things as Bourbon roses, rubies, and tropical midnights; her moods recalled lotus-eaters and the march in 'Athalie';[199] her motions, the ebb and flow of the sea; her voice, the viola. In a dim light, and with a slight rearrangement of her hair, her general figure might have stood for that of either of the higher female deities.

The Return of the Native

The 'night-side of sentiment' was something Hardy often recognized — for example the fears of the Boer War soldiers' wives 'in the night-time when life-beats are low';[200] *or in*

The Peace-Offering

It was but a little thing,
Yet I knew it meant to me
Ease from what had given a sting
To the very birdsinging
    Latterly.

But I would not welcome it;
And for all I then declined
O the regrettings infinite
When the night-processions flit
    Through the mind!

Night is the fate of humanity — most cruelly, after it has been shown the day.[201] *Night also is death:*

'And night-time calls,
And the curtain falls!'[202]

Night above all is the time of apocalypse and nightmare — 'midnight dreams of flight and disaster'[203] *— and again Hardy's underlinings in the fourth chapter of Job are telling:*

'In thoughts from the visions of the night, when deep sleep falleth on men,
Fear came upon me, and trembling, which made all my bones to shake.
Then a spirit passed before my face; the hair of my flesh stood up:
It stood still, but I could not discern the form thereof...'

A New Year's Eve in War Time

I

Phantasmal fears,
And the flap of the flame,
And the throb of the clock,
And a loosened slate,
And the blind night's drone,
Which tiredly the spectral pines intone!

II

And the blood in my ears
Strumming always the same,

198

And the gable-cock
With its fitful grate,
And myself, alone.

III

The twelfth hour nears
Hand-hid, as in shame;
I undo the lock,
And listen, and wait
For the Young Unknown.

IV

In the dark there careers —
As if Death astride came
To numb all with his knock —
A horse at mad rate
Over rut and stone.

V

No figure appears,
No call of my name,
No sound but 'Tic-toc'
Without check. Past the gate
It clatters — is gone.

VI

What rider it bears
There is none to proclaim;
And the Old Year has struck,
And, scarce animate,
The New makes moan.

VII

Maybe that 'More tears! —
More Famine and Flame —
More Severance and Shock!'
Is the order from Fate
That the Rider speeds on
To pale Europe; and tiredly the pines intone.
1915-1916

The Great War profoundly depressed Hardy, and his vision for the future of humanity became often dark and nightmarish. It had not been so when in 1870, having met Emma Gifford, he

199

'came back from Lyonnesse / With magic in my eyes!'[204] This was a light no darkness could quench.

'In the seventies'
'Qui deridetur ab amico suo sicut ego.' – JOB[205]

In the seventies I was bearing in my breast,
                    Penned tight,
Certain starry thoughts that threw a magic light
On the worktimes and the soundless hours of rest
In the seventies; aye, I bore them in my breast
                    Penned tight.

In the seventies when my neighbours – even my friend –
                    Saw me pass,
Heads were shaken, and I heard the words, 'Alas,
For his onward years and name unless he mend!'
In the seventies, when my neighbours and my friend
                    Saw me pass.

In the seventies those who met me did not know
                    Of the vision
That immuned me from the chillings of misprision
And the damps that choked my goings to and fro
In the seventies; yea, those nodders did not know
                    Of the vision.

In the seventies nought could darken or destroy it,
                    Locked in me,
Though as delicate as lamp-worm's lucency;
Neither mist nor murk could weaken or alloy it
In the seventies! – could not darken or destroy it,
                    Locked in me.

LIGHT

The passages already chosen to show the importance of light to Hardy (pages 41ff) also show that he hardly ever gives a straight description of light: he always sees connections and metaphors, and uses light as yet another way of illuminating reality.

The most obvious connotations are of light with all that is good – love, joy, beauty and goodness, understanding, vision and creative imagination.

Clym and Eustacia, in their little house at Alderworth, beyond East Egdon, were living on with a monotony which was delightful to them. The heath and changes of weather were quite blotted out from their eyes for the present. They were enclosed in a sort of luminous mist, which hid from them surroundings of any inharmonious colour, and gave to all things the character of light.

The Return of the Native

Fidelity in love for fidelity's sake had less attraction for [Eustacia] than for most women: fidelity because of love's grip had much. A blaze of love, and extinction, was better than a lantern glimmer of the same which should last long years.

The Return of the Native

Jocelyn Pierston, in love again with the second Avice, found that in her 'effulgence. . .all sordid details were disregarded.'[206]

And love lit my soul, notwithstanding
My features' ill favour . . .

From *The Flirt's Tragedy*

The End of the Episode

Indulge no more may we
In this sweet-bitter pastime:
The love-light shines the last time
Between you, Dear, and me.

There shall remain no trace
Of what so closely tied us,
And blank as ere love eyed us
Will be our meeting-place.

The flowers and thymy air,
Will they now miss our coming?
The dumbles thin their humming
To find we haunt not there?

Though fervent was our vow,
Though ruddily ran our pleasure,
Bliss has fulfilled its measure,
And sees its sentence now.

Ache deep; but make no moans:
Smile out; but stilly suffer:
The paths of love are rougher
Than thoroughfares of stones.

Happiness (in "The Self-Unseeing") is in the glow and gleam of Hardy's own happy childhood, in the 'magic light' of Lyonnesse in 'the seventies', and in Emma's 'smiles [which] would have shone / With welcomings'.[207] *Happiness shows in the light on people's faces: George Melbury, learning that his daughter could divorce her husband, 'was irradiated with the project. . .with a face like the face of an angel'; and the lame boy tells of his longing to have a linnet of 'his very own':*

And as he breathed the cherished dream
To those whose secrecy was sworn,
His face was beautified by the theme,
And wore the radiance of the morn.

From *The Boy's Dream*

When the young Jude thinks he has the promise of some books which will start him on the magical road to Christminster:

Through the intervening fortnight he ran about and smiled outwardly at his inward thoughts, as if they were people meeting and nodding to him – smiled with that singularly beautiful irradiation which is seen to spread on young faces at the inception of some glorious idea, as if a supernatural lamp were held inside their transparent natures, giving rise to the flattering fancy that heaven lies about them then.

Jude the Obscure

Beauty is often symbolised by light:

They stood silently looking upon Eustacia, who, as she lay there still in death, eclipsed all her living phases. Pallor did not include all the quality of her complexion, which seemed more than whiteness; it was almost light.

– In death, Eustacia and Wildeve shared

. . . the same luminous youthfulness. . .and the least sympathetic observer would have felt at sight of him now that he was born for a higher destiny than this.

The Return of the Native

It was Egbert Mayne's 'luminousness of nature' which attracted Geraldine Allenville, and Florence Dugdale's 'large luminous living eyes' that attracted Hardy.[208] *Both beauty and light are often linked with the Good. (One of his favourite hymns was 'Lead, kindly Light'; and he marked*

202

in his Bible, for example, the verse from Isaiah 60 'Arise, shine; for thy light is come, and the glory of the Lord is risen upon thee.') So light is prominent in three successive poems celebrating the Hardys' happiest time, at Sturminster Newton – 'This best of life – that shines about / Your welcoming!'[209] "On Sturminster Foot-bridge" (page 141) shows Emma 'as a lattice-gleam when midnight moans.'

A few months after marrying his second wife, Hardy wrote of them both:

A Poet

Attentive eyes, fantastic heed,
Assessing minds, he does not need,
Nor urgent writs to sup or dine,
Nor pledges in the rosy wine.

For loud acclaim he does not care
By the august or rich or fair,
Nor for smart pilgrims from afar,
Curious on where his hauntings are.

But soon or later, when you hear
That he has doffed this wrinkled gear,
Some evening, at the first star-ray,
Come to his graveside, pause and say:

'Whatever his message – glad or grim –
Two bright-souled women clave to him;'
Stand and say that while day decays;
It will be word enough of praise.
July 1914

Hardy also described his 'poet's bower' as a place where

Figures dance to a mind with sight
And music and laughter like floods of light
Make all the precincts gleam.

From *The House of Silence*

The light that in many poems means life and immortality[210] is also a part of poetic vision and the creative imagination. Hardy tells of the Abbey Mason who invented the Perpendicular style at Gloucester Cathedral 'after his craft-wit got aglow';[211] and stresses that neither Nature, nor reality, but the inner light of the imagination, brings comfort to woman and man:

203

On a Fine Morning

I

Whence comes Solace? – Not from seeing
What is doing, suffering, being,
Not from noting Life's conditions,
Nor from heeding Time's monitions;
    But in cleaving to the Dream,
    And in gazing at the gleam
    Whereby gray things golden seem.

II

Thus do I this heyday, holding
Shadows but as lights unfolding,
As no specious show this moment
With its iris-hued embowment;
    But as nothing other than
    Part of a benignant plan;
Proof that earth was made for man.

February 1899

Light means, of course, illumination and the work of reason. Swithin, after 'a time of cloudy mental weather', suddenly understood something about Viviette:

The sun, in sending its rods of yellow fire into his room, sent, as he suddenly thought, mental illumination with it.

A Laodicean

The child who, at Fiesole, gave Hardy a Roman coin identical to those he had picked up in Dorset, enlightened him 'better than all books', as

              her act flashed home
In that mute moment to my opened mind
The power, the pride, the reach of perished Rome.

From *In the Old Theatre, Fiesole*

In a deceptively simple-looking poem Hardy, as usual revisiting his experience in order to revise it, uses – negatively – the waning of light to symbolise his new understanding (and a stress on the word 'same' to highlight its difference)

Her Initials

Upon a poet's page I wrote
Of old two letters of her name;

Part seemed she of the effulgent thought
Whence that high singer's rapture came.
 – When now I turn the leaf the same
Immortal light illumes the lay,
But from the letters of her name
The radiance has waned away!
1869

When the full range of light is not present, there is misery or a lack of understanding. Jude, beginning to realise the immense obstacles to his acceptance by Christminster, had to come out of

. . . the imaginative world he had lately inhabited. . . .He was set regarding his prospects in a cold northern light.

Jude the Obscure

In Miss Aldclyffe's lawyer, too, understanding was limited:

Nyttleton was a man who surveyed everybody's character in a sunless and shadowless northern light.

Desperate Remedies

Knight equated truth and purity with light, and thought he saw in Elfride 'a soul truthful and clear as heaven's light'; but when, looking out at the sea, they reached one of the most damaging crises of their love:

   Two or three degrees above that melancholy and eternally level line the ocean horizon, hung a sun of brass, with no visible rays, in a sky of ashen hue. It was a sky the sun did not illuminate or enkindle, as is usual at sunsets.

A Pair of Blue Eyes

Certain lights, especially lurid ones, or 'that livid sad east', or 'a witch-flame's weirdsome sheen', or 'the nebulous light that lingers / In charnel-mould',[212] *have little good about them. They both reflect and affect our state, sometimes before we have become fully aware.*

At Henchard's sale of his wife, something happens when the money is actually put down:

Up to this moment it could not positively have been asserted that the man, in spite of his tantalizing declaration, was really in earnest. The spectators had indeed taken the proceedings throughout as a piece of mirthful irony carried to extremes; and had assumed that, being out of work he was, as a consequence, out of temper with the world, and society, and his nearest kin. But with the demand and response of real cash the jovial frivolity of the scene departed. A lurid colour seemed to fill the tent, and change the aspects of all therein. The mirth-wrinkles left the listeners' faces, and they waited with parting lips.

The Mayor of Casterbridge

Hardy has a kind of hierarchy of meaning or implication descending from 'bright' and 'glow' and 'gleam', to 'shine' which is often equivocally linked with death or unhappiness. Yet these are all lights which are part of a life lived to the full: it is the 'sunless and shadowless' light that is sterile.

LIGHT AND SHADOWS

Ruskin advised young architects to develop the habit of 'thinking in shadow.' He also required that architecture 'should express a kind of human sympathy by a measure of darkness as great as there is in human life.'[213] As many earlier-quoted passages about shadows show, Hardy came to see them as a very significant element in his patterns of darkness and light as revelations of the human condition and the workings of Fate.

The Later Autumn

Gone are the lovers, under the bush
    Stretched at their ease;
    Gone the bees,
Tangling themselves in your hair as they rush
    On the line of your track,
    Leg-laden, back
    With a dip to their hive
    In a prepossessed dive.

Toadsmeat is mangy, frosted, and sere;
    Apples in grass
    Crunch as we pass,
And rot ere the men who make cyder appear.
    Couch-fires abound
    On fallows around,
    And shades far extend
    Like lives soon to end.

Spinning leaves join the remains shrunk and brown
    Of last year's display
    That lie wasting away,
On whose corpses they earlier as scorners gazed down
    From their aery green height:

Now in the same plight
They huddle; while yon
A robin looks on.

As the patterns of life develop, a shadow is often seen to be growing alongside, at first imperceptibly, then fully revealed. After the brilliant early February sun the 'shadows of the October pine' reveal the undiscerned passing of time (page 160). The great ship Titanic *has been having 'a sinister mate' prepared for it by the Immanent Will:*

And as the smart ship grew
In stature, grace, and hue,
In shadowy silent distance grew the Iceberg too.

From *The Convergence of the Twain*

In November 1915 Hardy's beloved sister Mary died, and he wrote this poem – about the sundial recently installed at Talbothays, where she lived.

In the Garden
(M.H.)

We waited for the sun
To break its cloudy prison
(For day was not yet done,
And night still unbegun)
Leaning by the dial.

After many a trial –
We all silent there –
It burst as new-arisen,
Throwing a shade to where
Time travelled at that minute.

Little saw we in it,
But this much I know,
Of lookers on that shade,
Her towards whom it made
Soonest had to go.
1915

The shadow of money-matters creeps apace behind a debtor:

'I hope to be able to make that little bill-business right with you in the course of three weeks, Mr Barnet,' said Charlson with hail-fellow friendliness.

Barnet replied good-naturedly that there was no hurry.

This particular three weeks had moved on in advance of Charlson's present with the precision of a shadow for some considerable time.

Fellow-Townsmen

But Mr Barnet has other problems – an unloving wife, and a lost love, Lucy, he was mad to have forsaken for her. His friend Downe's charming wife tries to see how she could reconcile the Barnets, and proposes a seaside drive with the haughty Mrs Barnet. As they set out none knows the terrible tragedy to come – that the wrong one, Mrs Downe, will be drowned, and that Mr Downe will eventually supplant Barnet by marrying Lucy. But an ominous pattern prepares us:

The next day was as fine as the arrangement could possibly require. As the sun passed the meridian and declined westward, the tall shadows from the scaffold-poles of Barnet's rising residence streaked the ground as far as to the middle of the highway.

Fellow-Townsmen

Tess reveals her past to Angel after his own disclosure on their honeymoon:

Their hands were still joined. The ashes under the grate were lit by the fire vertically, like a torrid waste. Imagination might have beheld a Last Day luridness in this red-coaled glow, which fell on his face and hand, and on hers, peering into the loose hair about her brow, and firing the delicate skin underneath. A large shadow of her shape rose upon the wall and ceiling. She bent forward, at which each diamond on her neck gave a sinister wink like a toad's; and pressing her forehead against his temple she entered on her story of her acquaintance with Alec d'Urberville and its results, murmuring the words without flinching, and with her eyelids drooping down.

Tess of the d'Urbervilles

In a strange story of unconscious witchcraft[214], Mrs Lodge (whose arm has been inexplicably withered in a dream by her husband's former lover Rhoda) takes a crucial decision which will affect the course of subsequent events. As she arrives to implement it:

. . . a shadow intruded into the window-pattern thrown on Rhoda Brook's floor by the afternoon sun.

The Withered Arm

Elizabeth diffidently and uncertainly goes to see High-Place Hall, where she may take employment as Lucetta's companion:

At night the forms of passengers were patterned by the lamps in black shadows upon the pale walls.

Self-contradictions, and the dissonance between mental and external reality, are imaged with light and shadow:

Of the many contradictory particulars consituting a woman's heart, two had shown their vigorous contrast in Cytherea's bosom just at this time.

    It was a dark morning. . . . Having risen an hour earlier than was usual with her, Cytherea sat at the window of an elegant little sitting-room on the ground-floor. . . . She leant with her face on her hand, looking out into the gloomy grey air. A yellow glimmer from the flapping flame of the newly-lit fire fluttered on one side of her face and neck like a butterfly about to settle there, contrasting warmly with the other side of the same fair face, which received from the window the faint cold morning light, so weak that her shadow from the fire had a distinct outline on the window-shutter in spite of it. There the shadow danced like a demon, blue and grim.

Desperate Remedies

The Halborough brothers, condemned by a drunken father's squandering of their inheritance to achieve ordination without benefit of university, are first seen in their bedroom, 'engaged in the untutored reading. . .of the idiomatic and difficult Epistle to the Hebrews.' Their fate, and their constant manoeuvring to avoid the worst effects of their father, are imaged in their setting:

The Dog-day sun in its decline reached the low ceiling with slanting sides, and the shadows of the great goat's-willow swayed and interchanged upon the walls like a spectral army manoeuvring.

A Tragedy of Two Ambitions

Hardy was quick to see the metaphor in 'foreshadowing' – as in "At the Word 'Farewell' ", and another poem about Emma, imagined on the fateful night when the visiting architect was first approaching St Juliot:

A Man was Drawing Near to Me

On that gray night of mournful drone,
Apart from aught to hear, to see,
I dreamt not that from shires unknown
    In gloom, alone,
      By Halworthy,
A man was drawing near to me.

I'd no concern at anything,
No sense of coming pull-heart play;
Yet, under the silent outspreading
    Of even's wing
      Where Otterham lay,
A man was riding up my way.

I thought of nobody – not of one,
But only of trifles – legends, ghosts –
Though, on the moorland dim and dun
　　　That Travellers shun
　　　About these coasts,
The man had passed Tresparret Posts.

There was no light at all inland,
Only the seaward pharos-fire,
Nothing to let me understand
　　　That hard at hand
　　　By Hennett Byre
The man was getting nigh and nigher.

There was a rumble at the door,
A draught disturbed the drapery,
And but a minute passed before,
　　　With gaze that bore
　　　My destiny,
The man revealed himself to me.

CHANGES IN LIGHT

The lighthouse here refused its illumination to the waiting woman. In "The Wind's Prophecy" (Page 39) – a poem in which at every point nature confounds the speaker's personal impression, clouding the star he thinks he wants to see – the lighthouses are part of a dramatic change of light occurring at the end. This is characteristic and significant in Hardy's vision of how surprise and realisation of change are sometimes forced upon us.

In Stephen's parallel journey by pony-trap to Endelstow Rectory:

The dusk had thickened into darkness while they thus conversed, and the outline and surface of the mansion gradually disappeared. The windows, which had before been as black blots on a lighter expanse of wall, became illuminated, and were transfigured to squares of light on the general dark body of the night landscape as it absorbed the outlines of the edifice into its gloomy monochrome.

A Pair of Blue Eyes

Just so had the rejected lover's understanding dawned as 'the black squares grew to be squares of light' ("In Her Precincts"[215]*). At a moment of change in the Carriford fire when the flames came to engulf the church:*

The crackling grew sharper. Long quivering shadows began to be flung from the stately trees at the end of the house; the square outline of the church tower, on the other side of the way, which had hitherto been a dark mass against a sky comparatively light, now began to appear as a light object against a sky of darkness; and even the narrow surface of the flag-staff at the top could be seen in its dark surrounding, brought out from its obscurity by the rays from the dancing light.

Desperate Remedies

At a dinner in London one summer Hardy noted:

We sat down by daylight, and as we dined the moon brightened the trees in the garden, and shone under them into the room.

The Life of Thomas Hardy

Egbert sits alone in the house, meditating after his grandfather's death:

The candles were not yet lighted, and Mayne abstractedly watched upon the pale wall the latter rays of sunset slowly changing into the white shine of a moon a few days old. The ancient family clock had stopped for want of winding. . . .

He was sitting with his back to the window, meditating in this minor key, when a shadow darkened the opposite moonlit wall.

An Indiscretion in the Life of an Heiress

FIRE

In the following poem the dying day is accompanied at every point by the dying fire – until with daylight gone the firelight's last glow rouses the speaker from his apathy. The theme of the wasted day, when some 'enkindling ardency' with its 'maturer glows' may have been stifled, meshes perfectly with the fire imagery of its setting (and with its rhythm):[216]

A Commonplace Day

The day is turning ghost,
And scuttles from the kalendar in fits and furtively,
To join the ominous host
Of those that throng oblivion; ceding his place, maybe,
To one of like degree.

I part the fire-gnawed logs,
Rake forth the embers, spoil the busy flames, and lay the ends
Upon the shining dogs;

Further and further from the nooks the twilight's stride extends,
And beamless black impends.

Nothing of tiniest worth
Have I wrought, pondered, planned; no one thing asking blame or praise
Since the pale corpse-like birth
Of this diurnal unit, bearing blanks in all its rays –
Dullest of dull-hued Days!

Wanly upon the panes
The rain slides, as have slid since morn my colourless thoughts; and yet
Here, while Day's presence wanes,
And over him the sepulchre-lid is slowly lowered and set,
He wakens my regret.

Regret – though nothing dear
That I wot of, was toward in the wide world at his prime,
Or bloomed elsewhere than here,
To die with his decease,and leave a memory sweet, sublime,
Or mark him out in Time. . . .

– Yet, maybe, in some soul,
In some spot undiscerned on sea or land, some impulse rose,
Or some intent upstole
Of that enkindling ardency from whose maturer glows
The world's amendment flows;

But which, benumbed at birth
By momentary chance or wile, has missed its hope to be
Embodied on the earth;
And undervoicings of this loss to man's futurity
May wake regret in me.

The young Wesleyan minister ("The Distracted Preacher") had found his landlady disconcertingly 'enkindling', and Fitzpiers found that, in trying to win Grace back to him, his restraint 'fed his flame'. But much more significantly fire images (which occur in over a hundred poems) are to do with a moment of burning revelation or crisis, and with memory.

At a critical moment when Tim Tangs, about to emigrate, is realising more about his wife's infatuation with Fitzpiers:

The firelight shone upon Suke's plump face and form as she stood looking into it, and upon the face of Tim seated in a corner, and upon the walls of his father's house, which he was beholding that night almost for the last time.

The Woodlanders

Eustacia is set on fire by the arrival (and voice, heard only answering his mother and cousin in the darkness) of the unknown Clym Yeobright:

With the departure of the figures the profuse articulations of the women wasted away from her memory; but the accents of the other stayed on. . . .

On such occasions as this a thousand ideas pass through a highly charged woman's head; and they indicate themselves on her face; but the changes, though actual, are minute. Eustacia's features went through a rhythmical succession of them. She glowed; remembering the mendacity of the imagination, she flagged; then she freshened; then she fired; then she cooled again. It was a cycle of aspects, produced by a cycle of visions.

Eustacia entered her own house; she was excited. Her grandfather was enjoying himself over the fire, raking about the ashes and exposing the red-hot surface of the turves, so that their lurid glare irradiated the chimney-corner with the hues of a furnace.

The Return of the Native

The soldier of "The Revisitation", who retraces his past steps to revive a spent love affair, meets his old flame at dusk on their old downland haunt. Joyfully they reminisce and fall asleep sitting together on the old Sarsen stone. It is the 'red upedging sun. . .blazing on my eyes' which shows him next morning in his lady's face

> That which Time's transforming chisel
> Had been tooling night and day for twenty years, and tooled too well.

The fiery revelation is enough to end it: 'Love is lame at fifty years.'

The tragedy of "The Withered Arm" begins over the embers:

One night, two or three weeks after the bridal return, when the boy was gone to bed, Rhoda sat for a long time over the turf ashes that she had raked out in front of her to extinguish them. She contemplated so intently the new wife, as presented to her in her mind's eye over the embers, that she forgot the lapse of time. . . .

But the figure which had occupied her so much. . .was not to be banished at night. For the first time Gertrude Lodge visited the supplanted woman in her dreams. . . .

The Withered Arm

Hardy rhymes 'embers' both actually and metaphorically with 'remembers'. As 'the fire advances along the log', he recalls his sister as they climbed the tree together; as the tinder box glows 'in fits from the dark' he sees his mother's face beside it; and

213

When the wasting embers redden the chimney-breast . . .
My perished people who housed them here come back to me.'[217]

"The Flirt's Tragedy" begins:

> Here alone by the logs in my chamber,
> > Deserted, decrepit –
> Spent flames limning ghosts on the wainscot
> > Of friends I once knew –
>
> My drama and hers begins weirdly
> > Its dumb re-enactment,
> Each scene, sigh, and circumstance passing
> > In spectral review.

*   *   *

If the 'stab of fire' or 'the burn of love' sear realisation onto our consciousness, another potent light symbol – the moon – has a very different temperature.

THE MOON

"At Rushy Pond" revealed[218] a moon that was connected with frigidity and death. The 'troubled orb' that became the woman's 'wraith' was also described as the wraith of another Hardy creation, the third Avice in The Well-Beloved. *Throughout the novel the three Avices who succeed each other as embodiments of Pierston's fantasied Beloved are accompanied by the moon.*

He looked out of his bedroom window, and began to consider in what direction from where he stood that darling little figure lay. It was straight across there, under the young pale moon. The symbol signified well. The divinity of the silver bow was not more excellently pure than she, the lost, had been. Under that moon was the island of Ancient Slingers, and on the island a house, framed from mullions to chimney-top like the isle itself, of stone. Inside the window, the moonlight irradiating her winding-sheet, lay Avice, reached only by the faint noises inherent in the isle; the tink-tink of the chisels in the quarries, the surging of the tides in the Bay, and the muffled grumbling of the currents in the never-pacified Race.

The Well-Beloved

More than twenty years later, Pierston, back in the Isle, passes the cottage where the third Avice had been born:

Pausing he saw near the west behind him the new moon growing distinct upon the glow.

He was subject to gigantic fantasies still. In spite of himself, the sight of the new moon, as representing one who, by her so-called inconstancy, acted up to his own idea of a migratory Well-beloved, made him feel as if his own wraith in a changed sex had suddenly looked over the horizon at him. In a crowd secretly, or in solitude boldly, he had often bowed the knee three times to this sisterly divinity on her first appearance monthly, and directed a kiss towards her shining shape.

The Well-Beloved

This passage was a revised version of the serial form published five years earlier (1892) in the Illustrated London News. *In 1897 the ending was completely rewritten and this passage (among others) was extensively revised. In the earlier version Hardy had called the moon Pierston's 'chosen tutelary goddess' which had 'made him start as if his sweetheart in the flesh had suddenly looked over the horizon at him': there was no mention of 'his wraith, in a changed sex'. The paragraph had continued: 'He feared Aphrodite, but Selene he cherished.'*

The sisterly relationship, the fear of the Goddess of Love, and the representation of the moon as himself suggest interesting connections — with Hardy's own life, with his favoured Shelley and the Platonic theme of the perfect lovers being a double of each other, twin androgynous halves (a theme contemporaneously explored in both Tess *and* Jude*); and in Pierston's own narcissistic realisation that the elusive Well-Beloved, flitting, without ever settling, from one woman to another, is really the image of himself, his 'wraith, in a changed sex'.*

Pierston was a sculptor, and it is clear that his erotic fantasy of the pursuit of the Well-Beloved is connected with his artistic creativity. When finally the fantasy dies, he finds that:

The artistic sense had left him, and he could no longer attach a definite sentiment to images of beauty recalled from the past.

The Well-Beloved

Hardy linked the death of love and of the creative art with the moon in a beautiful poem written only a few years later. The speaker fears the moon — and his own part in it, his own wraith — which has stolen love, and those beloved, and the creative impulse, so that all that the poet can now give is the 'mechanic speech' he so much deplored.

Shut Out That Moon

Close up the casement, draw the blind,
    Shut out that stealing moon,
She wears too much the guise she wore
    Before our lutes were strewn
With years-deep dust, and names we read
    On a white stone were hewn.

Step not forth on the dew-dashed lawn
    To view the Lady's Chair,

Immense Orion's glittering form,
   The Less and Greater Bear:
Stay in; to such sights we were drawn
   When faded ones were fair.

Brush not the bough for midnight scents
   That come forth lingeringly,
And wake the same sweet sentiments
   They breathed to you and me
When living seemed a laugh, and love
   All it was said to be.

Within the common lamp-lit room
   Prison my eyes and thought;
Let dingy details crudely loom,
   Mechanic speech be wrought:
Too fragrant was Life's early bloom,
   Too tart the fruit it brought!
1904[219]

The relation between love and art, and the lament that human beings seem condemned to repeat again and again their mistakes in love and in life – an endless mirrored series of experiences – are fundamental themes in Hardy's work: and the moon as image of the poet's double, his peering eye, a chill spirit outside the window watching in himself or others the fragility and sterility of love, or the futility of life, deeply underlies it.[220] This poem was written by Hardy when he was seventy-six.

The Pedigree

I

   I bent in the deep of night
Over a pedigree the chronicler gave
As mine; and as I bent there, half-unrobed,
The uncurtained panes of my window-square let in the watery light
   Of the moon in its old age;
And green-rheumed clouds were hurrying past where mute and cold it globed
   Like a drifting dolphin's eye seen through a lapping wave.

II

   So, canning my sire-sown tree,
And the hieroglyphs of this spouse tied to that,
With offspring mapped below in lineage,
   Till the tangles troubled me,

216

The branches seemed to twist into a seared and cynic face
Which winked and tokened towards the window like a Mage
      Enchanting me to gaze again thereat.

III

        It was a mirror now,
    And in it a long perspective I could trace
Of my begetters, dwindling backward each past each
        All with the kindred look,
    Whose names had since been inked down in their place
        On the recorder's book,
Generation and generation of my mien, and build, and brow.

IV

    And then did I divine
That every heave and coil and move I made
Within my brain, and in my mood and speech,
        Was in the glass portrayed
As long forestalled by their so making it;
    The first of them, the primest fuglemen of my line,   .
Being fogged in far antiqueness past surmise and reason's reach.

V

        Said I then, sunk in tone,
    'I am merest mimicker and counterfeit! —
        Though thinking, *I am I,
    And what I do I do myself alone.'*
    — The cynic twist of the page thereat unknit
Back to its normal figure, having wrought its purport wry,
    The Mage's mirror left the window-square,
And the stained moon and drift retook their places there.
1916

As often, the moon, (aged here like the poet), combined with water and window, is ominous and cold; the line patterns of both lineage and engraved experience wreath him round as he seeks to escape; but, childless himself, his only exit is backward into the past — though it may be that having passed on his identity to the moon, ('I' becoming 'eye'), he can thus guarantee the survival of his poetry, even if he himself will fade.[221]

Another poem continued the omens,[222] *the mirror reflecting past generations but breaking under the voyeuristic eye of the moon/poet so that no future scions shall be reflected:*

At the shiver of morning, a little before the false dawn,
    The moon was at the window-square,
      Deedily brooding in deformed decay –
      The curve hewn off her cheek as by an adze;
At the shiver of morning a little before the false dawn
    So the moon looked in there.

Her speechless eyeing reached across the chamber,
    Where lay two souls opprest,
      One a white lady sighing, 'Why am I sad!'
      To him who sighed back, 'Sad, my Love, am I!'
And speechlessly the old moon conned the chamber,
    And these two reft of rest.

While their large-pupilled vision swept the scene there,
    Nought seeming imminent,
      Something fell sheer, and crashed, and from the floor
      Lay glittering at the pair with a shattered gaze,
While their large-pupilled vision swept the scene there,
    And the many-eyed thing outleant.

With a start they saw that it was an old-time pier-glass
    Which had stood on the mantel near,
      Its silvering blemished, – yes, as if worn away
      By the eyes of the countless dead who had smirked at it
Ere these two ever knew that old-time pier glass
    And its vague and vacant leer.

As he looked, his bride like a moth skimmed forth, and kneeling
    Quick, with quivering sighs,
      Gathered the pieces under the moon's sly ray,
      Unwitting as an automaton what she did;
Till he entreated, hasting to where she was kneeling,
    'Let it stay where it lies!'

'Long years of sorrow this means!' breathed the lady
    As they retired. 'Alas!'
      And she lifted one pale hand across her eyes.
      'Don't trouble, Love; it's nothing,' the bridegroom said.
'Long years of sorrow for us!' murmured the lady,
    'Or ever this evil pass!'

And the Spirits Ironic laughed behind the wainscot,
    And the Spirits of Pity sighed.
  'It's good,' said the Spirits Ironic, 'to tickle their minds
With a portent of their wedlock's aftergrinds.'
And the Spirits of Pity sighed behind the wainscot,
    'It's a portent we cannot abide!

'More, what shall happen to prove the truth of the portent?'
    – 'Oh; in brief, they will fade till old,
  And their loves grow numbed ere by death, by the cark of care.'
    – 'But nought see we that asks for portents there? –
'Tis the lot of all.' – 'Well, no less true is a portent
    That it fits all mortal mould.'

For Hardy, the honeymoon period (in today's sense as used, for example, of politicians or new management) is often accompanied by the full moon while the experience waxes (and a new moon as love begins): the maimed moon in this poem is part of the early portent of its waning. Moon patterns, like shadow and light and branch patterns, which they often incorporate, frequently accompany events – perhaps unseen or unnoticed or ignored until the moment of revelation comes.[223]

I Looked Back

I looked back as I left the house,
And, past the chimneys and neighbour tree,
The moon upsidled through the boughs: –
I thought: 'I shall a last time see
This picture; when will that time be?'

I paused amid the laugh-loud feast,
And selfward said: 'I am sitting where,
Some night, when ancient songs have ceased,
"Now is the last time I shall share
Such cheer," will be the thought I bear.'

An eye-sweep back at a look-out corner
Upon a hill, as forenight wore,
Stirred me to think: 'Ought I to warn her'
That, though I come here times three-score,
One day 'twill be I come no more?'

Anon I reasoned there had been,
Ere quite forsaken was each spot,
Bygones whereon I'd lastly seen

That house, that feast, that maid forgot;
But when? – Ah, I remembered not!

Tranter Dewy comments on how his son Dick seems to be set in a new pattern of life – he's in love:

'I'm afraid Dick's a lost man,' said the tranter . . . 'Ay,' [he] said . . . still gazing at Dick's unconscious advance. 'I don't like at all what I see! There's too many o' them looks out of the winder without noticing anything; too much shining of boots; too much peeping round corners; too much looking at the clock; telling about clever things *she* did till you be sick of it, and then upon a hint to that effect a horrible silence about her. I've walked the path once in my life and know the country, neighbours; and Dick's a lost man!' the tranter turned a quarter round and smiled a smile of miserable satire at the setting new moon, which happened to catch his eye.

Under the Greenwood Tree

On the extraordinary first (and apparently last) night of Cytherea's service with Miss Aldclyffe, (and when she is in great perplexity over her love for Edward), her employer begs to be allowed to share the young woman's bed for the night:[224]

[Cytherea] continued, wakeful, ill at ease, and mentally distressed. She withdrew herself from her companion's embrace, turned to the other side, and endeavoured to relieve her busy brain by looking at the window-blind, and noticing the light of the rising moon – now in her last quarter – creep round upon it: it was the light of an old waning moon which had but a few days' longer to live.

The sight led her to think again of what had happened under the ray s of the same month's moon, a little before its full, the ecstatic evening scene with Edward: the kiss, and the shortness of those happy moments – maiden imagination bringing about the apotheosis of a *status quo* which had had several unpleasantnesses in its earthly reality.

But sounds were in the ascendant that night. Her ears became aware of a strange and gloomy murmur.

She recognized it: it was the gushing of the waterfall, faint and low, brought from its source to the unwonted distance of the House by a faint breeze which made it distinctly perceptible by reason of the utter absence of all disturbing noises. . .She began to fancy what the waterfall must be like at that hour, under the trees in the ghostly moonlight. Black at the head, and over the surface of the deep cold hole into which it fell; white and frothy at the fall; black and white, like a pall and its border; sad everywhere.

She was in the mood for sounds of every kind now. . .Another soon came.

The second was quite different from the first – a kind of intermittent whistle it seemed primarily: no, a creak, a metallic creak, ever and anon, like a plough, or a rusty wheelbarrow, or at least a wheel of some kind. Yes, it was a wheel – the water wheel in the shrubbery by the old manor-house, which the coachman had said would drive him mad.

She determined not to think any more of these gloomy things; but now that she had once noticed the sound there was no sealing her ears to it. She could not help timing its creaks, and putting on a dread expectancy just before the end of each half-minute that brought them. To imagine the inside of the engine-house, whence these noises proceeded, was now a necessity. No window, but crevices in the door, through which, probably, the moonbeams streamed in the most attenuated and skeleton-like rays, striking sharply upon portions of wet rusty cranks and chains; a glistening wheel, turning incessantly, labouring in the dark like a captive starving in a dungeon; and instead of a floor below, gurgling water, which on account of the darkness could only be heard; water which laboured up dark pipes almost to where she lay.

She shivered.

Desperate Remedies

On an earlier page the reader saw Clym Yeobright, in the full flood of his first love for Eustacia, making his way to meet her by a radiant moon: − 'his face towards the moon, which depicted a small image of her in each of his eyes.'[225] *Feeling miserable guilt in the totally new situation of deceiving his mother, he watched while the 'tawny stain' of the eclipse began. (The 'stained moon' of "The Pedigree" had also reflected some of the pain of humanity.) Eustacia comes; and their passionate meeting is fraught from first to last with foreboding.*

Then, holding each other's hand, they were again silent, and the shadow on the moon's disc grew a little larger. . . .

'. . . One thing is certain − I do love you − past all compass and description. I love you to oppressiveness − I, who have never before felt more than a pleasant passing fancy for any woman I have ever seen. Let me look right into your moonlit face, and dwell on every like and curve in it! Only a few hair-breadths make the difference between this face and faces I have seen many times before I knew you; yet what a difference − the difference between everything and nothing at all. One touch on the at mouth again! there, and there, and there. Your eyes seem heavy, Eustacia.'

'No, it is my general way of looking. I think it arises from my feeling sometimes an agonizing pity for myself that I ever was born.'

'You don't feel it now?'

'No. Yet I know that we shall not love like this always. Nothing can ensure the continuance of love. It will evaporate like a spirit, and so I feel full of fears.'

The gulf between their hopes for the future widen as they kiss and talk.

'Ah! but you don't know what you have got in me,' she said. 'Sometimes I think there is not that in Eustacia Vye which will make a good homespun wife. Well, let it go − see how our time is slipping, slipping, slipping!' She pointed towards the half-eclipsed moon.

'You are too mournful.'

'No. Only I dread to think of anything beyond the present. What is, we know. We are together now, and it is unknown how long we shall be so: the unknown always fills my mind with terrible possibilities, even when I may reasonably expect it to be cheerful. . . . Clym, the eclipsed moonlight shines upon your face with a strange foreign colour, and shows its shape as if it were cut out in gold. That means you should be doing better things than this.'

— But the shadow of Time moves on resistlessly:

'Must you go home yet?' she asked. 'Yes, the sand has nearly slipped away, I see, and the eclipse is creeping on more and more. . . .'

— and a reflection on his troubles ends the chapter:

Thus as his sight grew accustomed to the first blinding halo kindled about him by love and beauty, Yeobright began to perceive what a strait he was in.

The Return of the Native

The moon image is drawn together with the account of Eustacia's end — 'who, as she lay there still in death, eclipsed all her living phases.'

The young Jude, a baker's boy who, in his ambition to get to Christminster, taught himself Latin and Greek by reading on his delivery rounds, has a moment of illumination by moonlight, when he blames himself for 'inconsistency' and makes a change of direction:

On a day when Fawley was getting quite advanced, being now about sixteen, and had been stumbling through the *'Carmen Saeculare'* on his way home, he found himself to be passing over the high edge of the plateau by the Brown House. The light had changed, and it was the sense of this which had caused him to look up. The sun was going down, and the full moon was rising simultaneously behind the woods in the opposite quarter. His mind had become so impregnated with the poem that, in a moment of the same impulsive emotion which years before had caused him to kneel on the ladder, he stopped the horse, alighted, and glancing round to see that nobody was in sight, knelt down on the roadside bank with open book. He turned first to the shiny goddess, who seemed to look so softly and critically at his doings, then to the disappearing luminary on the other hand, as he began:

'Phoebe silvarumque potens Diana!'[226]

The horse stood still till he had finished the hymn, which Jude repeated under the sway of a polytheistic fancy that he would never have thought of humouring in broad daylight.

Jude the Obscure

The moon brings out the pattern of the mind, as it also brings out the pattern in external reality. In "A Cathedral Façade at Midnight" (page 56) moonlight blanches the still old figures just as Reason shows up the obsolescence of the old ideas.[227] It seems to have a double capacity: as it waxes it leads on the imagination to hope and expansion — and as it wanes, it is shown also as the external fate which 'prison[s] my eyes and thought'. The woman of "A Hurried Meeting" (*page 191*) *who slips 'to the moonshade' dogged by her clinging cobwebbed fate, emerges later 'from shade to the moonlight ray', her love in ruins. "On the Esplanade" begins:*

The broad bald moon edged up where the sea was wide,

and ends:

That, behind,
My Fate's masked face crept near me I did not know!

So as Dick and Fancy leave after their wedding festivities:

The moon was just over the full, rendering any light from lamps or their own beauties quite unnecessary to the pair.

Under the Greenwood Tree

— an ironically innocent moon (for a full moon can only wane); but in the following poem there is the characteristic setting for tragedy. 'The fulling moon' partners the 'wild distraction' of the bride, held in romantic thrall to her past lover, while her new groom's bitterness swells — both captives in their own mental pattern; and as it wanes it reveals how that pattern will develop into their future life in the wider setting of the world they live in, with the familiar leafless and loveless road:

The Telegram

'O he's suffering — maybe dying — and I not there to aid,
And smooth his bed and whisper to him! Can I nohow go?
Only the nurse's brief twelve words thus hurriedly conveyed,
    As by stealth, to let me know.

'He was the best and brightest! — candour shone upon his brow,
And I shall never meet again a soldier such as he,
And I loved him ere I knew it, and perhaps he's sinking now,
    Far, far removed from me!'

— The yachts ride mute at anchor and the fulling moon is fair,
And the giddy folk are strutting up and down the smooth parade,
And in her wild distraction she seems not to be aware
    That she lives no more a maid,

But has vowed and wived herself to one who blessed the ground she trod
To and from his scene of ministry, and thought her history known
In its last particular to him — aye, almost as to God,
    And believed her quite his own.

So rapt her mind's far-off regard she droops as in a swoon,
And a movement of aversion mars her recent spousal grace,
And in silence we two sit here in our waning honeymoon
    At this idle watering-place. . . .

What now I see before me is a long lane overhung
With lovelessness, and stretching from the present to the grave.
And I would I were away from this, with friends I knew when young,
    Ere a woman held me slave.

The moon figures in some seventy of Hardy's poems, often linked with himself, as with the human and the natural pattern. In the following poem the moon, with its sexual imagery − its shape/meaning hidden, changing, and only tantalisingly revealed after time − and its companionship with the poet through all the experiences of his life and mind, from the full to the skeletal, seems to be the dominating image of his life.

At Moonrise and Onwards

    I thought you a fire
    On Heath-Plantation Hill,
Dealing out mischief the most dire
    To the chattels of men of hire
    There in their vill.

    But by and by
    You turned a yellow-green,
Like a large glow-worm in the sky;
    And then I could descry
    Your mood and mien.

    How well I know
    Your furtive feminine shape!
As if reluctantly you show
    You nude of cloud, and but by favour throw
    Aside its drape. . . .

    − How many a year
    Have you kept pace with me,
Wan Woman of the waste up there,
    Behind a hedge, or the bare
    Bough of a tree!

No novelty are you,
O Lady of all my time,
Veering unbid into my view
Whether I near Death's mew,
Or Life's top cyme!

*   *   *

COLOUR IMAGERY IN NATURE

And in the night as I lay weak,
As I lay weak,
The leaves a-falling on my cheek,
The red moon low declined –
The ghost of him I'd die to kiss
Rose up and said: 'Ah, tell me this!
Was the child mine, or was it his?
Speak, that I rest may find!'

From *The Trampwoman's Tragedy*

Red is often a sinister colour for Hardy. It is the colour of blood and war, of the Battle-God's 'crimson form', of the 'red sunset' seen by the fallen; 'the sun lay west like a crimson wound'. It is the colour of Julie-Jane's 'peony lips', which brought her to no good.[228] It was a 'red upedging sun' which revealed his lover's ageing face to the soldier of The Revisitation *and when the vicar's young wife met her secret lover, 'the sun was low and crimson-faced' like their guilt.[229] The setting for "A Conversation at Dawn" is clearly ominous:*

Above the level horizon spread
The sunrise, firing them from foot to head
From its smouldering lair,
And painting their pillows with dyes of red.

Nature suffers 'that red ravage through her zones'.[230] And when Knight was hanging hopelessly by his hands on the dread cliff face:

Nobody would have expected the sun to shine on such an evening as this. Yet it appeared, low down upon the sea. Not with its natural golden fringe, sweeping the furthest ends of the landscape, not with the strange glare of whiteness which it sometimes puts on as an alternative to colour, but as a splotch of vermilion red upon a leaden ground – a red face looking on with a drunken leer.

A Pair of Blue Eyes

225

Christopher Julian dares to call upon Ethelberta:

There was a strange light in the atmosphere: the glass of the street-lamps, the varnished back of a passing cab, a milk-woman's cans, and a row of church-windows glared in his eyes like new-rubbed copper; and on looking the other way he beheld a bloody sun hanging among the chimneys at the upper end, as a danger-lamp to warn him off.

The Hand of Ethelberta

Grace waits for Giles to come to her in his little cabin in the woods:

The strain upon Grace's mind in various ways was so great on this the most desolate day she had passed there that she felt it would be well-nigh impossible to spend another in such circumstances. The evening came at last; the sun, when its chin was on the earth, found an opening through which to pierce the shade, and stretched irradiated gauzes across the damp atmosphere, making the wet trunks shine, and throwing splotches of such ruddiness on the leaves beneath the beech that they were turned to gory hues.

The Woodlanders

When Mrs Masters died, her fuchsias had to be cut down for her funeral (page 138); and other fuchsias were linked with the death at Gallipoli of Frank George, Hardy's cousin and chosen heir:

> When the heath wore the robe of late summer,
> And the fuchsia-bells, hot in the sun,
> Hung red by the door, a quick comer
> Brought tidings that marching was done
> For him who had joined in that game overseas
> Where Death stood to win, though his name was to borrow
> A brightness therefrom not to fade on the morrow.
> September 1915

From *Before Marching and After*

Going and Staying

I

> The moving sun-shapes on the spray,
> The sparkles where the brook was flowing,
> Pink faces, plightings, moonlit May,
> These were the things we wished would stay;
>   But they were going.

II

> Seasons of blankness as of snow,
> The silent bleed of a world decaying,

The moan of multitudes in woe,
These were the things we wished would go;
But they were staying.

III

Then we looked closelier at Time,
And saw his ghostly arms revolving
To sweep off woeful things with prime,
Things sinister with things sublime
Alike dissolving.

In this poem white, as well as red, is invoked as a symbol of misery. It was a 'white lady' who sighed 'Why am I sad!' on her honeymoon; and the years of war were a time of 'Care whitely watching, Sorrows manifold'.[231] One of Hardy's many characters who return to revise a past experience found his former love 'but a thing of flesh and bone':

And my dream was scared, and expired on a moan,
And I whitely hastened away.

The Dream-Follower

White is often linked with tombstones and 'the white-flowered mound',[232] and with death:

Or perhaps his bones are whiting
In the wind to their decay! . . .

Sitting on the Bridge

A figure lay stretched out whitely . . .

The Last Time

and at the icy death of a marriage one Christmas:

. . . their steps dimmed into white silence upon the slippery glaze
And the trees went on with their spitting amid the icicled haze.[233]

There was now a distinct manifestation of morning in the air, and presently the bleared white visage of a sunless winter day emerged like a dead-born child.

The Woodlanders

One of Hardy's most moving poems, "The Bird-Catcher's Boy", tells how Freddy, loathing his father's trade, disappears one night from home. His sorrowing parents, watching interminably, think one Christmas that they hear him, and press to his old room:

There on the empty bed
    White the moon shone,
As ever since they'd said,
    'Freddy is gone!'

That night at Durdle-Door
    Foundered a hoy,
And the tide washed ashore
    One sailor boy.
21 November 1912

After the terrible accident before dawn which killed Tess's horse Prince:

The atmosphere turned pale, the birds shook themselves in the hedges, arose, and twittered; the lane showed all its white features, and Tess showed hers, still whiter. The huge pool of blood in front of her was already assuming the iridescence of coagulation . . .

Tess of the d'Urbervilles

White and red were also linked (page 55) in "At Rushy Pond" when the moon was the woman's 'very wraith', and when, as in several moon contexts, ice wins over fire, frigidity over warmth. White often emphasises cold, particularly the cold aspect of the moon or sun, the sun frowning 'whitely in eye-trying flaps', and the 'white shine' of the moon as Egbert Mayne tries to come to terms with his grandfather's death.[234] *When Hardy went to St Juliot in 1916 to inspect the memorial which he had erected to Emma, his poem "The Marble Tablet" began:*

There it stands, though alas, what a little of her
    Shows in its cold white look!

In "Song to an Old Burden" he remembered others whose 'cheeks have wanned to whiteness'; and 'wan' is a characteristic word, like 'dun', 'ashen', 'dim', 'colourless' and all the other 'neutral-tinted haps' which fill his writings. 'Wanly. . . . have slid since morn my colourless thoughts'. . . .

After Marcia had left Pierston:

During the slow and colourless days he had to sit and behold the mournful departure of his Well-Beloved from the form he had lately cherished, till she had almost vanished away.

The Well-Beloved

For Hardy, the kind of time in which we are imprisoned in our daily life is one that is totally drained of colour. From 'the pale corpse-like birth' of a commonplace day we pass much of our time in a 'sad-coloured landscape', a 'muddy monochrome', a 'drab-aired afternoon',[235] *until, as he describes himself in "The Dead Man Walking":*

I am but a shape that stands here,

A pulseless mould,

A pale past picture, screening

Ashes gone cold.

Some of the metallic images already referred to[236] *share this monotony and negative view:*

One of the gentlemen . . . looked out upon the dreary prospect before him. The wide concave of cloud, of the monotonous hue of dull pewter, formed an unbroken hood over the level from horizon to horizon; beneath it, reflecting its wan lustre, was the glazed high-road which stretched, hedgeless and ditchless, past a directing-post where another road joined it . . .

The Hand of Ethelberta

Similar negatives, in a 'rayless' sun like 'a flameless fire', had accompanied Farmer Boldwood (now 'wan in expression') after he received Bathsheba's idle Valentine – and the 'wasting moon' hung in the sky 'like tarnished brass.' Jude when he was very unhappy saw 'the blue sky as zinc.'

Although Tess is blindingly happy, the (reflected) light is ominously bright:

Her feelings almost filled her ears like a babble of waves, and surged up to her eyes. She put her hand in his, and thus they went on, to a place where the reflected sun glared up from the river, under a bridge, with a molten-metallic glow that dazzled their eyes, though the sun itself was hidden by the bridge.

Tess of the d'Urbervilles

Neutral Tones

We stood by a pond that winter day

And the sun was white, as though chidden of God,

And a few leaves lay on the starving sod;

    – They had fallen from an ash, and were gray.

Your eyes on me were as eyes that rove

Over tedious riddles of years ago;

And some words played between us to and fro

    On which lost the more by our love.

The smile on your mouth was the deadest thing

Alive enough to have strength to die;

And a grin of bitterness swept thereby

    Like an ominous bird a-wing. . . .

Since then, keen lessons that love deceives,
And wrings with wrong, have shaped to me
Your face, and the God-curst sun, and a tree,
    And a pond edged with grayish leaves.
1867

'Gray' is another favourite Hardy word among these tones that is explicitly an image – 'grey shades, material and mental'; 'the grey gaunt days dividing us'; 'tragic, gruesome, gray'; and the tree, bereft of his lady, 'icicles grieving me gray'.[237]

   But of course this is only part of the picture; and there are many antidotes, many moments of brilliant light and vibrant greens – both 'green and gray times'. For Hardy, many colours are good and full of delight. He uses an interesting colour simile when writing of 'the typical Hodge', who would soon be seen as an individual by anyone taking the trouble to look:

As, to the eye of the diver, contrasting colours shine out by degrees from what has originally painted itself of an unrelieved earthy hue, so would shine out the characters, capacities, and interests of these people to him.

                                                              The Dorsetshire Labourer

He Fears His Good Fortune

There was a glorious time
At an epoch of my prime;
Mornings beryl-bespread,
And evenings golden-red;
        Nothing gray:
And in my heart I said,
'However this chanced to be,
It is too full for me,
Too rare, too rapturous, rash,
Its spell must close with a crash
        Some day!'

The radiance went on
Anon and yet anon,
And sweetness fell around
Like manna on the ground.
        'I've no claim,',
Said I, 'to be thus crowned:
I am not worthy this: –
Must it not go amiss? –
Well. . . let the end foreseen
Come duly! – I am serene,
        – And it came.

230

Green is usually one of the 'hope-hues growing gayer and yet gayer' in Hardy's palette. For the young lover/bird the 'evergreen nesting-tree' was security and love; and a young woman told her lover she was content to wait for whenever he could come:

> blissful ever to abide
> In this green labyrinth . . .[238]

Similarly the poem "Concerning His Old Home"[239] speaks of

> That friendly place
> With its green low door –

Green symbolises or accompanies both youth and happiness – the 'green years' when 'grasses and grove shone', when 'life was green'.[240] And in the haunting poem "Under the Waterfall":

> My lover and I
> Walked under a sky
> Of blue with a leaf-wove awning of green.

It is also the colour of hope and immortality. The Souls of the Slain are thankful 'that hearts keep us green'; and the misanthropic old Sir Nameless thanked God he had no children:

> 'For green remembrance there are better means
> Than offspring, who but wish their sires away.'

'Summer's green wonderwork' – when 'the May month flaps its glad green leaves like wings' and 'lush summer lit the trees to green'[241] – is of course symbolic, as all Hardy's seasons are. In the following poem the pattern of branches across his vision again images his mind's life and perceptions growing over the years until he cannot see out beyond them.

At Day-Close in November

> The ten hours' light is abating,
> And a late bird wings across,
> Where the pines, like waltzers waiting,
> Give their black heads a toss.
>
> Beech leaves, that yellow the noon-time,
> Float past, like specks in the eye;
> I set every tree in my June time,
> And now they obscure the sky.

And the children who ramble through here
Conceive that there never has been
A time when no tall trees grew here,
That none will in time be seen.

Joys of Memory

When the spring comes round, and a certain day
Looks out from the brume by the eastern copsetrees
And says, Remember,
I begin again, as if it were new,
A day of like date I once lived through,
Whiling it hour by hour away;
So shall I do till my December,
When spring comes round.

I take my holiday then and my rest,
Away from the dun life here about me,
Old hours re-greeting
With the quiet sense that bring they must
Such throbs as at first, till I house with dust,
And in the numbness my heartsome zest
For things that were, be past repeating
When spring comes round.

Hardy's 'secret light of greens', however, shades off into less favourable portents as it yellows. The moon's light 'as a witch-flame's weirdsome sheen' influenced the lovers' vision; 'turned a yellow-green' and revealed more of itself; coloured the 'green-rheumed clouds' in its watery old age as it prepared to enchant the poet into the tangles of his lineage.[242] 'When yellow begins to show in the leaf' is always the beginning of the end, 'the yellowing years'; and in one of Hardy's most ironically resentful poems about the speed with which the dead are forgotten, we move from the opening 'sunny tree' under which he lies, through the yellow corn, to the last bitter scene:

And mourn not me
Beneath the yellowing tree;
For I shall mind not, slumbering peacefully.

From Regret Not Me

Apart from the gold of sunset, the other end of the spectrum seemed a happier one for Hardy. Rainbows suggest joy or beauty or love.[243] In March 1913 he was looking at a picture of his late wife:

But don't you know it, my dear,
    Don't you know it,
That this day of the year
(What rainbow-rays embow it!)
We met, strangers confessed,
    But parted — blest?

From Looking at a Picture on an Anniversary

Fitzpiers expounds his sophisticated view of love:

Human love is a subjective thing — the essence itself of man, as that great thinker Spinoza says. . . . — it is joy accompanied by an idea which we project against any suitable object in the line of our vision, just as the rainbow iris is projected against an oak, ash, or elm tree indifferently. So that if any other young lady had appeared instead of the one who did appear, I should have felt just the same interest in her. . . .

The Woodlanders

When the Swancourts arrive at the wharf for their voyage to Plymouth by coaster, they are appalled at the chaos:

'Never saw such a dreadful scene in my life — never!' said Mr Swancourt, floundering into the boat. 'Worse than Famine and Sword upon one. I thought such customs were confined to continental ports. Aren't you astonished, Elfride?'

'O no,' said Elfride, appearing amid the dingy scene like a rainbow in a murky sky. 'It is a pleasant novelty, I think.'

A Pair of Blue Eyes

As an old man Hardy looked back on the love-lit past:

There were those songs, a score times sung,
    With all their tripping tunes,
There were the laughters once that rung,
    There those unmatched full moons,
        Those idle noons:

There fadeless, fixed, were dust-dead flowers
    Remaining still in blow;
Elsewhere, wild love-makings in bowers;
    Hard by, that irised bow
        Of years ago.

From The Absolute Explains

233

Her Apotheosis
'Secretum meum mihi'[244]
(Faded Woman's Song)

There were years vague of measure,
  Needless the asking when;
No honours, praises, pleasure
  Reached common maids from men.

And hence no lures bewitched them,
  No hand was stretched to raise,
No gracious gifts enriched them,
  No voices sang their praise.

Yet an iris at that season
  Amid the accustomed slight
From denseness, dull unreason,
  Ringed me with living light.

Of all colours for Hardy, one has a metaphysical quality:

Out of the past there rises a week
  Enringed with a purple zone.

From *The Change*

As a young man he had annotated in his copy of The Golden Treasury *a line from Gray's* Progress of Poesy, *describing the goddess Venus/Cytherea: 'the bloom of young Desire and purple light of Love.'*

Early in his stay, Stephen waits for Elfride in the church he is to restore:

Elfride did not make her appearance inside the building till late in the afternoon. . . . She looked so intensely *living* and full of movement in the old silent place that young Smith's world began to be lit by 'the purple light' in all its definiteness. Worm was got rid of by sending him to measure the height of the tower . . .

A Pair of Blue Eyes

(Describing his first attraction to Emma Gifford at St Juliot, Hardy wrote:

She was so *living*, he used to say . . .

The Life of Thomas Hardy

The purples and blues, and the limpid radiance, of the sea as Edward and Cythera rowed together (page 143), were not fortuitous:

234

Then he kissed her again with a longer kiss.

It was the supremely happy moment of their experience. The 'bloom' and the 'purple light' were strong on the lineaments of both. Their hearts could hardly believe the evidence of their lips.

'I love you, and you love me, Cytherea!' he whispered.

Desperate Remedies

(After he had confessed that their love's progress could not yet be plain sailing, the sun had set, and:

She surveyed the long line of lamps on the sea-wall of the town, now looking small and yellow, and seeming to send long tap-roots of fire quivering down deep into the sea . . .)

Shortly before her wedding-day, Grace reviews the state of her feelings:

What an attentuation this cold pride was of the dream of her youth, in which she had pictured herself walking in state towards the altar, flushed by the purple light and bloom of her own passion, without a single misgiving as to the sealing of the bond . . .

The Woodlanders

Hardy always saw the purple light in his Cornish experience – as in "Beeny Cliff" (page 145) and:

> I found her out there
> On a slope few see,
> That falls westwardly
> To the salt-edged air,
> Where the ocean breaks
> On the purple strand,
> And the hurricane shakes
> The solid land . . .

From *I Found Her Out There*

The 'bloom of dark purple cast' of the Preface (page 40) appears in the novel:

The precipice may be called the Cliff without a Name.

What gave an added terror to its height was its blackness. And upon this dark face the beating of ten thousand west winds had formed a kind of bloom, which had a visual effect not unlike that of a Hambro' grape. Moreover the bloom seemed to float off into the atmosphere, and inspire terror through the lungs.

A Pair of Blue Eyes

This 'bloom' which was exhaled, and 'floated off', and inspired both terror and ecstasy, was a figure for love.[245] *But it had other sources for Hardy than Gray's lines alone. Virgil's Aeneid had been a significant influence since his mother gave him Dryden's translation as a small boy.*

He must have absorbed Virgil's (and Dryden's yet more) frequent use of the word 'purpureus',which in poetic use meant 'bright, brilliant, beautiful . . . or glowing'. Hardy often re-read the Aeneid; A Pair of Blue Eyes *and* Desperate Remedies *are particularly full of references to it or to Virgil; and the epigraph to the* Poems of 1912-13 *came from Book IV, when the widowed Dido tells of how she now feels for Aeneas 'the sparks of an ancient flame' – 'veteris vestigia flammae'.*

In the Sixth Book, Aeneas goes to visit the soul of his father, privileged to be in Elysium – a state where, more than anywhere else, 'a purple light, a more abundant air / Invest the meadows.'[246] *It seems more than likely that Hardy, in his total disarray after Emma's death, linked this purple light of love with the light of heaven as he searched reality – including the landscape – for signs of her continuing spiritual existence, preferably in the Fields of the Blessed.*

> Where drives she now? It may be where
>   No mortal horses are,
> But in a chariot of the air
>   Towards some radiant star.

From *A Woman Driving*

THE IMAGE OF THE LANDSCAPE

It is easy to see that locality and landscape are very important to Hardy. His childhood environment, absorbed like air, his probing mind, his observant sensitivity and his training as an architect and artist are some contributory factors.

On taking up *The Woodlanders* and reading it after many years I think I like it, as a story, the best of all. Perhaps that is owing to the locality and scenery of the action, a part I am very fond of.

The Life of Thomas Hardy

[1922] *Aug.* I am convinced that it is better for a writer to know a little bit of the world remarkably well than to know a great part of the world remarkably little.

Memoranda II

His reflections start from a precise setting in time and space:

An August Midnight

I

> A shaded lamp and a waving blind,
> And the beat of a clock from a distant floor:
> On this scene enter – winged, horned, and spined –
> A longlegs, a moth, and a dumbledore;

236

While 'mid my page there idly stands
A sleepy fly, that rubs its hands. . . .

II

Thus meet we five, in this still place,
At this point of time, at this point in space.
 – My guests besmear my new-penned line,
Or bang at the lamp and fall supine.
'God's humblest, they!' I muse. Yet why?
They know Earth-secrets that know not I.
Max Gate, 1899

Hardy's central preoccupation is the exploration of reality – which for human beings is made up of their own genus and individual selves plus the universe in which they are set. The human mind is set in a body as well as in a wider environment; the human being is a complex creature both of matter and of spirit, of reason and of emotion. Both can fail us; every possible facet of life must be enrolled in the search for understanding, so an attempt to 'read' the landscape (which here I shall confine to the natural landscape rather than the industrial or urban) is a necessary part, and becomes an image, in the search.

When Stephen, greatly changed, returns from India to an even more changed Elfride, he needs to orientate himself:

For a reason of his own he made this spot his refuge from the storm, and turning his face to the left, conned the landscape as a book.
  He was overlooking the valley containing Elfride's residence.

A Pair of Blue Eyes

In his search for the truth about Emma and his relationship with her, Hardy in his Poems of 1912-13 *(and in physical fact) travels from Dorset to Cornwall and Plymouth and back. Having begun with the 'traces of an old fire' and experienced many changes of feeling, he ends scanning the landscape, a spot circled with the ashes of a fire lit before she died: a burnt circle, like the circle of friends now broken, a charred relic (like Hardy) of an experience which has to be revised and remade in understanding against the background of unchanging Nature:*

Where the Picnic Was

Where we made the fire
In the summer time
Of branch and briar
On the hill to the sea,
I slowly climb
Through winter mire,

237

And scan and trace
The forsaken place
Quite readily.

Now a cold wind blows,
And the grass is gray,
But the spot still shows
As a burnt circle — aye,
And stick-ends, charred,
Still strew the sward
Whereon I stand,
Last relic of the band
Who came that day!

Yes, I am here
Just as last year,
And the sea breathes brine
From its strange straight line
Up hither, the same
As when we four came.

— But two have wandered far
From this grassy rise
Into urban roar
Where no picnics are,
And one — has shut her eyes
For evermore.

In his exploration Hardy tries out the landscape in a variety of different rôles.

The pilgrim or journeying lover, and the traveller who returns to an old haunt, are frequent characters for whom the environing landscape naturally has particular significance. But in all human life the environment plays a large part — at Hardy's point in time and space this, externally, was largely a natural landscape, (though the domestic environment was also an image for him of life's restrictions, family joys, or endlessly mirrored and time-worn failures.) Places trigger memories; most of us — as we saw in "Neutral Tones" — remember vividly our surroundings at a moment of crisis (with or without the help of fire, colour imagery, or a change in light):

Stephen, after his return, meets Elfride for the first time with Knight, in the vault where Lady Luxellian's tomb is being prepared:

There was a silence. The blackened coffins were now revealed more clearly than at first, the whitened walls and arches throwing them forward in strong relief. It was a scene which was remembered by all three as an indelible mark in their history.

A Pair of Blue Eyes

Later it was Knight's turn, as Elfride confessed what seemed the worst:

The scene was engraved for years on the retina of Knight's eye: the dead and brown stubble, the weeds among it, the distant belt of beeches shutting out the view of the house, the leaves of which were now red and sick to death.

A Pair of Blue Eyes

As a small boy Hardy had accompanied his mother on a visit to her sister in Hatfield – a memorable first journey away from home. Seventeen years later:

[1866]*June 6.* Went to Hatfield. Changed since my early visit. A youth thought the altered highway had always run as it did. Pied rabbits in the Park, descendants of those I knew. The once children are quite old inhabitants. I regretted that the beautiful sunset did not occur in a place of no reminiscences, that I might have enjoyed it without their tinge.

The Life of Thomas Hardy

> So, the map revives her words, the spot, the time,
> And the thing we found we had to face before the next year's prime;
> The charted coast stares bright,
> And its episode comes back in pantomime.

From The Place on the Map

The environment actually affects human lives – an expression of chance and change and all the mechanistic forces of the universe that condition us. It may be that a clock wakes us from a reverie, or the fog rolls in, or rain and storm wash away our handiwork; Tess's seduction was largely made possible by the distances in her life over which she had no control.

Knight is suspended against the towering cliff-face in a persecuting rain and wind:

The wind, though not intense in other situations, was strong here. It tugged at his coat and lifted it. We are mostly accustomed to look upon all opposition which is not animate as that of the stolid, inexorable hand of indifference, which wears out the patience more than the strength. Here, at any rate, hostility did not assume that slow and sickening form. It was a cosmic agency, active, lashing, eager for conquest; determination; not an insensate standing in the way.

A Pair of Blue Eyes

Hardy's novels show how their work and surroundings really made the life of his rural characters. Far from the Madding Crowd is structured around the occupations of the farming year, as Under the Greenwood Tree was around the seasons, and The Woodlanders patterned by copsework and the woodland tracks like the maze of problems in personal and social relationships. Much of Henchard's downfall was due to his failure to judge the harvest aright – a part of his general problem as a spent force, an obsolescent Darwinian species trying, bewildered and in vain, to fight against inevitable progress.

This is perhaps worked out most carefully in Tess of the d'Urbervilles. *The localities in which she lived and worked both matched or imaged, and actually conditioned, her life. At Marlott she struggled for any kind of individual existence or fulfilment:*

A field-man is a personality afield; a field-woman is a portion of the field; she has somehow lost her own margin, imbibed the essence of her surrounding, and assimilated herself with it.

Tess of the d'Urbervilles

In the lush Froom valley she blossomed; in the starve-acre Flintcomb-Ash her life was pinched, stunted, and shrivelled to mere survival;[247] *in the stifling luxury of Sandbourne her own individual self was smothered almost to death. Hardy further manipulates his seasons to point the link of environment to life. After the débâcle of their marriage, Clare and Tess return to Talbothays, where the withy-bed is cut to mere stumps, and*

. . . the gold of the summer picture was now gray, the colours mean, the rich soil mud, and the river cold.

They then separate, each to their parents' houses, from where Clare goes to Brazil. In the ensuing narrative Hardy obliterates the whole spring and summer: so that Tess leaves again in October and, after the hunted birds incident (page 186), gets to Flintcomb-Ash in the time of winter 'morning frosts and afternoon rains'.

Wet to the skin, Tess and Marian

. . . lived all this afternoon in memories of green, sunny, romantic Talbothays.
   'You can see a gleam of a hill within a few miles o' Froom Valley from here when 'tis fine,' said Marian.
   'Ah! Can you?' said Tess, awake to the new value of this locality.
   So the two forces were at work here as everywhere, the inherent will to enjoy, and the circumstantial will against enjoyment.

Tess of the d'Urbervilles

When the threshing happens, it is in March — soon after which comes Old Lady-Day, the time of new work contracts and new beginnings. Tess's little siblings in their innocence were 'rejoicing in the idea of a new place', unknowing that their removal was forced by the lifehold laws on the death of their father and that Tess's own new beginning was frustrated. Again Alec d'Urberville exemplifies the Darwinian truth:

'The old order changeth. The little finger of the sham d'Urberville can do more for you than the whole dynasty of the real . . .'

Tess of the d'Urbervilles

Since Hardy explores in turn all the 'series of seemings' or impressions which reach him about the landscape, they are, like life, full of paradox. Although in one sense the landscape/environment/universe conditions human life and often obliterates all trace, there is another way in which it can enhance individuality and give it lasting value. The crucial importance of that individual value is imaged in the description of the young girls at the Marlott club-walking:

And as each and all of them were warmed without by the sun, so each had a private little sun for her soul to bask in; some dream, some affection, some hobby, at least some remote and distant hope which, though perhaps starving to nothing, still lived on, as hopes will.

Tess of the d'Urbervilles

The young Drummer Hodge buried in South Africa is carefully shown isolated among the features of a strange country where even the stars are at first foreign — but by the end they have become 'his' stars and seem only to highlight his intrinsic worth.[248] Another of Hardy's most tender evocations of an individual locates her firmly in space at Hermitage, her beloved (and beloved's) home: its lack of mention in the middle stanza only emphasises her dislocation and suffering.

The Inquiry

And are ye one of Hermitage –
Of Hermitage, by Ivel Road,
And do ye know, in Hermitage,
A thatch-roofed house where sengreens grow?
And does John Waywood live there still –
He of the name that there abode
When father hurdled on the hill
      Some fifteen years ago?

Does he now speak o' Patty Beech,
The Patty Beech he used to – see
Or ask at all if Patty Beech
Is known or heard of out this way?
– Ask ever if she's living yet,
And where her present home may be,
And how she bears life's fag and fret
      After so long a day?

In years agone at Hermitage
This faded face was counted fair,
None fairer; and at Hermitage
We swore to wed when he should thrive.
But never a chance had he or I,

And waiting made his wish outwear,
And Time, that dooms man's love to die,
Preserves a maid's alive.

Emma is seen time and again as 'the figure in the scene', the genius loci, *against the local background (pages 71 and 137) — the 'ghost-girl-rider' enhanced and immortalised by the Cornish landscape:*

The Phantom Horsewoman

I

Queer are the ways of a man I know:
He comes and stands
In a careworn craze,
And looks at the sands
And the seaward haze
With moveless hands
And face and gaze,
Then turns to go . . .
And what does he see when he gazes so?

II

They say he sees as an instant thing
More clear than to-day,
A sweet soft scene
That was once in play
By that briny green;
Yes, notes alway
Warm, real, and keen,
What his back years bring —
A phantom of his own figuring.

III

Of this vision of his they might say more:
Not only there
Does he see this sight,
But everywhere
In his brain — day, night,
As if on the air
It were drawn rose-bright —
Yea, far from that shore
Does he carry this vision of heretofore:

IV

A ghost-girl-rider. And though, toil-tried,
    He withers daily,
    Time touches her not,
    But she still rides gaily
    In his rapt thought
    On that shagged and shaly
    Atlantic spot,
    And as when first eyed
Draws rein and sings to the swing of the tide.
1913

An important role for the landscape is also to reflect or figure man or woman's inner state. On the night of terrible storm and foreboding[249] when:

The moon and stars were closed up by cloud and rain to the degree of extinction. . . . Eustacia at length reached Rainbarrow, and stood still there to think. Never was harmony more perfect than that between the chaos of her mind and the chaos of the world without. . . . Between the drippings of the rain from her umbrella to her mantle, from her mantle to the heather, from the heather to the earth, very similar sounds could be heard coming from her lips; and the tearfulness of the outer scene was repeated upon her face.

The Return of the Native

Fitzpiers lingers in the woods as the sun goes down:

He dreamed and mused till his consciousness seemed to occupy the whole space of the woodland round, so little was there of jarring sight or sound to hinder perfect mental unity with the sentiment of the place.

The Woodlanders

It was a cloudy afternoon. Elfride was often diverted from a purpose by a dull sky; and though she used to persuade herself that the weather was as fine as possible on the other side of the clouds, she could not bring about any practical result from this fancy. Now, her mood was such that the humid sky harmonized with it.

A Pair of Blue Eyes

When Edward and Cytherea's reflections meet in the river, from opposite banks, just after she has unhappily married Manston, and they rediscover all their old love, the river is the image of all that separates them:

'I wish I could be near and touch you, just once,' said Springrove, in a voice which he vainly endeavoured to keep firm and clear.

They looked at the river, then into it; a shoal of minnows was floating over the sandy

bottom, like the black dashes on miniver; though narrow, the stream was deep, and there
was no bridge.

'Cytherea, reach out your hand that I may just touch it with mine.'

She stepped to the brink and stretched out her hand and fingers towards his, but not
into them. The river was too wide.

They do manage at last to clasp hands; then, 'her heart. . .near to breaking':

. . . She . . . ran up the garden without looking back. All was over between them. The
river flowed on as quietly and obtusely as ever, and the minnows gathered again in their
favourite spot as if they had never been disturbed.

Desperate Remedies

*Over the several pages which Hardy takes to describe the tumult caused by Swithin's proposal
of marriage to Lady Constantine, the wind is repeatedly an active partner:*

'Dear Lady Constantine, allow me to marry you.'

She started, and the wind without shook the building, sending up a yet intenser moan
from the firs. . . .

'Dearest, agree to my proposal, as you love both me and yourself!'

He waited, while the fir trees rubbed and prodded the base of the tower, and the wind
roared around and shook it; but she could not find words to reply. . . .

She sat on with suspended breath, her heart wildly beating, while he waited in
open-mouthed expectation. Each was swayed by the emotion within them, much as the
candle-flame was swayed by the tempest without. It was the most critical evening of
their lives.

*Lady Constantine agrees to marry him; and shortly after, Swithin (whose grandmother's house
has suffered in the storm) has to leave her alone in the observatory tower while he goes to the rescue:*

Lights began to move to and fro in the hollow where the house stood, and shouts
occasionally mingled with the wind, which retained some violence yet, playing over the
trees beneath her as on the strings of a lyre. But not a bough of them was visible, a
cloak of blackness covering everything netherward; while overhead the windy sky looked
down with a strange and disguised face, the three or four stars that alone were visible
being so dissociated by clouds that she knew not which they were. Under any other
circumstances Lady Constantine might have felt a nameless fear in thus sitting aloft on
a lonely column, with a forest groaning under her feet, and palaeolithic dead men feeding
its roots; but the recent passionate decision stirred her pulses to an intensity beside which
the ordinary tremors of feminine existence asserted themselves in vain. The apocalyptic

effect of the scene surrounding her was, indeed, not inharmonious, and afforded an appropriate background to her intentions.

Two on a Tower

At another apocalyptic moment – "A New Year's Eve in War Time" – when 'nightmare / Rides upon sleep'[250], and the poet finds no answer to his hope for revelation but the ruin of everything, the inner weather and throbbing pulse is mirrored by the outer (page 198).

*   *   *

This reflection by nature of a person's inner state seems to symbolise the relation of the human mind to the surrounding world it inhabits. The descriptions quoted above have a figurative application, but they are not falsifications of nature, as in Ruskin's terms of the pathetic fallacy – 'a falseness in. . .impressions of external things' – the tendency to ascribe human feelings or qualities to inanimate objects.

However, mindful of the Darwinian thesis that 'we all are one with creeping things'[251] – mere dots, with other species, on the landscape of evolution – Hardy does often engage in the pathetic fallacy (and in its denial too.) It is another way of exploring reality.

The world fell like a bolt, and the very land and sky seemed to suffer.[252]

A Pair of Blue Eyes

In the face of his son-in-law's infatuation with Mrs Charmond, a perplexed and troubled Melbury seeks advice:

He set out to look for Giles on a rimy evening when the woods seemed to be in a cold sweat; beads of perspiration hung from every bare twig; the sky had no colour, and the trees rose before him as haggard, grey phantoms whose days of insubstantiality were passed.

The Woodlanders

– and when Grace and Mrs Charmond (wife and 'other woman') cling to each other, lost in the woods:

. . . each one's body, as she breathed, alternately heaved against that of her companion; while the funereal trees rocked and chanted dirges unceasingly.

The Woodlanders

Just so on Eustacia's last night alive had nature taken on human characteristics:

The gloom of the night was funereal; all nature seemed clothed in crape.

The Return of the Native

When Jude set out to see Sue:

The trees overhead deepened the gloom of the hour, and they dripped sadly upon him, impressing him with forebodings. . .for though he knew that he loved her he also knew that he could not be more to her than he was.

Jude the Obscure

— and Egbert Mayne, rising early by the 'sad and yellow' light of a candle to seek his fortune in London, in the hopes of one day winning Geraldine, found that:

The morning was dark, and the raw wind made him shiver till walking warmed him. 'Good Heavens, here's an undertaking!' he sometimes thought. Old trees seemed to look at him through the gloom, as they rocked uneasily to and fro; and now and then a dreary drop of rain beat upon his face as he went on. The dead leaves in the ditches, which could be heard but not seen, shifted their position with a troubled rustle, and flew at intervals with a little rap against his walking-stick and hat.

An Indiscretion in the Life of an Heiress

A numbed Grace and her parents walk home after Giles's death in the woods:

It was just in the blue of the dawn, and the chilling tone of the sky was reflected in her cold, wet face. The whole wood seemed to be a house of death, pervaded by loss to its uttermost length and breadth. Winterborne was gone, and the copses seemed to show the want of him.

The Woodlanders

It is not always tragic. The four dairymaids at Talbothays love Angel Clare to a woman; and they suddenly learn that he has gone away for a few days:

For four impassioned ones around that table the sunshine of the morning went out at a stroke, and the birds muffled their song. But neither girl by word or gesture revealed her blankness.

Tess of the d'Urbervilles

The original title for this poem had been "The Pathetic Fallacy":

The Seasons of Her Year

I

Winter is white on turf and tree,
    And birds are fled;
But summer songsters pipe to me,
    And petals spread,
For what I dreamed of secretly
    His lips have said!

O 'tis a fine May morn, they say,
    And blooms have blown;
But wild and wintry is my day,
    My song-birds moan;
For he who vowed leaves me to pay
    Alone – alone!

In the following poem – a moving plea for unity and 'lovingkindness' in the creation – Hardy turns round the pathetic fallacy by making the pain of the universe felt in himself, rather than in the rest of Nature:

The Wind Blew Words

The wind blew words along the skies,
    And these it blew to me
Through the wide dusk: 'Lift up your eyes,
    Behold this troubled tree,
Complaining as it sways and plies;
    It is a limb of thee.

'Yea, too, the creatures sheltering round –
    Dumb figures, wild and tame,
Yea, too, thy fellows who abound –
    Either of speech the same
Or far and strange – black, dwarfed and browned,
    They are stuff of thy own frame.'

I moved on in a surging awe
    Of inarticulateness
At the pathetic Me I saw
    In all his huge distress
Making self-slaughter of the law
    To kill, break, or suppress.

Nature has its own laws and paradoxes; and another of the 'fugitive impressions' he explores[253] is the very reversal of the pathetic fallacy: the way in which Nature can totally ignore the human insect crawling over its surface.

There shall remain no trace
Of what so closely tied us,
And blank as ere love eyed us
Will be our meeting-place.[254]

At Emma's death the poet seems to castigate her own landscape for remaining unmoved and unchanged.

> Why did not Valency
>   In his purl deplore
> One whose haunts were whence he
>   Drew his limpid store?
> Why did Bos not thunder,
>   Targan apprehend
> Body and Breath were sunder
>   Of their former friend?

From *A Death-Day Recalled*

Tess found the same; after her 'trouble', 'the past was past':

Whatever its consequences, time would close over them; they would all in a few years be as if they had never been, and she herself grassed down and forgotten. Meanwhile the trees were just as green as before; the birds sang and the sun shone as clearly now as ever. The familiar surroundings had not darkened because of her grief, nor sickened because of her pain.

Tess of the D'Urbervilles

When a rather perplexed Somerset follows Paula on her European tour:

In a state of indecision Somerset strolled into the gardens of the Casino, and looked out upon the sea. There it still lay, calm yet lively; of an unmixed blue, yet variegated; hushed, but articulate even to melodiousness. Everything about and around this coast appeared indeed jaunty, tuneful, and at ease, reciprocating with heartiness the rays of the splendid sun; everything, except himself. The palms and flowers on the terraces before him were undisturbed by a single cold breath. The marble work of parapets and steps was unsplintered by frosts.

A Laodicean

In one of his best-known (but often not fully plumbed) poems, Hardy again looks to see what is 'written on terrestrial things'. A poem 'on the Century's End', 'it expressed, for him, the bankruptcy of the Romantic pastoral lyric.'[255] *Here, surrounded by a bleak Nature seeming to mirror his own uncreative mood, the poet finds the one contradiction (or pathetic fallacy reversed) to be in the thrush – whose apparent joy is inexplicable to him, showing up yet again his nescience in the universe, and leaving him still 'unaware'.*

The Darkling Thrush

> I leant upon a coppice gate
>   When Frost was spectre-gray,

And Winter's dregs made desolate
    The weakening eye of day.
The tangled bine-stems scored the sky
    Like strings of broken lyres,
And all mankind that haunted nigh
    Had sought their household fires.

The land's sharp features seemed to be
    The Century's corpse outleant,
His crypt the cloudy canopy,
    The wind his death-lament.
The ancient pulse of germ and birth
    Was shrunken hard and dry,
And every spirit upon earth
    Seemed fervourless as I.

At once a voice arose among
    The bleak twigs overhead
In a full-hearted evensong
    Of joy illimited;
An aged thrush, frail, gaunt, and small,
    In blast-beruffled plume,
Had chosen thus to fling his soul
    Upon the growing gloom.

So little cause for carolings
    Of such ecstatic sound
Was written on terrestrial things
    Afar or nigh around,
That I could think there trembled through
    His happy good-night air
Some blessed Hope, whereof he knew
    And I was unaware.
31 December 1900

The landscape, then, — our setting in the universe — is to be read in the search for an understanding of reality. It is an indelible part of human experience, and conditions our lives; it can enhance individuality and reflect our inner state; it can even seem sometimes to take on human feelings and characteristics — and sometimes just the opposite.

However the landscape is, man and woman must learn from it. It is always teaching us, if we will listen to the voice of things and look at the background and the figure. The sun flashed Barnes's last signal to his friend, as it revealed reality, in his lover's wrinkles, to the soldier of "The Revisitation".[256]

[Mr Barnet] merely said that the afternoon was fine, and went on his way.

As he went a sudden blast of air came over the hill as if in contradiction to his words, and spoilt the previous quiet of the scene. The wind had already shifted violently, and now smelt of the sea.

Fellow-Townsmen

Here, as often, the warning of ensuing events (the boating accident[257]) comes from nature. Sometimes it actually prompts our actions.

Farmer Darton decides to journey a second time to ask for Sally's hand:

Darton was not a man to act rapidly, and the working out of his reparative designs might have been delayed for some time. But there came a winter evening precisely like the one that had darkened over that former ride to Hintock, and he asked himself why he should postpone longer, when the very landscape called for a repetition of that attempt. . . .

To make the journey a complete parallel to the first, he would fain have had his old acquaintance Japheth Johns with him. But Johns, alas! was missing. . . .He screwed himself up to as cheerful a pitch as he could without his former crony, and became content with his own thoughts as he rode, instead of the words of a companion. The sun went down; the boughs appeared scratched in like an etching against the sky; old crooked men with faggots at their backs said 'Good-night, sir,' and Darton replied 'Good-night' right heartily.

Interlopers at the Knap

So the words of his companion were the pattern of his life etched on the sky, added to the (similarly shaped) human words of fellowship – words which were to be unfulfilled, as Sally refused him again.

The patterns of nature, as we saw earlier,[258] were a vital part of the artist's inspiration.

Nature taught the Abbey Mason, both metaphorically and actually. Trying to build Gloucester Cathedral in the new 'Perpendicular' style, he met unseen snags in the construction of the transept – and all work stopped.

'The upper archmould nohow serves
To meet the lower tracery curves:

'The ogees bend too far away
To give the flexures interplay.

'This it is causes my distress. . . .
So will it ever be unless

'New forms be found to supersede
The circle when occasions need.'

And he acknowledges defeat, spending many days vainly attempting to solve the technical problem. After one particularly sleepless night, rising early to look again at his drawing-board, left out on site, he finds that the night's freezing rain has added to the lines of his diagrams:

> Whose icicled drops deformed the lines
> Innumerous of his lame designs,
>
> So that they streamed in small white threads
> From the upper segments to the heads
>
> Of arcs below, uniting them
> Each by a stalactitic stem.
>
> — At once, with eyes that struck out sparks,
> He adds accessory cusping-marks,
>
> Then laughs aloud. The thing was done
> So long assayed from sun to sun. . . .

Over the years the building rose, abbot and mason alike being replaced by successors, and even the mason's identity being forgotten. It was a later abbot who, commenting on such anonymity,

> Replied: 'Nay; art can but transmute;
> Invention is not absolute;
>
> 'Things fail to spring from nought at call,
> And art beginnings most of all.
>
> 'He did but what all artists do,
> Wait upon Nature for his cue.'

From *The Abbey Mason*

Nature is not always so friendly.

Elfride became imprisoned by her own landscape, uncomfortably revisiting the same spots, the same failures, with successive lovers — perhaps a symbol for Hardy of the Victorian restriction of women which he recognised. Knight felt to the full 'the inveterate antagonism of these black precipices to all strugglers for life.' These precipices dwarf them all, including Stephen in the steamboat many hundreds of feet below; and they image the knife-edge on which Elfride in her inexperience lives throughout the story.[259]

Tess, telling Angel of her past, suffered the cruel hostility of fire and light:

The complexion even of external things seemed to suffer transmutation as her announcement progressed. The fire in the grate looked impish — demoniacally funny, as if it did not care in the least about her strait. The fender grinned idly, as if it too did not care. The light from the water-bottle was merely engaged in a chromatic problem. All material objects around announced their irresponsibility with terrible iteration.

Tess of the d'Urbervilles

It is perhaps the most bitter lesson of Hardy's landscape that it puts humanity in its place — a place of no special value which Darwin had shown to be governed by chance and mechanistic laws. Tess and Marian hacked swedes in an upland field between the drab 'upper and nether visages' of earth and sky, 'the two girls crawling over the surface of the former like flies.' Jude, a young bird-scarer, worked in a lonely field 'deprived of all history':

The brown surface of the field went right up towards the sky all round, where it was lost by degrees in the mist that shut out the actual verge and accentuated the solitude.[260]

Jude the Obscure

Mrs Yeobright, pausing in the heat to rest, watched something that reminded her of the mass insignificance of humanity:

In front of her a colony of ants had established a thoroughfare across the way, where they toiled a never-ending and heavy-laden throng. To look down upon them was like observing a city street from the top of a tower. She remembered that this bustle of ants had been in progress for years at the same spot . . .[261]

The Return of the Native

When Cytherea left Edward 'the river flowed on as quietly and obtusely as ever . . .' The study of astronomy, says Swithin of Two on a Tower, *will reduce your troubles 'by reducing the importance of everything. So that the science is still terrible, even as a panacea'.[262] The last word on Napoleon in* The Dynasts *is that men like him:*

> Are in the elemental ages' chart
> Like meanest insects on obscurest leaves
> But incidents and grooves of Earth's unfolding . . .
> The moon sinks, and darkness blots out Napoleon and the scene.

The Dynasts

Egdon Heath, probably the most potent of all Hardy's landscapes, was never to be finally conquered by man. At Mistover Knap

. . . was a paddock in an uncultivated state, though bearing evidence of having once been tilled; but the heath and fern had insidiously crept in and were reasserting their old supremacy.

Though farmers tended to ignore the heath and congratulate themselves on all they had cultivated, Clym knew Egdon was invincible:

. . . observing that, in some of the attempts at reclamation from the waste, tillage, after holding on for a a year or two, had receded again in despair, the ferns and furze-tufts stubbornly reasserting themselves.

The sea changed, the fields changed, the rivers, the villages, and the people changed, yet Egdon remained.[263]

The Return of the Native

After Clym learnt of Eustacia's rejection of his mother he was in agony:

Yeobright went forth from the little dwelling. The pupils of his eyes, fixed steadfastly on blankness, were vaguely lit with an icy shine; his mouth had passed into the phase more or less imaginatively rendered in studies of Oedipus. The strangest deeds were possible to his mood. But they were not possible to his situation. Instead of there being before him the pale face of Eustacia, and a masculine shape unknown, there was only the imperturbable countenance of the heath, which, having defied the cataclysmal onsets of centuries, reduced to insignificance by its seamed and antique features the wildest turmoil of a single man.

The Return of the Native.

That same antiquity of the countryside contributed to the diminishing of the human species. Hardy, surrounded at home in Dorset by prehistoric and Roman remains, was particularly conscious of the past and careful to use it as a telling background. Knight hanging from the cliff eye to eye with 'mean' fossils 'was to be with the small in his death.' Henchard meets his former wife Susan after dark in the Ring, which was a Roman amphitheatre and had seen many terrible encounters with fire and wild animals; Farfrae and Elizabeth-Jane meet by the great earthwork of Mai-Dun.[264] There are barrows and Ancient Britons in the poems, and allusions to what is now grassed over, which all set a time-scale that reduces the importance of the living. And it was on the altar stone where once were made sacrifices to the sun that Tess lay before her death.

And yet . . .

– of one of his novels Hardy wrote:

This slightly-built romance was the outcome of a wish to set the emotional history of two infinitesimal lives against the stupendous background of the stellar universe, and to impart to readers the sentiment that of these contrasting magnitudes the smaller might be the greater to them as men.

1895 Preface, Two on a Tower

Foremost in my vision
Everywhere goes she;

Change dissolves the landscapes,
    She abides with me.

From *In the Mind's Eye*

For Hardy the individual human being is more to be valued than anything on earth; the figure, above the scene:

Yet her rainy form is the Genius still of the spot,
        Immutable, yea,
Though the place now knows her no more, and has known her not
        Ever since that day.[265]   .

When he thinks of the Roman road across the heath, it is not the helmed legionaries that rise in his mind, but his mother, as she and the small boy he once was walked along it together.[266] His sister too is indelibly present, engraved upon the scene:

'Sacred to the Memory'
(Mary H.)

That 'Sacred to the Memory'
Is clearly carven there I own,
And all may think that on the stone
The words have been inscribed by me
In bare conventionality.

They know not and will never know
That my full script is not confined
To that stone space, but stands deep lined
Upon the landscape high and low
Wherein she made such worthy show.

The watcher who surmises that the man with basket and spade by the Roman Gravemounds is there to dig relics soon learns the truth; it's to bury his dead cat. 'The furred thing is all to him – nothing Rome!'[267] And though primaeval rocks line the roadside, their antiquity is as nothing compared with the significance of the lovers who passed.

At Castle Boterel

As I drive to the junction of lane and highway,
    And the drizzle bedrenches the waggonette,
I look behind at the fading byway,
    And see on its slope, now glistening wet,
        Distinctly yet

Myself and a girlish form benighted
    In dry March weather. We climb the road
Beside a chaise. We had just alighted
    To ease the sturdy pony's load
      When he sighed and slowed.

What we did as we climbed, and what we talked of
    Matters not much, nor to what it led, –
Something that life will not be balked of
    Without rude reason till hope is dead,
      And feeling fled.

It filled but a minute. But was there ever
    A time of such quality, since or before,
In that hill's story? To one mind never,
    Though it has been climbed, foot-swift, foot-sore,
      By thousands more.

Primaeval rocks form the road's steep border,
    And much have they faced there, first and last,
Of the transitory in Earth's long order;
    But what they record in colour and cast
      Is – that we two passed.

And to me, though Time's unflinching rigour,
    In mindless rote, has ruled from sight
The substance now, one phantom figure
    Remains on the slope, as when that night
      Saw us alight.

I look and see it there, shrinking, shrinking,
    I look back at it amid the rain
For the very last time; for my sand is sinking,
    And I shall traverse old love's domain
      Never again.
March 1913

In this deceptively simple, yet profoundly moving and profoundly organised poem, Hardy links the landscape with time. It is Time which, in a double function, has both illuminated on this second visit that 'time of such quality', and also has destroyed the original sharer in it. In the same way the rain by its glistening on the slope shows up the scene 'distinctly yet'; but by the end it shares in Time's function of obliteration. The darkness and the distance have similar properties; there is one supreme moment when the picture seems lit with the finest clarity before it fades for ever. (Hardy's cast of mind, seeing connections and complexities in every sphere of life and language, may not have ruled out a double meaning in 'Saw us alight' – 'when you were all aglow.') This is one of his finest poems.

If individual human beings are of first importance, the landscape or setting, although it may condition them, is yet necessarily in second place. More, it suggests humanity's ultimate greatness – in that for Hardy, one of the most enduring of his 'impressions' is that the landscape only exists as each individual sees it.

[1865] *Aug. 23.* The poetry of a scene varies with the minds of the perceivers. Indeed, it does not lie in the scene at all.

The Life of Thomas Hardy

We colour according to our moods the objects we survey.

A Pair of Blue Eyes

Jude suffers when Sue has married Phillotson:

The oppressive strength of his affection for Sue showed itself on the morrow and following days yet more clearly. He could no longer endure the light of the Melchester lamps; the sunshine was as drab paint; and the blue sky as zinc.

Jude the Obscure

Tess walks across country to seek help from her parents-in-law:

In time she reached the edge of the vast escarpment below which stretched the loamy Vale of Blackmoor, now lying misty and still in the dawn. Instead of the colourless air of the uplands the atmosphere down there was a deep blue. Instead of the great enclosures of a hundred acres in which she was now accustomed to toil there were little fields below her of less than half-a-dozen acres, so numerous that they looked from this height like the meshes of a net. Here the landscape was whitey-brown; down there, as in Froom Valley, it was always green. Yet it was in that vale that her sorrow had taken shape, and she did not love it as formerly. Beauty to her, as to all who have felt, lay not in the thing, but in what the thing symbolized.

Tess of the d'Urbervilles

Having agreed to marry (on that night of probing wind[268]) Lady Constantine and Swithin discuss practical details:

While these tactics were under discussion the two-and-thirty winds of heaven continued, as before, to beat about the tower, though their onsets appeared to be somewhat lessening in force. Himself now calmed and satisfied, Swithin, as is the wont of humanity, took serener views of Nature's crushing mechanics without, and said, 'The wind doesn't seem disposed to put the tragic period to our hopes and fears that I spoke of in my momentary despair.'

'The disposition of the wind is as vicious as ever,' she answered, looking into his face with pausing thoughts on, perhaps, other subjects than that discussed. 'It is your mood of viewing it that has changed. "There is nothing either good or bad, but thinking makes it so." '

Two on a Tower

Tess, when she is pregnant, goes out only by night:

On these lonely hills and dales her quiescent glide was of a piece with the element she moved in. Her flexuous and stealthy figure became an integral part of the scene. At times her whimsical fancy would intensify natural processes around her till they seemed a part of her own story. Rather they became a part of it; for the world is only a psychological phenomenon, and what they seemed they were. The midnight airs and gusts, moaning amongst the tightly-wrapped buds and bark of the winter twigs, were formulae of bitter reproach. A wet day was the expression of irremediable grief at her weakness in the mind of some vague ethical being whom she could not class definitely as the God of her childhood, and could not comprehend as any other.

Tess of the d'Urbervilles

Hardy himself was not greatly interested in a landscape that had no deeper meaning:

[1887] *January.* After looking at the landscape ascribed to Bonington in our drawing-room I feel that Nature is played out as a Beauty, but not as a Mystery. I don't want to see landscapes, *i.e.,* scenic paintings of them, because I don't want to see the original realities — as optical effects, that is. I want to see the deeper reality underlying the scenic, the expression of what are sometimes called abstract imaginings.

The "simply natural" is interesting no longer. The much-decried, mad, late-Turner rendering is now necessary to create my interest.

The Life of Thomas Hardy

[1889] *January 9.* At the Old Masters, Royal Academy. Turner's water-colours each is a landscape *plus* a man's soul. . . .

The Life of Thomas Hardy

[1924] [*Various passages recalled by the Byron centenary.*]
"Nature, in her most dazzling aspects or stupendous parts, is but the background & theatre of the tragedy of man."
(Morley, *Critical Miscellanies.*) "*Byron*"

Memoranda II

Many of Hardy's characters hardly notice their landscape: the landscape of the mind (and soul) is so much more absorbing.

For many it is simply a blank screen on which to focus their own thoughts. Yeobright's eyes, a few pages ago, were 'fixed steadfastly on blankness' as he went out to find Eustacia; Fitzpiers talked of projecting the idea of love on to a particular woman like a rainbow on a tree.[269]

[Christopher Julian] was a man who often, when walking abroad, and looking as it were at the scene before his eyes, discerned successes and failures, friends and relations, episodes of childhood, wedding feasts and funerals, the landscape suffering greatly by these visions, until it became no more than the patterned wall-tints about the paintings in a gallery; something necessary to the tone, yet not regarded.

The Hand of Ethelberta

When Knight learned of Elfride's death, he

. . . stood staring blindly at where the hearse had been; as if he saw it, or some one, there.

A Pair of Blue Eyes

After a Romantic Day

The railway bore him through
An earthen cutting out from a city:
There was no scope for view,
Though the frail light shed by a slim young moon
Fell like a friendly tune.

Fell like a liquid ditty,
And the blank lack of any charm
Of landscape did no harm.
The bald steep cutting, rigid, rough,
And moon-lit, was enough
For poetry of place: its weathered face
Formed a convenient sheet whereon
The visions of his mind were drawn.

Mrs Crickett, making Manston's bed, is transfixed by something she finds:

She looked closely – more closely – very closely. 'Well, to be sure!' was all she could say. The clerk's wife stood as if the air had suddenly set to amber, and held her fixed like a fly in it.

The object of her wonder was a trailing brown hair, very little less than a yard long, which proved it clearly to be a hair from some woman's head. She drew it off the pillow, and took it to the window; there holding it out she looked fixedly at it, and became utterly lost in meditation: her gaze, which had at first actively settled on the hair, involuntarily dropped past its object by degrees and was lost on the floor, as the inner vision obscured the outer one.

Desperate Remedies

The Reverend Mr Raunham is exercised by Cytherea's legal marriage problems:

The rector of Carriford trotted homewards under the cold and clear March sky, its countless stars fluttering like bright birds. He was unconscious of the scene.

Desperate Remedies

The speaker in the long poem "In Front of the Landscape" tells how he walked with 'the customed landscape . . . / Blotted to feeble mist' by the visions of his inner sight — 'the intenser / Stare of the mind' — as not only past scenes and people, but other landscapes filled his thoughts and sight as if they were present. It is only now that they are dead that he truly sees them — therefore that constant Hardy lament, Too Late!

The Rambler

I do not see the hills around,
Nor mark the tints the copses wear;
I do not note the grassy ground
And constellated daisies there.

I hear not the contralto note
Of cuckoos hid on either hand,
The whirr that shakes the nighthawk's throat
When eve's brown awning hoods the land.

Some say each songster, tree, and mead —
All eloquent of love divine —
Receives their constant careful heed:
Such keen appraisement is not mine.

The tones around me that I hear,
The aspects, meanings, shapes I see,
Are those removed ones missed when near,
And now perceived too late by me!

Amongst those 'removed ones' must not be forgotten the purple light of love and its spiritual connotations for Hardy after Emma's death.

So the landscape, in this last manifestation, is something essential to woman and man – the air they breathe – 'something necessary to the tone, but not regarded'.

The paradoxes seen by Hardy in the landscape faithfully mirror the paradoxes and contradictions of life. To both he knows that there is no final answer.

> Thus things around. No answerer I. . . .
> Meanwhile the winds, and rains,
> And Earth's old glooms and pains
> Are still the same, and Life and Death are neighbours nigh.

From *Nature's Questioning*

In later years Hardy began to wonder whether there might be a condition after death in which some of the answers might be known. The following poem lives up to its name in directly contradicting "Sacred to the Memory"'s theme that Mary was 'deep lined' upon the landscape – in favour of something better:

Paradox

(MH)

> Though out of sight now, and as 'twere not the least to us;
> Comes she in sorrows, as one bringing peace to us?
> Lost to each meadow, each hill-top, each tree around,
> Yet the whole truth may her largened sight see around?
>> Always away from us
>> She may not stray from us!
> Can she, then, know how men's fatings befall?
> Yea indeed, may know well; even know thereof all.

Two final passages clearly state the paradox of humanity and the universe – the priceless worth of the individual woman or man, who can alter the aspect of the landscape and leave in the world an indelible mark; and yet the inexorable way in which, in a physical universe, Nature constantly interrupts our human activities and, with its steady drip, finally obliterates humanity's personal pattern with its own.

Angel Clare found at Talbothays that:

A personality within it was so far-reaching in her influence as to spread into and make the bricks, mortar, and whole overhanging sky throb with a burning sensibility. Whose was this mighty personality? A milkmaid's. . . .

Many besides Angel have learnt that the magnitude of lives is not as to their external displacements, but as to their subjective experiences. . . .

Tess was no insignificant creature to toy with and dismiss; but a woman living her precious life – a life which, to herself who endured or enjoyed it, possessed as great a dimension as the life of the mightiest to himself. Upon her sensations the whole world depended to Tess; through her existence all her fellow-creatures existed, to her. The universe itself only came into being for Tess on the particular day in the particular year in which she was born.

Tess of the d'Urbervilles

They sing their dearest songs –
He, she, all of them – yea,
Treble and tenor and bass,
      And one to play;
With the candle mooning each face. . . .
      Ah, no; the years O!
How the sick leaves reel down in throngs!

They clear the creeping moss –
Elders and juniors – aye,
Making the pathways neat
      And the garden gay;
And they build a shady seat. . . .
      Ah, no; the years, the years;
See, the white storm-birds wing across!

They are blithely breakfasting all –
Men and maidens – yea,
Under the summer tree,
      With a glimpse of the bay,
While pet fowl come to the knee. . . .
      Ah, no; the years O!
And the rotten rose is ript from the wall.

They change to a high new house,
He, she, all of them – aye,
Clocks and carpets and chairs
      On the lawn all day,
And brightest things that are theirs. . . .
      Ah, no: the years, the years;
Down their carved names the rain-drop ploughs.

IV

HARDY'S

'IMPRESSIONS' ABOUT NATURE

[*December 31, 1901*]. After reading various philosophic systems, and being struck with their contradictions and futilities, I have come to this: *Let every man make a philosophy for himself out of his own experience.* He will not be able to avoid using terms and phraseology from earlier philosophers, but let him avoid adopting their theories if he values his own mental life. Let him remember the fate of Coleridge, and save years of labour by working out his own views as given him by his surroundings.

The Life of Thomas Hardy

– here again the environment is his teacher.

[1917] *January 6*. I find I wrote in 1888 that "Art is concerned with seemings only", which is true.

The Life of Thomas Hardy

Commenting on an article on his writings which had appeared in the Fortnightly Review *of April 1917:*

Like so many critics, Mr Courtney treats my works of art as if they were a scientific system of philosophy, although I have repeatedly stated in prefaces and elsewhere that the views in them are *seemings*, provisional impressions only, used for artistic purposes because they represent approximately the impressions of the age, and are plausible, till somebody produces better theories of the universe.

The Life of Thomas Hardy

December 19th, 1920. . . . It seems strange that I should have to remind [Mr Alfred Noyes] . . . of the vast difference between the expression of fancy and the expression of belief. . . . My sober opinion – so far as I have any definite one – of the Cause of Things, has been defined in scores of places, and is that of a great number of ordinary thinkers: that the said Cause is neither moral nor immoral, but *unmoral*: "loveless and hateless" I have called it, "which neither good nor evil knows" – etc., etc., – (you will find plenty of these definitions in *The Dynasts* as well as in short poems). . . .In my fancies, or poems of the imagination, I have of course called this Power all sorts of names – never supposing they would be taken for more than fancies. I have even in prefaces warned readers to take them as such – as mere impressions of the moment, exclamations in fact.

Letter to Mr Alfred Noyes

Although Hardy always disclaimed having a coherent philosophy, his 'impressions', especially when conveyed in letters, notes, or articles rather than in his poetry, seem constant enough to form a fairly clear pattern of his 'theories of the universe'. From young manhood he seems to have felt

265

strongly that human life was at the mercy, not usually of wilful enmity in the Power, but of sheer, unpredictable, pointless chance.

Postscript to a letter to Florence Henniker, 18 July 1893:

P.S. What I meant about your unfaithfulness to the Shelley cult referred not to any lack of poetic emotion, but to your view of things: e.g., you are quite out of harmony with this line of his in *Epipsychidion*: "The sightless tyrants of our fate." which beautifully expresses one's consciousness of blind circumstance beating upon one, without any feeling, for or against.

T.H.

Hap

If but some vengeful god would call to me
From up the sky, and laugh: 'Thou suffering thing,
Know that thy sorrow is my ecstasy,
That thy love's loss is my hate's profiting!'

Then would I bear it, clench myself, and die,
Steeled by the sense of ire unmerited;
Half-eased in that a Powerfuller than I
Had willed and meted me the tears I shed.

But not so. How arrives it joy lies slain,
And why unblooms the best hope ever sown?
— Crass Casualty obstructs the sun and rain,
And dicing Time for gladness casts a moan. . .
These purblind Doomsters had as readily strown
Blisses about my pilgrimage as pain.
1866
16 Westbourne Park Villas

The images of nature here seem to show it as the happy background of life against which the Power's henchmen of Chance and Time so successfully militate. A lengthy study of this Power or First Cause(s) as glimpsed by Hardy is not within the scope of this book; but seen as one of its chief vassals is Nature herself — already met (page 180) as 'the Mother, naturing Nature . . . All racked and wrung by her unfaithful lord.'

Doom and She

I

There dwells a mighty pair —
Slow, statuesque, intense —
Amid the vague Immense:
None can their chronicle declare,
Nor why they be, nor whence.

II

Mother of all things made,
Matchless in artistry,
Unlit with sight is she, —
And though her ever well-obeyed
Vacant of feeling he.

III

The Matron mildly asks —
A throb in every word —
'Our clay-made creatures, lord,
How fare they in their mortal tasks
Upon Earth's bounded bord?

IV

'The fate of those I bear,
Dear lord, pray turn and view,
And notify me true;
Shapings that eyelessly I dare
Maybe I would undo.

V

'Sometimes from lairs of life
Methinks I catch a groan,
Or multitudinous moan,
As though I had schemed a world of strife,
Working by touch alone.'

VI

'World-weaver!' he replies,
'I scan all thy domain;
But since nor joy nor pain
It lies in me to recognize,
Thy questionings are vain.

VII

'World-weaver! what *is* Grief?
And what are Right, and Wrong,
And Feeling, that belong
To creatures all who owe thee fief?
Why is Weak worse than Strong?'. . .

VIII

– Unanswered, curious, meek,
She broods in sad surmise. . . .
– Some say they have heard her sighs
On Alpine height or Polar peak
When the night tempests rise.

But She is not entirely blame-free. In "The Bullfinches", the birds tell how 'queenly Nature' never lifts a finger to protect her creatures: and

Busy in her handsome house
Known as Space, she falls a-drowse;
Yet, in seeming, works on dreaming,
While beneath her groping hands
Fiends make havoc in her bands.

They speak of her moods; and in A Pair of Blue Eyes *(1873) she is seen as capricious and heartless:*

To those musing weather-beaten West-country folk who pass the greater part of their days and nights out of doors, Nature seems to have moods in other than a poetical sense; predilections for certain deeds at certain times, without any apparent law to govern or season to account for them. She is read as a person with a curious temper; as one who does not scatter kindnesses and cruelties alternately, impartially, and in order, but heartless severities or overwhelming generosities in lawless caprice. Man's case is always that of the prodigal's favourite or the miser's pensioner. In her unfriendly moments there seems a feline fun in her tricks, begotten by a foretaste of her pleasure in swallowing the victim.

Such a way of thinking had been absurd to Knight, but he began to adopt it now.

A Pair of Blue Eyes

She appears to have some responsibility for the creation both of the universe and of human beings. In "The Mother Mourns" she laments their dawning criticism of her, as their insight and capabilities develop — beyond what she had intended.

> Man's mountings of mindsight I checked not,
>   Till range of his vision
> Now tops my intent, and finds blemish
>   Throughout my domain.

She ends:

> Let me grow, then, but mildews and mandrakes,
>   And slimy distortions,
> Let nevermore things good and lovely
>   To me appertain;
>
> 'For Reason is rank in my temples,
>   And Vision unruly,
> And chivalrous laud of my cunning
>   Is heard not again!'

The mildews and mandrakes, distortions and horrid growths, cramps, blights, and decay, are a recurrent Hardy image in thinking of Nature — an image of the blemished domain in which we are set. In "The Lacking Sense" his speaker questions Time about the Mother:

III

> — 'And how explains thy Ancient Mind her crimes upon her creatures,
>   These fallings from her fair beginnings, wounding where she loves,
> Into her would-be perfect motions, modes, effects, and features
>   Admitting cramps, black humours, wan decay, and baleful blights,
>   Distress into delights?'

Hardy grouped several such poems about Nature in his second volume, Poems of the Past and Present, *published in 1901.*

The Sleep-Worker

When wilt thou wake, O Mother, wake and see —
As one who, held in trance, has laboured long
By vacant rote and prepossession strong —
The coils that thou hast wrought unwittingly;

Wherein have place, unrealized by thee,
Fair growths, foul cankers, right enmeshed with wrong,
Strange orchestras of victim-shriek and song,
And curious blends of ache and ecstasy! —

Should that morn come, and show thy opened eyes
All that Life's palpitating tissues feel,
How wilt thou bear thyself in thy surprise? —

Wilt thou destroy, in one wild shock of shame,
The whole high heaving firmamental frame,
Or patiently adjust, amend, and heal?

The mandrake, with all its complex legendary associations with fertility and aphrodisiacs, death and sleep and screams when uprooted, must have fascinated Hardy.[270] Cytherea, by the ruins of an old mill in a flat, humid meadow where the gnats wailed,[271] is disturbed by Manston's apparent love for her and the decisions she may have to make:

Should she withdraw her hand? She would think whether she would. Thinking, and hesitating, she looked as far as the autumnal haze on the marshy ground would allow her to see distinctly. There was the fragment of a hedge — all that remained of a 'wet old garden' — standing in the middle of the mead, without a definite beginning or ending, purposeless and valueless. It was overgrown, and choked with mandrakes, and she could almost fancy she heard their shrieks. . . . Should she withdraw her hand?. . . . She felt as one in a boat without oars, drifting with closed eyes down a river — she knew not whither.

Desperate Remedies

Henchard's garden — once, maybe, like Eden — images his outmoded clinging to the old ways — and perhaps suggests that Farfrae is a Trojan horse he is taking into his fortress:

The garden was silent, dewy, and full of perfume. It extended a long way back from the house, first as lawn and flower-beds, then as fruit-garden, where the long-tied espaliers, as old as the old house itself, had grown so stout, and cramped, and gnarled that they had pulled their stakes out of the ground and stood distorted and writhing in vegetable agony, like leafy Laocoöns.[272]

The Mayor of Casterbridge

Margery, the romantic milkmaid, changes into her ball-gown inside a decayed elm in the wood – 'huge, hollow, distorted, and headless, with a rift in its side' – on the occasion of the ball which is such a fruitless contrast with her normal life. Similarly for Lady Constantine:

A fog defaced all the trees of the park that morning; the white atmosphere adhered to the ground like a fungoid growth from it, and made the turfed undulations look slimy and raw. But Lady Constantine settled down in her chair to await the coming of the late curate's son with a serenity which the vast blanks outside could neither baffle nor destroy.

Two on a Tower

After the Austrian defeat at Ulm, Napoleon talks of chance – and fungi:

> War, general, ever has its ups and downs,
> And you must take the better and the worse
> As impish chance or destiny ordains.
> Come near and warm you here. A glowing fire
> Is life on these depressing, mired, moist days
> Of smitten leaves down-drooping clammily,
> And toadstools like the putrid lungs of men.

The Dynasts

Rot, decay and distortions everywhere underlie the futility of life in the fallen world, where Chance or Time destroy all. At Stancy Castle the new owner was removing the rotten gates bearing the old family's initials – and 'alongside were the hollow and fungous boles of trees sawn down in long past years.' The same phrase is used of one of Hardy's preoccupations – the old families that had gone 'down, down, down' – 'some family, hollow and fungous with antiquity . . .'[273]

On the night which evoked 'all that is terrible and dark in history . . .':

Skirting the pool [Eustacia] followed the path towards Rainbarrow, occasionally stumbling over twisted furze-roots, tufts of rushes, or oozing lumps of fleshy fungi, which at this season lay scattered about the heath like the rotten liver and lungs of some colossal animal. The moon and stars were closed up by cloud and rain to the degree of extinction.

The Return of the Native

After Troy's final betrayal Bathsheba flees into the night and sleeps among the ferns and 'red and yellow leaves', which disperse in the breeze 'like ghosts from an enchanter fleeing':

From her feet, and between the beautiful yellowing ferns with their feathery arms, the ground sloped downwards to a hollow, in which was a species of swamp, dotted with fungi. A morning mist hung over it now – a fulsome yet magnificent silvery veil, full of light from the sun, yet semi-opaque – the hedge behind it being in some measure

271

hidden by its hazy luminousness. Up the sides of this depression grew sheaves of the common rush, and here and there a peculiar species of flag, the blades of which glistened in the emerging sun, like scythes. But the general aspect of the swamp was malignant. From its moist and poisonous coat seemed to be exhaled the essences of evil things in the earth, and in the waters under the earth. The fungi grew in all manner of positions from rotting leaves and tree stumps, some exhibiting to her listless gaze their clammy tops, others their oozing gills. Some were marked with great splotches, red as arterial blood, others were saffron yellow, and others tall and attenuated, with stems like macaroni. Some were leathery and of richest browns. The hollow seemed a nursery of pestilences small and great, in the immediate neighbourhood of comfort and health, and Bathsheba arose with a tremor at the thought of having passed the night on the brink of so dismal a place.

Far from the Madding Crowd

When Grace realises her marriage may be in ruins through Fitzpiers' infatuation with Mrs Charmond, she and her father go to look for him:

They halted beneath a half-dead oak, hollow and disfigured with white tumours, its roots spreading out like claws grasping the ground. A chilly wind circled round them, upon whose currents the seeds of a neighbouring lime-tree, supported parachute-wise by the wing attached, flew out of the boughs downwards like fledglings from their nest. The vale was wrapped in a dim atmosphere of unnaturalness,and the east was like a livid curtain edged with pink.

The Woodlanders

And as Grace waits in the wood for Winterborne – though he is dying:

She continually peeped out through the lattice, but could see little. In front lay the brown leaves of last year, and upon them some yellowish green ones of this season that had been prematurely blown down by the gale. Above stretched an old beech, with vast arm-pits, and great pocket-holes in its sides where branches had been removed in past times; a black slug was trying to climb it. Dead boughs were scattered about like ichthyosauri in a museum, and beyond them were perishing woodbine stems resembling old ropes.

From the other window all she could see were more trees, in jackets of lichen and stockings of moss. At their roots were stemless yellow fungi like lemons and apricots, and tall fungi with more stem than stool. Next were more trees close together, wrestling for existence, their branches disfigured with wounds resulting from their mutual rubbings and blows. It was the struggle between these neighbours that she had heard in the night. Beneath them were the rotting stumps of those of the group that had been vanquished long ago, rising from their mossy setting like black teeth from green gums.

The Woodlanders

The Woodlanders makes particularly clear how decay and distortion in Nature image the woeful frustration (and defiance) of humanity in 'a world conditioned thus'.

Fitzpiers, newly enamoured of Mrs Charmond, visits her at Hintock House:

He went on foot across the wilder recesses of the park, where slimy streams of fresh moisture, exuding from decayed holes caused by old amputations, ran down the bark of the oaks and elms, the rind below being coated with a lichenous wash as green as emerald. They were stout-trunked trees, that never rocked their stems in the fiercest gale, responding to it only by crooking their limbs. Wrinkled like an old crone's face, and antlered with dead branches that rose above the foliage of their summits, they were nevertheless still green – though yellow had invaded the leaves of other trees.

– He finds closed curtains even in broad daylight; and she explains:

'O', she murmured, 'it is because the world is so dreary outside! Sorrow and bitterness in the sky, and floods of agonized tears beating against the panes. . . .O! Why were we given hungry hearts and wild desires if we have to live in a world like this? Why should Death alone lend what Life is compelled to borrow – rest?'

The Woodlanders

Early in the novel Hardy describes 'the Unfulfilled Intention':

They went noiselessly over mats of starry moss, rustled through interspersed tracts of leaves, skirted trunks with spreading roots whose mossed rinds made them like hands wearing green gloves; elbowed old elms and ashes with great forks, in which stood pools of water that overflowed on rainy days and ran down their stems in green cascades. On older trees still than these huge lobes of fungi grew like lungs. Here, as everywhere, the Unfulfilled Intention, which makes life what it is, was as obvious as it could be among the depraved crowds of a city slum. The leaf was deformed, the curve was crippled, the taper was interrupted; the lichen ate the vigour of the stalk, and the ivy slowly strangled to death the promising sapling.

– Melbury and Grace arrive at the timber-auction, where they see:

. . . mostly woodland men, who on that account could afford to be curious in their walking-sticks, which consequently exhibited various monstrosities of vegetation, the chief being corkscrew shapes in black and white thorn, brought to that pattern by the slow torture of an encircling woodbine during their growth, as the Chinese have been said to mould human beings into grotesque toys by continued compression in infancy . . .

The Woodlanders

Even the glorious autumn is marred, and human life shares its canker:

And so the infatuated surgeon went along through the gorgeous autumn landscape of White-Hart Vale, surrounded by orchards lustrous with the reds of apple-crops, berries, and foliage, the whole intensified by the gilding of the declining sun. The earth this year had been prodigally bountiful, and now was the supreme moment of her bounty. In the poorest spots the hedges were bowed with haws and blackberries; acorns cracked underfoot, and the burst husks of chestnuts lay exposing their auburn contents as if arranged by anxious sellers in a fruit-market. In all this proud show some kernels were unsound as her own situation, and [Grace] wondered if there were one world in the universe where the fruit had no worm, and marriage no sorrow.

The Woodlanders

The world is awry. Nature is spoiled and imperfect. All promising life is strangled; 'why unblooms the best hope ever sown?'

March 21, 1897 . . . the unalterable laws of nature are based upon a wrong . . .

Letter to Lady Grove

February 27, 1902 . . . Well: what we gain by science is, after all, sadness, as the Preacher saith.[274] The more we know of the laws & nature of the Universe the more ghastly a business we perceive it all to be − & the non-necessity of it. As some philosopher says, if nothing at all existed, it would be a completely natural thing; but that the world exists is a fact absolutely logicless & senseless . . .

Letter to Edward Clodd

So the two forces were at work here as everywhere, the inherent will to enjoy, and the circumstantial will against enjoyment.[275]

Tess of the d'Urbervilles

Some people would like to know whence the poet whose philosophy is in these days deemed as profound and trustworthy as his song is breezy and pure, gets his authority for speaking of 'Nature's holy plan'.[276]

Tess of the d'Urbervilles

The Last Chrysanthemum

Why should this flower delay so long,
To show its tremulous plumes?
Now is the time of plaintive robin-song,
When flowers are in their tombs.

Through the slow summer, when the sun
Called to each frond and whorl
That all he could for flowers was being done,
Why did it not uncurl?

It must have felt that fervid call
Although it took no heed,

Waking but now, when leaves like corpses fall,
        And saps all retrocede.

Too late its beauty, lonely thing,
        The season's shine is spent,
Nothing remains for it but shivering
        In tempests turbulent.

Had it a reason for delay,
        Dreaming in witlessness
That for a bloom so delicately gay
        Winter would stay its stress?

    – I talk as if the thing were born
        With sense to work its mind;
Yet it is but one mask of many worn
        By the Great Face behind.

This is the nub of Hardy's stricture:

Yell'ham-Wood's Story

Coomb-Firtrees say that Life is a moan,
        And Clyffe-hill Clump says 'Yea!'
But Yell'ham says a thing of its own:
        It's not 'Gray, gray
        Is Life alway!'
        That Yell'ham says,
Nor that Life is for ends unknown.

It says that Life would signify
        A thwarted purposing:
That we come to live, and are called to die.
        Yes, that's the thing
        In fall, in spring,
        That Yell'ham says: –
'Life offers – to deny!'
1902

On the evening when, in the church, Manston persuaded Cytherea to accept him:

Everything in the place was the embodiment of decay: the fading red glare from the setting
sun, which came in at the west window, emphasising the end of the day and all its cheerful

275

doings, the mildewed walls, the uneven paving-stones, the wormy pews, the sense of recent occupation, and the dank air of death which had gathered with the evening, would have made grave a lighter mood than Cytherea's was then.

'What sensations does the place impress you with?' she said at last, very sadly.

'I feel imperatively called upon to be honest, from very despair of achieving anything by stratagem in a world where the materials are such as these.' He, too, spoke in a depressed voice, purposely or otherwise.

'I feel as if I were almost ashamed to be seen walking such a world,' she murmured.

Desperate Remedies

Her Dilemma
(In – Church)

The two were silent in a sunless church,
Whose mildewed walls, uneven paving-stones,
And wasted carvings passed antique research;
And nothing broke the clock's dull monotones.

Leaning against a wormy poppy-head,
So wan and worn that he could hardly stand,
– For he was soon to die, – he softly said,
'Tell me you love me!' – holding long her hand.

She would have given a world to breathe 'yes' truly,
So much his life seemed hanging on her mind,
And hence she lied, her heart persuaded throughly
'Twas worth her soul to be a moment kind.

But the sad need thereof, his nearing death,
So mocked humanity that she shamed to prize
A world conditioned thus, or care for breath
Where Nature such dilemmas could devise.
1866

Angel Clare talks to Tess about 'this hobble of being alive'.[277] *Hardy tells more:*

[1883] *November 17.* Poem. We [human beings[278]] have reached a degree of intelligence which Nature never contemplated when framing her laws, and for which she consequently has provided no adequate satisfactions.' [This which he had adumbrated before, was clearly the germ of the poem entitled "The Mother Mourns" and others.]

The Life of Thomas Hardy

[1889] *April* 7. A woeful fact – that the human race is too extremely developed for its corporeal conditions, the nerves being evolved to an activity abnormal in such an environment. Even the higher animals are in excess in this respect. It may be questioned if Nature, or what we call Nature, so far back as when she crossed the line from vertebrates to invertebrates, did not exceed her mission. This planet does not supply the materials for happiness to higher existences. Other planets may, though one can hardly see how.

The Life of Thomas Hardy

Before Life and After

A time there was – as one may guess
And as, indeed, earth's testimonies tell –
Before the birth of consciousness,
    When all went well.

None suffered sickness, love, or loss,
None knew regret, starved hope, or heart-burnings,
None cared whatever crash or cross
    Brought wrack to things.

If something ceased, no tongue bewailed,
If something winced and waned, no heart was wrung;
If brightness dimmed, and dark prevailed,
    No sense was stung.

But the disease of feeling germed,
And primal rightness took the tint of wrong;
Ere nescience shall be reaffirmed
    How long, how long?

(This poem may not release its full treasure at one reading, with its gentle, dignified, suffering, conscious human speaker in tension against the unfeeling universe, its careful word-choice and pregnant alternations between negatives and affirmatives. 'When the cry of protest . . . is passionate enough to shape substance and style from the philosophy, a major poem is born'.[279])

Hardy had already published Nature's view of humanity's over-development in "The Mother Mourns" – how she found 'Reason is rank in my temples, / And Vision unruly'. This 'rankness' must be noted as another element somewhat similar to the fungoid and distorted unpleasantnesses of Nature's world.

Cytherea disliked Miss Aldclyffe's love for her:

This vehement imperious affection was in one way soothing, but yet it was not of the kind that Cytherea's instincts desired. Though it was generous, it seemed too rank, [sensuous,] and capricious for endurance.

Desperate Remedies

(The word 'sensuous' in the first edition was permanently dropped in and after the 1896 one.)

As the action progressed,

Miss Aldclyffe's tenderness towards Cytherea, between the hours of her irascibility, increased till it became no less than doting fondness. Like Nature in the tropics, with her hurricanes and the subsequent luxuriant vegetation effecting their ravages, Miss Aldclyffe compensated for her outbursts by excess of generosity afterwards.

Desperate Remedies

Tess, too, on her wedding-day, felt that:

Her idolatry of this man was such that she herself almost feared it to be ill-omened. She was conscious of the notion expressed by Friar Laurence:[280] 'These violent delights have violent ends.' It might be too desperate for human conditions – too rank, too wild, too deadly.

Tess of the d'Urbervilles

Hardy had already painted Tess in the rank garden of 'blooming weeds emitting offensive smells', where she had been stained with 'slug-slime, and. . .sticky blights' at the time of her exaltation in music, love and her senses (page 104). (The weeds had been carefully noted too in the scene engraved for years on Knight's retina – page 239). There was a long interlopation earlier in A Pair of Blue Eyes *about 'the horrid Jacob's ladders. . . .weeds, and not flowers at all' (page 138). The mist over Bathsheba's 'nursery of pestilences' was 'fulsome'. Nature's excesses – her exuberant growths and fruitings which become 'mangy, frosted, and sere', which 'rot. . . .shrunk and brown' until they are 'corpses' are all part of the fault in the universe, and the abundance that lures men and women to desolation. 'Life offers – to deny!'[281]*

In 1902 Hardy wrote the following letter about a review of Maeterlinck's Apology for Nature. *It was published in* The Academy and Literature *on May 17, and Hardy thought it worth including in the* Life.

Sir,

In your review of M. Maeterlinck's book you quote with seeming approval his vindication of Nature's ways, which is, (as I understand it) to the effect that, though she does not appear to be just from our point of view, she may practise a scheme of morality unknown to us, in which she is just. Now, admit but the bare possibility of such a hidden morality, and she would go out of court without the slightest stain on her character, so certain should we feel that indifference to morality was beneath her greatness.

Far be it from my wish to distrust any comforting fantasy, if it can be barely tenable. But alas, no profound reflection can be needed to detect the sophistry in M. Maeterlinck's argument, and to see that the original difficulty recognized by thinkers like Schopenhauer, Hartmann, Haeckel, etc., and by most of the persons called pessimists, remains unsurmounted.

Pain has been, and pain is: no new sort of morals in Nature can remove pain from the past and make it pleasure for those who are its infallible estimators, the bearers thereof. And no injustice, however slight, can be atoned for by her future generosity, however ample, so long as we consider Nature to be, or to stand for, unlimited power. The exoneration of an omnipotent Mother by her retrospective justice becomes an absurdity when we ask, what made the foregone injustice necessary to her Omnipotence?

So you cannot, I fear, save her good name except by assuming one of two things: that she is blind and not a judge of her actions, or that she is an automaton, and unable to control them: in either of which assumptions, though you have the chivalrous satisfaction of screening one of her sex, you only throw responsibility a stage further back.

But the story is not new. It is true, nevertheless, that, as M. Maeterlinck contends, to dwell too long amid such reflections does no good, and that to model our conduct on Nature's apparent conduct, as Nietzsche would have taught, can only bring disaster to humanity.

Yours truly,
Thomas Hardy.

Max Gate, Dorchester.

Hardy continued to criticise Nature on several counts. First, her indifference:

18 May 1910 . . . my own conclusion − the difficulty of carrying out to its logical extreme the principle of equal justice to all the animal kingdom. Whatever humanity may try to do, there remains the stumbling-block that nature herself is absolutely indifferent to justice, & how to instruct nature is rather a large problem.

Letter to Mr Sidney Trist, Editor of The Animals' Guardian

Tess and her younger brother Abraham travel to market in the small hours:

He leant back against the hives, and with upturned face made observations on the stars, whose cold pulses were beating amid the black hollows above, in serene dissociation from those two wisps of human life. He asked how far away those twinklers were, and whether God was on the other side of them. . .

Tess of the d'Urbervilles

Swithin to Lady Constantine:

'Whatever the stars were made for, they were not made to please our eyes. It is just the same in everything; nothing is made for man.'[282]

Two on a Tower

279

[1902] *June 2.* Nature's indifference to the advance of her species along what we are accustomed to call civilized lines makes the late war of no importance to her, except as a sort of geological fault in her continuity.

The Life of Thomas Hardy

At A Bridal
Nature's Indifference

When you paced forth, to await maternity,
A dream of other offspring held my mind,
Compounded of us twain as Love designed;
Rare forms, that corporate now will never be!

Should I, too, wed as slave to Mode's decree,
And each thus found apart, of false desire,
A stolid line, whom no high aims will fire
As had fired ours could ever have mingled we;

And, grieved that lives so matched should miscompose,
Each mourn the double waste; and question dare
To the Great Dame whence incarnation flows,
Why those high-purposed children never were:
What will she answer? That she does not care
If the race all such sovereign types unknows.
1866

Nature can also be actively hostile to woman and man. In the damp hollow of Hintock Park, 'the situation of the house, prejudicial to humanity, was a stimulus to vegetation'.[283] Knight, hanging on the cliff-face:

. . . could think of no future, nor of anything connected with his past. He could only look sternly at Nature's treacherous attempt to put an end to him, and strive to thwart her.

A Pair of Blue Eyes

As Geraldine Allenville lies dying:

Everything was so still that her weak act of trying to live seemed a silent wrestling with all the powers of the universe.

An Indiscretion in the Life of an Heiress

The authorial voice:

Men are too often harsh with women they love; women with men. And yet these harshnesses are tenderness itself when compared with the universal harshness out of which they grow; the harshness of the position towards the temperament, of the means towards the aims, of to-day towards yesterday, of hereafter towards to-day.

Tess of the d'Urbervilles

Nature is cruel, both to her own lesser creatures, and to human beings. As morning broke in Little Hintock:

Owls that had been catching mice in the outhouses, rabbits that had been eating the winter-greens in the gardens, and stoats that had been sucking the blood of the rabbits, discerning that their human neighbours were on the move discreetly withdrew from publicity, and were seen and heard no more till nightfall.

The Woodlanders

17 October, 1906. . . . In regard of [blood] Sport, for instance, will ever the great body of human beings. . .ever see its immorality? Worse than that, supposing they do, when will the still more numerous terrestrial animals – our kin, having the same ancestry – learn to be merciful? The fact is that when you get to the bottom of things you find no bed-rock of righteousness to rest on – nature is *unmoral* – & our puny efforts are those of people who try to keep their leaky house dry by wiping the waterdrops from the ceiling.

Letter to Mr Frederic Harrison

In a Wood
See 'The Woodlanders'

Pale beech and pine so blue,
    Set in one clay,
Bough to bough cannot you
    Live out your day?
When the rains skim and skip,
Why mar sweet comradeship,
Blighting with poison-drip
    Neighbourly spray?

Heart-halt and spirit-lame,
    City-opprest,
Unto this wood I came
    As to a nest;
Dreaming that sylvan peace
Offered the harrowed ease –
Nature a soft release
    From men's unrest.

But, having entered in,
    Great growths and small
Show them to men akin –
    Combatants all!
Sycamore shoulders oak,
Bines the slim sapling yoke,
Ivy-spun halters choke
    Elms stout and tall.

Touches from ash, O wych,
    Sting you like scorn!
You, too, brave hollies, twitch
    Sidelong from thorn.
Even the rank poplars bear
Lothly a rival's air,
Cankering in black despair
    If overborne.

Since, then, no grace I find
    Taught me of trees,
Turn I back to my kind,
    Worthy as these.
There at least smiles abound,
There discourse trills around,
There, now and then, are found
    Life-loyalties.
1887: 1896

'Life-loyalties' were found among the milkmaids at Talbothays, united in their love for Angel Clare:

The air of the sleeping-chamber seemed to palpitate with the hopeless passion of the girls. They writhed feverishly under the oppressiveness of an emotion thrust on them by cruel Nature's law – an emotion which they had neither expected nor desired. The incident of the day had fanned the flame that was burning the inside of their hearts out, and the torture was almost more than they could endure. The differences which distinguished them as individuals were abstracted by this passion, and each was but portion of one organism called sex. There was so much frankness and so little jealousy because there was no hope. Each one was a girl of fair common sense, and she did not delude herself with any vain conceits, or deny her love, or give herself airs, in the idea of outshining the others. The full recognition of the futility of their infatuation, from a social point of view; its purposeless beginning; its self-founded outlook; its lack of everything to justify its existence in the eye of civilization (while lacking nothing in the eye of Nature); the one fact that it did exist, ecstasizing them to a killing joy; all this imparted to them a resignation, a dignity, which a practical and sordid expectation of winning him as a husband would have destroyed.

Tess of the d'Urbervilles

Yet here is another of Life's paradoxes: Nature is in some ways an ally of her creature, humanity. Often it is the laws of society which have subverted her, and turned human life into misery.

[1889] *May 5* . . . That which, socially, is a great tragedy, may be in Nature no alarming circumstance.

The Life of Thomas Hardy

The schoolmaster Egbert Mayne reflects on the class barriers that divide him from Squire Allenville's daughter:

That the habits of men should be so subversive of the law of nature as to indicate that he was not worthy to marry a woman whose own instincts said that he was worthy, was a great anomaly, he thought, with some rebelliousness; but this did not upset the fact or remove the difficulty.

An Indiscretion in the Life of an Heiress

Tess had felt shame 'based on nothing more tangible than a sense of condemnation under an arbitrary law of society which had no foundation in Nature' (page 187). She had a 'natural side of her which knew no social law.'[284] Earlier her mother, trying in the face of Tess's unlooked-for pregnancy to make sense of these two opposing forces, had

. . . murmured, wiping her eyes with her apron[:] 'Well, we must make the best of it, I suppose. 'Tis nater, after all, and what do please God!'

Tess of the d'Urbervilles

If she could have been but just created, to discover herself as a spouseless mother, with no experience of life except as the parent of a nameless child, whould the position have caused her to despair? No, she would have taken it calmly, and found pleasures therein. Most of the misery had been generated by her conventional aspect, and not by her innate sensations.

Tess of the d'Urbervilles

But her baby was not to live,

. . . luckily perhaps for himself, considering his beginnings. . . . So passed away Sorrow the Undesired − that intrusive creature, that bastard gift of shameless Nature who respects not the social law; a waif to whom eternal Time had been a matter of days merely, who knew not that such things as years and centuries ever were; to whom the cottage interior

283

was the universe, the week's weather climate, new-born babyhood human existence, and the instinct to suck human knowledge.

Tess of the d'Urbervilles

Hardy recognised the unstoppable power of the 'innate sensations', implanted by Nature, over the 'conventional aspect' decreed by society: this was part of life's pain. And so when at last Tess agreed to marry Angel:

The 'appetite for joy' which pervades all creation, that tremendous force which sways humanity to its purpose, as the tide sways the helpless weed, was not to be controlled by vague lucubrations over the social rubric.

Tess of the d'Urbervilles

To the fraught human being, unconscious Nature could sometimes be restful – as Grace found, gazing from the window of Giles's hut in the woods:

She could see various small members of the animal community that lived unmolested there – creatures of hair, fluff, and scale; the toothed kind and the billed kind; underground creatures jointed and ringed – circumambulating the hut under the impression that, Giles having gone away, nobody was there; and eyeing it inquisitively with a view to winter quarters. Watching these neighbours who knew neither law or sin distracted her a little from her trouble. . .

The Woodlanders

In other ways Nature has healing gifts – the benison of fresh air and sunlight, or of peace in its beauty. After her disaster Tess wondered:

Was once lost always lost really true of chastity? . . . The recuperative power which pervaded organic nature was surely not denied to maidenhood alone.

Tess of the d'Urbervilles

Hardy the architect, in a paper read to the Society for the Protection of Ancient Buildings, reinforced this idea of Nature's creative power:

The true architect, who is first of all an artist and not an antiquary, is naturally most influenced by the aesthetic sense, his desire being, like Nature's, to retain, recover, or recreate the idea which has become damaged. . .Few occupations are more pleasant than that of endeavouring to re-capture an old design from the elusive hand of annihilation.

Memories of Church Restoration

*　　　*　　　*

So Tess's creator, possessing likewise the appetite for joy, continued, despite what he thought his better judgement, to wish that Humankind and Nature ('or what we call Nature') could live in partnership. Much of the imagery already noted shows nature in harmony with woman and man; there are frequent references to 'Nature's teeming family' of which they are a part. Clym's 'familiars were creeping and winged things, and they seemed to enroll him in their band'. Hardy himself often felt one with his fellow-creatures — 'Blank as I am even is he' was the bird in the pine outside his window.[285] And, as seen in "The Abbey Mason" and other examples, for him Nature had another essential function: it is vital for the artist and poet. It is a springboard for the understanding and interpretation of life:

[1877] *June.* If Nature's defects must be looked in the face and transcribed, whence arises the *art* in poetry and novel-writing? which must certainly show art, or it becomes merely mechanical reporting. I think the art lies in making these defects the basis of a hitherto unperceived beauty, by irradiating them with "the light that never was" on their surface, but is seen to be latent in them by the spiritual eye.

The Life of Thomas Hardy

The poet's task is similar to Nature's:

[1886] *January 2* . . . Cold weather brings out upon the faces of people the written marks of their habits, vices, passions, and memories, as warmth brings out on paper a writing in sympathetic ink. The drunkard looks still more a drunkard when the splotches have their margins made distinct by frost, the hectic blush becomes a stain now, the cadaverous complexion reveals the bone under, the quality of handsomeness is reduced to its lowest terms.

January 3. My art is to intensify the expression of things, as is done by Crivelli, Bellini, etc., so that the heart and inner meaning is made vividly visible.

The Life of Thomas Hardy

Christopher Julian was

. . . a born musician, artist, poet, seer, mouthpiece — whichever a translator of Nature's oracles into simple speech may be called.

The Hand of Ethelberta

Ethelberta ironically explains how she herself has joined art and nature:

'I drew the outlines, and designed the tiles round the fire. The flowers, mice and spiders are done very simply, you know: you only press a real flower, mouse, or spider out flat under a piece of glass, and then copy it, adding a little more emaciation and angularity at pleasure.'

'In that "at pleasure" is where all the art lies,' said [Christopher].

The Hand of Ethelberta

I lived in quiet, screened, unknown,
Pondering upon some stick or stone. . . .

From A Private Man on Public Men[286]

There are some who can achieve a special rapport with Nature; and this seems to give them, or accompany in them, a moral superiority. (Grace says of Giles: 'he was pure and perfect in his heart'.) Gabriel Oak is one, Clym Yeobright, in a different way, another. Giles and Marty exemplified the perfect relationship with Nature:

He had a marvellous power of making trees grow. Although he would seem to shovel in the earth quite carelessly there was a sort of sympathy between himself and the fir, oak, or beech that he was operating on; so that the roots took hold of the soil in a few days. When, on the other hand, any of the journeymen planted, although they seemed to go through an identically similar process, one quarter of the trees would die away during the ensuing August. . . . Marty, who turned her hand to anything, was usually the one who performed the part of keeping the trees in a perpendicular position whilst he threw in the mould.

. . . The holes were already dug, and they set to work. Winterborne's fingers were endowed with a gentle conjuror's touch in spreading the roots of each little tree, resulting in a sort of caress under which the delicate fibres all laid themselves out in their proper directions for growth.

The Woodlanders

Marty South alone, of all the women in Hintock and the world, had approximated to Winterborne's level of intelligent intercourse with Nature. In that respect she had formed his true complement in the other sex, had lived as his counterpart, had subjoined her thoughts to his as a corollary.

The casual glimpses which the ordinary population had bestowed upon that wondrous world of sap and leaves called the Hintock woods had been with these two, Giles and Marty, a clear gaze. They had been possessed of its finer mysteries as of commonplace knowledge; had been able to read its hieroglyphs as ordinary writing; to them the sights and sounds of night, winter, wind, storm, amid those dense boughs, which had to Grace a touch of the uncanny, and even of the supernatural, were simple occurrences whose origin, continuance, and laws they foreknew. They had planted together, and together they had felled; together they had, with the run of the years, mentally collected those remoter signs and symbols which seen in few were of runic obscurity, but all together made an alphabet. From the light lashing of the twigs upon their faces when brushing through them in the dark either could pronounce upon the species of the tree whence they stretched; from the quality of the wind's murmur through a bough either could in like manner name its sort afar off. They knew by a glance at a trunk if its heart were sound, or tainted with incipient decay; and by the state of its upper twigs the stratum that had been reached by its roots. The artifices of the seasons were seen by them from the conjuror's own point of view, and not from that of the spectator.

The Woodlanders

For a brief period in his later years Hardy himself seemed to enjoy a more relaxed attitude or relationship to Nature, allowing his imagination to float without the usual restrictions of his mind. As he wrote of William Barnes's poetry:

His rustics are, as a rule, happy people, and very seldom feel the painful sting of the rest of modern mankind, the disproportion between the desire for serenity and the power of obtaining it.

An Unsigned Review of Barnes' Poems of Rural Life in the Dorset Dialect

Reviewing his life and work during his last two decades, in order to compile the Life, *Hardy picked up many of the pastoral images of his early novels – of his Dorset youth – as if to round his end with his beginnings. Some of the poems in* Human Shows *(published late in 1925) concern, like his description of Giles and Marty, an actual and felt harmony with Nature more in tune with what Hardy himself, in the same review, called 'the pervading instinct of the nineteenth century', than he had written or would write. This harmony had everything to do with Nature being a working setting; with*

. . . the peasant's . . . absolute dependence on the moods of the air, earth, and sky. Sun, rain, wind, snow, dawn, darkness, mist, are to him, now as ever, personal assistants and obstructors, masters and acquaintances, with whom he comes directly into contact, whose varying tempers must be well-considered before he can act with effect.[287]

An Unsigned Review of Barnes's Poems of Rural Life in the Dorset Dialect

In some poems, Hardy shows himself integrated to a surprising degree with Nature. In "Afterwards" he is a part of Nature at each passing stage of day and season – May month, dusk, nocturnal blackness, winter; and at the end, as the tollings sound 'as they were a new bell's boom', he seems to have crossed the boundary of death without separation, into some new beginning. As in "Proud Songsters"[288] he seems to have become part of that cycle of 'earth, and air, and rain', beyond the 'painful sting' of either life or death.

This cycle is suggested in many poems already quoted, like "Joys of Memory", "If It's Ever Spring Again" – where it seems as if we can recall at timeless will, in a hypnotic hum, those 'bees a-chime'; and in "A Bird-Scene at a Rural Dwelling",[289]

> Where for a hundred summers there have been
> Just such enactments, just such daybreaks seen.

Many of these poems are full of grammatical ambiguities which heighten the blending of humanity and Nature. In "The Later Autumn" one doesn't know if it is bees or men who are 'leg-laden' with Nature's fruits – and in this new-found tranquillity, whether the lovers are 'stretched at their ease' in love or death hardly matters. The cider-maker's hair,[290] like that of the man in "A Light Snow-Fall after Frost", is white with either frost or years – who knows? In "Snow in the Suburbs" we are delightfully uncertain whether it is sparrow or 'lodging lump' of snow which 'lights on a nether twig' – so much are the two comically confounded. In "The Fallow Deer at the Lonely House", the humans who sit and think indoors are hardly different from the deer

287

who is 'wondering' without; and both, humans within and deer's eyes without, seem 'Lit by lamps of rosy dyes'.[291]

In these late pastoral poems there is a manifest unity between the daily activities of humans and Nature. "Life and Death at Sunrise"[292] (its very title expressive) enjoys the ludicrously scrambled awakening noises of birds and animals, and the more leisurely stirring of the hills 'like awakened sleepers on one elbow lifted', while the human cycle of birth and death proceeds alongside. In "Last Look round St Martin's Fair"[293] there are many parallels between the sun and 'the woman in red' at the nut-stall: she is 'redder in the flare-lamp than the sun' which, 'like an open furnace door', opened the poem. She

> Tosses her ear-rings,and talks ribaldry
> To the young men around as natural gaiety,

and Nature seems like her, 'the fickle unresting earth', the stars flickering, the breeze twitching the trees.
In April 1884, Hardy noted a 'curious scene. A fine poem in it.' Four sisters — itinerant musicians — were playing in the street; he noted that

. . . The eldest had a fixed, old, hard face, and wore white roses in her hat . . . The next sister. . .had rather bold dark eyes, and a coquettish smirk . . . The next, with her hair in ringlets, beat the tambourine. The youngest, a mere child, dinged the triangle. . . .

I saw them again in the evening, the silvery gleams from Saunders's [silver-smith's] shop shining out upon them. They were now sublimed to a wondrous charm. The hard face of the eldest was flooded with soft solicitous thought; the coquettish one was no longer bold but archly tender . . . the third child's face that of an angel; the fourth that of a cherub . . . *Now* they were what Nature made them, before the smear of "civilization" had sullied their existences.

The Life of Thomas Hardy

(The poem he links with this scene was "Music in a Snowy Street"; but it contained none of this tribute to Nature.)

Tess knew that it was from 'social sophistication, and. . .manners other than rural', that 'Black Care had come' to her.[294] *So at Talbothays, wounded in herself, as in her future life, by Alec's assault, she is puzzled and defensive about life when she talks to Clare; but one thing she knows:*

'What makes you draw off in that way, Tess?' said he. 'Are you afraid?'
'Oh no, sir. . .not of outdoor things; especially just now when the apple-blooth is falling, and everything so green.'

Tess of the d'Urbervilles

Her unsophisticated open-air existence required no varnish of conventionality to make it palatable to him.

Tess of the d'Urbervilles

And when Grace saw Giles appearing with his cidermaking equipment, and saw that 'he looked and smelt like Autumn's very brother',[295]

Her heart rose from its late sadness like a released bough; her senses revelled in the sudden lapse back to Nature unadorned.

The Woodlanders

('Bough' was another of Hardy's late inspirations, and perfected his metaphor: in the early editions it had been a 'released spring'.)

With the same surge of feeling as this nostalgia for the innocent past, she had addressed Marty South after Giles's death:

'Yet you and he could speak in a tongue that nobody else knew — not even my father, though he came nearest knowing — the tongue of the trees and fruits and flowers themselves.'

She could indulge in mournful fancies like this to Marty . . .

The Woodlanders

At once Hardy shows his inner thought: these indulgences were only 'fancies', with no basis in reasoning. Grace herself was not in tune with her natural surroundings. ('The woods were uninteresting, and Grace stayed indoors a good deal'.) There is no room for either sentimentality or ignorance (like Matilda's[296]*) in our approach to Nature. The real world is the world awry, the world of the blemished domain, the world of Nature's indifference. We may forget it for a time, and enjoy the pastoral idyll, but for* homo sapiens *there is no going back.*

Freed the Fret of Thinking

Freed the fret of thinking,
    Light of lot were we,
Song with service linking
    Like to bird or bee:
Chancing bale unblinking,
Freed the fret of thinking
    On mortality!

Had not thought-endowment
    Beings ever known,
What Life once or now meant
    None had wanted shown —
Measuring but the moment —
Had not thought-endowment
    Caught Creation's groan!

Loosed from wrings of reason,
We might blow like flowers,
Sense of Time-wrought treason
Would not then be ours
In and out of season;
Loosed from wrings of reason
We should laud the Powers!

[Bale — woe, evil]

Just as Cytherea had entered into the labyrinth of 'Taking Thought' (page 169) so Angel Clare was aware of something precious in Tess:

. . . something which carried him back into a joyous and unforeseeing past, before the necessity of taking thought had made the heavens gray.

Tess of the d'Urbervilles

Among the most far-reaching reasons for 'taking thought' were the theories of Darwin.

During his stay in London he attended, on April 26, [1882] the funeral of Darwin in Westminster Abbey. As a young man he had been among the earliest acclaimers of *The Origin of Species.*

The Life of Thomas Hardy

[*Summer* 1909]. About this time he wrote to a lady of New York in answer to an enquiry she made:
'The discovery of the law of evolution, which revealed that all organic creatures are of one family, shifted the centre of altruism from humanity to the whole conscious world collectively. Therefore the practice of vivisection, which might have been defended while the belief ruled that men and animals are essentially different, has been left by that discovery without any logical argument in its favour. And if the practice, to the extent merely of inflicting slight discomfort now and then, be defended [as I sometimes hold it may] on grounds of it being good policy for animals as well as men, it is nevertheless in strictness a wrong, and stands precisely in the same category as would stand its practice on men themselves.'

The Life of Thomas Hardy

To the Secretary of the Humanitarian League
The Athenaeum, Pall Mall, S.W.   *10th April, 1910*

. . . Few people seem to perceive fully as yet that the most far-reaching consequence of the establishment of the common origin of all species is ethical; that it logically involved a readjustment of altruistic morals by enlarging as a *necessity of rightness* the application of what has been called "The Golden Rule" beyond the area of mere mankind to that of the whole animal kingdom. Possibly Darwin himself did not wholly perceive it, though he alluded to it. While man was deemed to be a creation apart from all other creations, a secondary or tertiary morality was considered good enough towards the "inferior" races; but no person who reasons nowadays can escape the trying conclusion that this is not maintainable. And though I myself do not at present see how the principle of equal justice all round is to be carried out in its entirety, I recognize that the League is grappling with the question.'

It will be seen that in substance this agrees with a letter written earlier, and no doubt the subject was much in his mind just now.

The Life of Thomas Hardy

The Reminder

While I watch the Christmas blaze
Paint the room with ruddy rays,
Something makes my vision glide
To the frosty scene outside.

There, to reach a rotting berry,
Toils a thrush, – constrained to very
Dregs of food by sharp distress,
Taking such with thankfulness.

Why, O starving bird, when I
One day's joy would justify,
And put misery out of view,
Do you make me notice you!

In or before September 1909 Hardy prepared this poem for publication; poems like "The Blinded Bird" and "The Wind Blew Words" appeared in 1917. 'The subject' – the essential unity of all creation – had in fact been in his mind for many years, his intellectual acceptance of the Darwinian revolution only reinforcing a natural inclination to 'lovingkindness' to all living things as the basis of all morality. All Nature is fundamentally one. (See "A Thought in Two Moods", on page 112.)

Indeed, an 'impression' which took this idea to its extreme is expressed in a poem called "Voices from Things Growing in a Churchyard", and in the following:

Transformations

Portion of this yew
Is a man my grandsire knew,
Bosomed here at its foot:

This branch may be his wife,
A ruddy human life
Now turned to a green shoot.

These grasses must be made
Of her who often prayed,
Last century, for repose;
And the fair girl long ago
Whom I often tried to know
May be entering this rose.

So, they are not underground,
But as nerves and veins abound
In the growths of upper air,
And they feel the sun and rain,
And the energy again
That made them what they were!

Other elements of Darwin's thesis, however, were important to Hardy. He accepted in principle that the make-up of both individuals and the human race itself is predetermined by chance and other factors, like environment and heredity, which are beyond human control. (He would have been tremendously interested in the discovery of DNA later in the century.[297]) This we have seen in poems like "Hap" and "The Pedigree", and many events in the novels. Authorial comments like the following are plentiful:

That old-fashioned revelling in the general situation grows less and less possible as we uncover the defects of natural laws, and see the quandary that man is in by their operation.

The Return of the Native

Evolution, obsolescence, and the 'survival of the fittest' (in Spencer's phrase) are important themes. Clym Yeobright is a man 'of the future', who is ahead of the environment to which he returns: Egdon Heath was 'an obsolete thing, and few cared to study it' – yet Clym was 'its product' and he loved it. Michael Henchard and Tess have to struggle for survival, she against her all-powerful environment and heredity, he as a superseded species unable to learn new ways. Giles Winterborne, despite his communion with Nature, is caught up in a vanishing way of life (which Hardy is careful to point out in his 1912 addition to The Woodlanders' Preface*).[298] The passages already quoted describing Giles's death (page 272) surround it with the violent turmoil of the natural order – gales prematurely blowing down leaves, and trees 'wrestling for existence, their boughs disfigured with wounds'. Moreover all the images of death, not just Giles's but the death – 'rotting', 'perishing' – of old growths 'vanquished long ago', 'where branches had been removed in past times', are images of obsolescence: 'like ichthyosauri in a museum'.*

Indeed The Woodlanders *is in itself a kind of lament for the passing of the old view of nature. It is worth lingering on how Hardy developed this theme in this particular novel – which is as near the poetic pastoral elegy as a novel could be. It has particularly interesting resonances with Giles Winterborne.*

In ancient and Renaissance pastoral, the Arcadian state of rustic simplicity was idealised, and the genre was also used as a vehicle for moral criticism – of, for example, the corruption of cities. (The later pastoral elegy, such as "Lycidas", "Adonais", and "Thyrsis", which Hardy knew well, had similar preoccupations.) It had too a strong religious connection: 'in the classical pastoral elegy', writes Northrop Frye, 'the subject of the elegy is not treated as an individual but as a representative of a dying spirit of nature'.[299]

Adonis, for example, (originally worshipped by the Phoenicians) was the subject of the archetypal Laments by the classical poets Bion and Moschus – on which Shelley based his "Adonais". Adonis, beloved of the goddess Aphrodite, and god-like in his beauty, was killed by a boar, and so mourned by the goddess that he was finally allowed a yearly resurrection from the Underworld. Because of this he symbolised the coming of spring after winter and was worshipped as a god of both the seasons' and vegetation's renewal.

In some versions of the Adonis legend his unusual birth is told; for his mother Myrrha, after conceiving him, was turned into a tree, and in due course he burst out of her – a kind of tree-spirit.

Another connection is interesting: he was worshipped mainly by women and girls, in ceremonies somewhat analogous to the Midsummer Eve celebrations in The Woodlanders.[300]

Giles Winterborne must be seen against this background, part of Hardy's elegy for the passing of the old, safe, uncomplicated acceptance of a bountiful Nature, fulfilling the beneficent will of God.

He is high up, lopping branches off the tree which so obsesses John South as having a supernatural power to 'dash me into my grave'. It is at such a time, from the ground, that Grace tries to tell Giles they cannot marry.[301]

With a sudden start he worked on, climbing higher into the sky, and cutting himself off more and more from all intercourse with the sublunary world. At last he had worked himself so high up the elm, and the mist had so thickened, that he could only just be discerned as a dark grey spot on the light grey zenith. . . .

(She returns and tries to talk again; but the circumstances hardly favour it.)
He continued motionless and silent in that gloomy Niflheim[302] or fogland which involved him, and she proceeded on her way. . . .

A quarter of an hour passed, and all was blackness overhead. Giles had not yet come down.

Then the tree seemed to shiver, then to heave a sigh: a movement was audible, and Winterborne dropped almost noiselessly to the ground.

The Woodlanders

When Fitzpiers leaves her for Mrs Charmond, Grace becomes ill, and with the possibility of the new divorce laws, she thinks of Giles:

He rose upon her memory as the fruit-god and the wood-god in alternation: sometimes leafy and smeared with green lichen, as she had seen him amongst the sappy boughs of the plantations: sometimes cider-stained and starred with apple-pips, as she had met him on his return from cider-making in Blackmoor Vale. . .

The Woodlanders

There are many more religious overtones in Grace's relationship with Giles. During her second night in his hut the wind was

. . . springing out of the trees . . . and shrieking and blaspheming. . . . She had never before been so struck with the devilry of a gusty night in a wood, because she had never been so entirely alone in spirit as she was now.

She begins to realise that he is dying: (. . . 'a dying spirit of nature' . . .)

The purity of his nature, his freedom from the grosser passions, his scrupulous delicacy, had never been fully understood by Grace till this strange self-sacrifice in lonely juxtaposition to her own person was revealed. The perception of it added something that was little short of reverence to the deep affection for him of a woman who, herself, had more of Artemis than of Aphrodite in her constitution.

As she ran through the wood to find help,

. . . the spirit of Winterborne seemed to keep her company and banish all darkness from her mind.

After his death, she laid 'her hand reverently on the dead man's eyelids'; and visited his grave, in a 'memorial act to which she and Marty had devoted themselves'. Hardy continues to use such suggestive words when Grace tells Fitzpiers:

'I go with Marty South to Giles's grave. I almost worship him. We swore we would show him that devotion.'

– and again when he reverts to their visits being

. . . kept up with pious strictness for the purpose of putting snowdrops, primroses, and other vernal flowers thereon as they came.

The vernal flowers, symbols of resurrection, appear in "Lycidas", in "Adonais", in "Thyrsis", and, of course, in Cymbeline,[303] *to which Hardy alludes as he compares Grace and Marty to its 'two mourners . . . [as they] sweetened his sad grave with their flowers and their tears'. (In that play Imogen, who appeared dead but was only drugged, came to life again.)*

Winterborne died without issue – like Hardy, Henchard, Elfride, the Trumpet-Major, Pierston, Tess and Jude (their children being dead). The old securities die and a harsher regime takes their place. Heredity, love, beauty and fulfilment can be thwarted by environment and chance. Those who survive are not necessarily the best, but they are often (like Fitzpiers) the fittest for an inclement world.

Hardy's thinking, as we have seen, is permeated with Darwin's; he has been called 'the most honest and sensitive recorder of the shock-wave from the evolutionary discoveries'[304]: 'loss, instability, disorientation, incoherence and, above all, the reduction of man's significance in his own sight.'

Yet it is also clear that although Hardy accepted intellectually that Darwin's analysis was correct – the human being was only one in a chain of evolving life, ruled by chance and other uncontrollable forces – at the same time he knew that it was incomplete. The human, sentient individual mattered more, in his view, than any other part of creation. The complexity of the human personality and condition could not, from our own experience, be sufficiently explained by merely mechanistic laws. He wrote The Dynasts *(with its different Spirits voicing alternative philosophical theories of the universe) to show that science alone had not the answers to these enigmas.[305]*

[1876] *June 26.* If it be possible to compress into a sentence all that a man learns between 20 and 40, it is that all things merge in one another – good into evil, generosity into justice, religion into politics, the year into the ages, the world into the universe. With this in view the evolution of species seems but a minute and obvious process in the same movement.

The Life of Thomas Hardy

In a dictated letter declining to be included in a Biographical Dictionary of Modern Rationalists:

February 18, 1920. . . . [Mr Hardy] says he thinks he is rather an irrationalist than a rationalist, on account of his inconsistencies. He has, in fact, declared as much in prefaces to some of his poems, where he explains his views as being mere impressions that frequently change. Moreover, he thinks he could show that no man is a rationalist, and that human actions are not ruled by reason at all in the last resort.

Letter to Mr Joseph McCabe

As I have tried to show elsewhere,[306] Hardy exemplified the dilemmas of much post-Enlightenment thinking about the laws of cause and effect in the universe, over against the ruling of some kind of purpose; and about the recognition of truly human values in society. Men and women make a spiritual or ethical response to life which marks them out from inanimate Nature. Faced with the place of humanity in the natural world, he was unhesitating:

[1877] *September 28.* An object or mark raised or made by man on a scene is worth ten times any such formed by unconscious Nature. Hence clouds, mists, and mountains are unimportant beside the wear on a threshold, or the print of a hand.

The Life of Thomas Hardy

Writing to an American publisher who wished to visit 'the Wessex country':

8 June, 1911 ... The heath part is not so attractive now as at some other seasons, &, indeed, at all times it appeals rather to the sentiment than to the eye.

Letter to Mr George Putnam

[1878] *April 22* . . . The beauty of association is entirely superior to the beauty of aspect, and a beloved relative's old battered tankard to the finest Greek vase. Paradoxically put, it is to see the beauty in ugliness.

The Life of Thomas Hardy

Under the Waterfall

'Whenever I plunge my arm, like this,
In a basin of water, I never miss
The sweet sharp sense of a fugitive day
Fetched back from its thickening shroud of gray.
   Hence the only prime
   And real love-rhyme
   That I know by heart,
   And that leaves no smart,
Is the purl of a little valley fall
About three spans wide and two spans tall
Over a table of solid rock,
And into the scoop of the self-same block;
The purl of a runlet that never ceases
In stir of kingdoms, in wars, in peaces;
With a hollow boiling voice it speaks
And has spoken since hills were turfless peaks.'

'And why gives this the only prime
Idea to you of a real love-rhyme?
And why does plunging your arm in a bowl
full of spring water, bring throbs to your soul?'

'Well, under the fall, in a crease of the stone,
Though where precisely none ever has known,
Jammed darkly, nothing to show how prized,
And by now with its smoothness opalized,
   Is a drinking-glass:
   For, down that pass
   My lover and I
   Walked under a sky
Of blue with a leaf-wove awning of green,
In the burn of August, to paint the scene,

And we placed our basket of fruit and wine
By the runlet's rim, where we sat to dine;
And when we had drunk from the glass together,
Arched by the oak-copse from the weather,
I held the vessel to rinse in the fall,
Where it slipped, and sank, and was past recall,
Though we stooped and plumbed the little abyss
With long bared arms. There the glass still is.
And, as said, if I thrust my arm below
Cold water in basin or bowl, a throe
From the past awakens a sense of that time,
And the glass we used, and the cascade's rhyme.
The basin seems the pool, and its edge
The hard smooth face of the brook-side ledge,
And the leafy pattern of china-ware
The hanging plants that were bathing there.

'By night, by day, when it shines or lours,
There lies intact that chalice of ours,
And its presence adds to the rhyme of love
Persistently sung by the fall above.
No lip has touched it since his and mine
In turns therefrom sipped lovers' wine.'

The spot may have beauty, grandeur, salubrity, convenience; but if it lack memories it will ultimately pall upon him who settles there without opportunity of intercourse with his kind.

The Woodlanders

Hardy cared deeply for his kind. (In a not uncritical reminiscence of him, his parlourmaid, Miss Titterington, made a point of saying 'He was a man of very great compassion.'[307]*) The thought of these uniquely precious individuals being born into a world of injustice, poverty, emotional frustration and death, burns through him until a poem is made.*

To an Unborn Pauper Child

I

Breathe not, hid Heart; cease silently,
And though thy birth-hour beckons thee,
Sleep the long sleep:
The Doomsters heap
Travails and teens around us here,
And Time-wraiths turn our songsingings to fear.

II

Hark, how the peoples surge and sigh,
And laughters fail, and greetings die:
    Hopes dwindle; yea,
    Faiths waste away,
Affections and enthusiasms numb;
Thou canst not mend these things if thou dost come.

III

Had I the ear of wombèd souls
Ere their terrestrial chart unrolls,
    And thou wert free
    To cease, or be,
Then would I tell thee all I know,
And put it to thee: Wilt thou take Life so?

IV

Vain vow! No hint of mine may hence
To theeward fly: to thy locked sense
    Explain none can
    Life's pending plan:
Thou wilt thy ignorant entry make
Though skies spout fire and blood and nations quake.

V

Fain would I, dear, find some shut plot
Of earth's wide wold for thee, where not
    One tear, one qualm,
    Should break the calm,
But I am weak as thou and bare;
No man can change the common lot to rare.

VI

Must come and bide. And such are we –
Unreasoning, sanguine, visionary –
    That I can hope
    Health, love, friends, scope
In full for thee; can dream thou wilt find
Joys seldom yet attained by humankind!

Hardy's tenderness for this child never spills over into whining pity or sentimentality. Nor does it become self-pity on the occasions when he speaks directly of himself, faced with the frustrating laws of a hostile Nature.

[1892] *October 18.* Hurt my tooth at breakfast-time. I look in the glass. Am conscious of the humiliating sorriness of my earthly tabernacle, and of the sad fact that the best of parents could do no better for me. . . . Why should a man's mind have been thrown into such close, sad, sensational, inexplicable relations with such a precarious object as his own body!

The Life of Thomas Hardy

These 'inexplicable relations' were felt also by Knight, as he stood with Elfride and Stephen in the Luxellian vault:

'Such occasions as these seem to compel us to roam outside ourselves, far away from the fragile frame we live in, and to expand till our perception grows so vast that our physical reality bears no sort of proportion to it. We look back upon the weak and minute stem on which this luxuriant growth depends, and ask, Can it be possible that such a capacity has a foundation so small? Must I again return to my daily walk in that narrow cell, a human body, where worldy thoughts can torture me?. . . . One has a sense of wrong, too, that such an appreciative breadth as a sentient being possesses should be committed to the frail casket of a body. What weaken's one's intentions regarding the future like the thought of this?. . . .'

A Pair of Blue Eyes

They were revealed (also by the glass) to Jocelyn Pierston:

The person he appeared was too grievously far, chronologically, in advance of the person he felt himself to be. Pierston did not care to regard the figure confronting him so mockingly. Its voice seemed to say 'There's tragedy hanging on to this!' . . . Never had he seemed so aged by a score of years as he was represented in the glass in that cold grey morning light. While his soul was what it was, why should he have been encumbered with that withering carcase, without the ability to shift it off for another, as his ideal Beloved had so frequently done?

The Well-Beloved

One thing it passed him to understand: on what field of observation the poets and philosophers based their assumption that the passion of love was intensest in youth and burnt lower as maturity advanced.

The Well-Beloved

Time was against him and love, and time would probably win.

The Well-Beloved

When was it to end — this curse of his heart not ageing while his frame moved naturally onward? Perhaps only with life.

The Well-Beloved

I Look Into My Glass

I look into my glass,
And view my wasting skin,
And say, 'Would God it came to pass
My heart had shrunk as thin!'

For then, I, undistrest
By hearts grown cold to me,
Could lonely wait my endless rest
With equanimity.

But Time, to make me grieve,
Part steals, lets part abide;
And shakes this fragile frame at eve
With throbbings of noontide.

A stoic dignity, a belief in the primacy of truth, and an unfailing promotion of the human values of 'loving-kindness' as set out in St Paul's letter to the Corinthians[308] – one of his most frequent Biblical allusions – was Hardy's answer to the cruel laws of Nature and the universe. This was his own form of rebellion.[309] There were others – typified by the November bonfires lit in the benighted heath:

To light a fire is the instinctive and resistant act of man when, at the winter ingress, the curfew is sounded throughout Nature. It indicates a spontaneous, Promethean rebelliousness against the fiat that this recurrent season shall bring foul times, cold darkness, misery and death. Black chaos comes, and the fettered gods of the earth say, Let there be light.[310]

The Return of the Native

His first description of the heath in that novel bracketed it with humanity; it was 'like man, slighted but enduring.'[311]

Hardy helps other characters to rebel by asserting their own individuality and right to live – or die. We have read about the 'mighty personality' of Tess, 'a woman living her precious life'; and we can never forget her. Nor can one forget characters like Julie-Jane, or Patty Beech of "The Inquiry",[312] or many others in story, novel and poem. Michael Henchard – who remains the 'Man of Character' of Hardy's sub-title even after every loss, including life – leaves his own indelible, undefeated mark:

MICHAEL HENCHARD'S WILL

That Elizabeth-Jane Farfrae be not told of my death, or made to grieve on account of me.

& that I be not bury'd in consecrated ground.
& that no sexton be asked to toll the bell.

& that nobody is wished to see my dead body.
& that no murners walk behind me at my funeral
& that no flours be planted on my grave.
& that no man remember me.
To this I put my name.

MICHAEL HENCHARD.

Cytherea Graye, the heroine of Hardy's first published novel, after her agonised decision to marry Manston in order to save her brother Owen, is then chided by him when she admits she still loves Edward:

'Yes – my duty to society,' she murmured. 'But ah, Owen, it is difficult to adjust our outer and inner life with perfect honesty to all! Though it may be right to care more for the benefit of the many than for the indulgence of your own single self, when you consider that the many, and duty to them, only exist to you through your own existence, what can be said? What do our own acquaintances care about us? Not much. . . . And perhaps, far in time to come, when I am dead and gone, some other's accent, or some other's song, or thought, like an old one of mine, will carry them back to what I used to say, and hurt their hearts a little that they blamed me so soon. And they will pause just for an instant, and give a sigh to me, and think, ''Poor girl!'' believing they do great justice to my memory by this. But they will never, never realize that it was my single opportunity of existence, as well as of doing my duty, which they are regarding; they will not feel that what to them is but a thought, easily held in those two words of pity, ''Poor girl!'' was a whole life to me; as full of hours, minutes, and peculiar minutes, of hopes and dreads, smiles, whisperings, tears, as theirs: that it was my world, what is to them their world, and they in that life of mine, however much I cared for them, only as the thought I seem to them to be.

Desperate Remedies

Fortunately for Cytherea, a wise old man, Parson Raunham, realised too, that

. . . the gentle, defenceless girl, whom it seemed nobody's business to help or guard . . . had but one life, and the superciliousness with which all the world now regarded her should be compensated in some measure by the man whose carelessness – to set him in the best light – had caused it.

Desperate Remedies

Even the anonymous Milkmaid (page 146) rebels against reader's and poet's false assumptions about her, their categorising of her in a way that destroys her individuality; and she asserts it, over them and over Nature.
  Tess similarly refused to be somebody she was not, as Clare tried to make her:

301

She was no longer the milkmaid, but a visionary essence of woman — a whole sex condensed into one typical form. He called her Artemis, Demeter, and other fanciful names half teasingly, which she did not like because she did not understand them.

'Call me Tess,' she would say askance; and he did.

Tess of the d'Urbervilles

Like Elfride, and Emma Gifford when Hardy first met her, Tess was 'so intensely living' *that she needed no other personality than her own. With many handicaps and few weapons she fought simply to be: and brought to the struggle two qualities which Hardy knew would always spring, unquenchably, in the human heart. As she travelled to begin a new life at Talbothays:*

Some spirit within her rose automatically as the sap in the twigs. It was unexpended youth, surging up anew after its temporary check, and bringing with it hope, and the invincible instinct towards self-delight.

Tess of the d'Urbervilles

By briefest meeting something sure is won;
　　It will have been:
Nor God nor Daemon can undo the done,
　　Unsight the seen,
Make muted music be as unbegun,
　　Though things terrene
Groan in their bondage till oblivion supervene.

So, to the one sweeping symphony
　　From times remote
Till now, of human tenderness, shall we
　　Supply one note,
Small and untraced, yet that will ever be
　　Somewhere afloat
Amid the spheres, as part of sick Life's antidote.

From To Meet, or Otherwise

The two factors — the sick Life, and the invincible instinct towards self-delight — are inseparable; and like the light shining in the darkness, neither can put the other out. The poem "Let Me Enjoy", from which this book takes its title, is tuned likewise, and inevitably with Hardy, in both minor and major keys. As so often, he tried to distance himself from the sentiments of the poem:

[*December 29, 1909*] . . . Some good judges agree with you in liking "Let Me Enjoy". I fear I am not clear on the precise mental state of the singer of that lyric.

Letter to Lady Grove

Yet it encapsulates so much of Hardy himself. Though he made many changes in the last three stanzas,[313] *the first, with its joy in the beauty of the earth around him, pointed (but not qualified)*

302

by a theological statement, is entirely characteristic; and it seems to have come without hindrance. The last is no less typical: agnostic, the human pilgrim spirit accepting with steadiness whatever its fate may be — and yet, still glad, still joyful in the 'great things' of life, and sure of 'the invincible instinct towards self-delight.' Who knows if the echo of Psalm 121 near the end (and possibly even of both father and son in the parable called The Prodigal Son) is not a hidden hope?

Let Me Enjoy
(Minor Key)

I

Let me enjoy the earth no less
Because the all-enacting Might
That fashioned forth its loveliness
Had other aims than my delight.

II

About my path there flits a Fair,
Who throws me not a word or sign;
I'll charm me with her ignoring air,
And laud the lips not meant for mine.

III

From manuscripts of moving song
Inspired by scenes and dreams unknown
I'll pour out raptures that belong
To others, as they were my own.

IV

And some day hence, toward Paradise
And all its blest — if such should be —
I will lift glad, afar-off eyes,
Though it contain no place for me.

Notes

ABBREVIATIONS USED IN THE NOTES

TH: Thomas Hardy
Life   F.E. Hardy, *The Life of Thomas Hardy 1840-1928* (in one volume, London 1962)
Lit. Notes *The Literary Notebooks of Thomas Hardy*, ed. Lennart Björk (London 1985);
            original documents in the Dorset County Museum.
Materials   *Materials for the Study of the Life, Times and Works of Thomas Hardy*, 72
            monographs, ed. J.S. Cox, (Guernsey, various dates from 1962).
Millgate   Michael Millgate, *Thomas Hardy: A Biography* (Oxford, 1982)
Orel   *Thomas Hardy's Personal Writings*, ed. H. Orel (Kansas 1966, London 1977)
FWL   *Figures in a Wessex Landscape*, ed. J. Cullen Brown (London 1987)

(Since the present volume is the companion to FWL I have not generally duplicated relevant passages, but have indicated their location therein.)

TEXTS USED

Letters: *The Collected Letters of Thomas Hardy*, ed. Purdy & Millgate (Oxford, seven vols., 1978-); *Life* (see above).

Notes: *Memoranda: The Personal Notebooks of Thomas Hardy*, ed. R.H. Taylor (Macmillan 1978); *Lit. Notes* (see above); *Life.*

Novels and stories: the New Wessex edition (Macmillan, 1974-77)

Poems and their Prefaces: *The Complete Poetical Works of Thomas Hardy*, ed. Samuel Hynes, (3 vols, Oxford, 1982-5); *Thomas Hardy: The Complete Poems*, ed. James Gibson (London 1976). Poem titles are given below in italics.

Various essays, articles, etc: *Orel* (see above).

Markings in TH's own books are noted from his copies in the Dorset County Museum.

INTRODUCTION

1 'An Unsigned Review of *Poems of Rural Life in the Dorset Dialect*, by William Barnes', *Orel*, 98; *After the Visit.*
2 ''The Last Chrysanthemum'', p 274
3 *The Hand of Ethelberta*, ch 2 (p 257)
4 *Real Conversations*, *FWL*, 277
5 *Life*, 229 (p 145)
6 Such a judgment however may ignore the freak variations which occur.
7 See pp 214-225
8 *Under the Greenwood Tree*, II ch 3 (p 220); letter to Arthur Moule, 19 October 1903
9 Letter to Florence Henniker, 22 December 1916; George Gissing to Algernon Gissing, 22 September 1895, quoted in R.L. Purdy, 'George Gissing at Max

Gate', Yale University Library Gazette 17, iii (1943) p 52, and in Millgate, *Thomas Hardy: His Career as a Novelist*, 342-3. See, however, pages 137-8, and the testimony about his love of wild flowers of both his gardener and parlourmaid (note 11)

10 *Life*, 403. See also *FWL*, 5, 282.

11 B.N. Stephens, 'Thomas Hardy in his Garden'; E.E. Titterington, 'The Domestic Life of Thomas Hardy (1921-28)'; W.M. Parker, 'A Visit to Thomas Hardy', all in *Materials*, I nos. 6, 4, 24.

12 *Life*, 285. The *Spectator* review of *Desperate Remedies* in 1871, though critical, yet paid tribute to this new writer's 'talent of a remarkable kind – sensitiveness to scenic and atmospheric effects, and to their influence on the mind, and the power of rousing similar sensitiveness in his readers.'

13 See the passage from *The Woodlanders* quoted on pages 134–5.

14 Letters to Edward Clodd, 3 March 1909, 9 September 1908. To Mrs Henniker, newly settled in Shoreham, he wrote on 2 November 1903: 'I hope you do not feel dull there when the weather is bad. That makes an enormous difference to my feeling about places.'

15 *Life*, 13, 21

16 See p 22

17 *Life*, 137

18 *Life*, 397

19 Hermann Lea, letter to E.N. Sanders, 29 November 1943, *Materials* I no. 20; H.L. Voss, 'Motoring with Thomas Hardy', *Materials* I no. 7

20 p 84

21 *Dorset County Chronicle*, 15 February 1912; D.N.H. & A.F. Club's *Proceedings*, 1912; D.F. Barter, *Concerning Thomas Hardy*, 126

22 *Lit. Notes*, vol I, entries 321, 322 (TH mistakenly transposed Wood's initials); *The Return of the Native*, I ch 10

23 *The Return of the Native*, II ch 2

24 "Night-Time in Mid-Fall", p 41

25 *FWL*, 194

26 *Far from the Madding Crowd:* ch 37 (see page 80); ch 33 (page 64)

27 See *The Woodlanders*, ch 3. Gosse had asked where he could find this reference in the novels; TH could not remember but promised to look it up.

28 *Tess of the d'Urbervilles*, ch 58; *Daily Chronicle*, 24 August 1903, Orel, 200

29 'The Science of Fiction', Orel, 134

30 'Candour in English Fiction', Orel, 125

31 'The Science of Fiction', Orel, 135-6, 137, 138

32 *ibid*, 136

33 *The Trumpet-Major*, ch 3; *Desperate Remedies*, ch I, 5; *The Trumpet-Major*, ch 36

34 P 71; p 137

35 *A Pair of Blue Eyes*, chs 3 and 38. Grace too 'looked so lovely in the green world about her.' (*Woodlanders*, ch 24).

36 *The Dynasts*, Pt III, Act VI Sc 8

37 See pp 179; 244; 243-4

38 See *FWL* 176-8

39 See p 293

40 *The Woodlanders*, ch 28, 42. See pp 292-4

41 *The Return of the Native*, I ch 3

42 *Far from the Madding Crowd*, ch 28

43 'A Tradition of 1804' *(Wessex Tales); A Pair of Blue Eyes*, ch 22 (*FWL* 288); *The Hand of Ethelberta*, ch43: see p 143

44 *The Return of the Native*, IV ch 5; see p 98

45 See pp 265, 290-2; and in *FWL* e.g. "Winter Night in Woodland" (42), "The Spring Call" (98), and the blushing sheep, 232.

46 "On a Fine Morning", p 204; *The Mayor of Casterbridge*, ch19; *Far from the Madding Crowd*, ch 5 (*FWL*, 225)

47 *A Pair of Blue Eyes*, ch 10, see p 146; *Two on a Tower*, ch 24

48 *The Return of the Native*, III ch 6, see p 134; "Drinking Song". In *The Woodlanders*, ch 17, Hardy also ironically describes some of Nature's 'strange mistakes'.

49 *A Journey into Hardy's Poetry*, (Allison & Busby, 1989) ch XII

50 "At a Bridal", p 280

51 *The Mayor of Casterbridge*, ch 19; "The Mother Mourns", p 269

52 Note, *Life*, : see p 277

53 Wordsworth, "The Small Celandine", in *The Woodlanders*, ch 3

54 *Life*, 116: see p 295
55 *Life*, 185: see p 257; *Life*, 50: see p 255.
56 "The Phantom Horsewoman", p 242
57 *Life*, 315: see p 279
58 "Julie-Jane"; *FWL*, 75; "The Inquiry", p 241; "The Bedridden Peasant to an Unknowing God", "To an Unborn Pauper Child", p 297
59 In *A Journey into Thomas Hardy's Poetry* I have also mentioned Hardy's affinities with Camus and the philosophy of 'the Absurd'. (Ch XII)
60 *Tess of the d'Urbervilles*, II ch 15; see pp 302
61 "A Backward Spring", p 93; "The Year's Awakening", p 92; "An August Midnight", p 236
62 "On a Fine Morning", p 204
63 p 300. 'I was a child till I was 16; a youth till I was 25; a young man till I was 40 or 50.' (*Life*, 378)
64 *Satires of Circumstance*, November 1914. "A Poet" is placed at the end of the main part of the collection, followed only by a set of fifteen poems already published, which he rather regretted having to include. (See his letter to Gosse of 16 April 1918).
65 *FWL*, 10
66 "Surview" (*Late Lyrics and Earlier*)
67 Dennis Taylor, *Hardy's Poetry: 1860-1928* (London 1981) 137-8
68 e.g. *Life*, 368
69 *Gospel of St John*, ch 8 v32, quoted by TH in "He Resolves to Say No More"

I   THE COUNTRY OF HARDY'S CHILDHOOD

70 See also "A Bird-Scene at a Rural Dwelling", *FWL*, 18
71 A block of wood or similar hobble
72 St Sebastian was martyred in 288, tied to a tree and shot by arrows
73 Other poems such as "By the Barrows" commemorate the place. Hardy sought out and talked to the descendants of the beacon-keepers Whiting and Purchess who figure in *The Dynasts*, Part First, Act II, sc 5
74 *FWL*, 181, 68
75 *Revelation*, ch 22, v1

II   HARDY AS NATURAL OBSERVER

76 See e.g. pp 21-22, and notes quoted throughout this book
77 See the passage from *The Return of the Native* on p 252
78 Faggot: the bundle of gorse, or furze, sticks he had been collecting for firewood
79 Ishmael, eldest son of Abraham, was banished to the wilderness: his name has come to represent an outcast.
80 See Hardy's note, quoted p 22
81 *Millgate*, 94, 100

Light

82 *FWL*, 36

Shadows

83 See p 206

Sunset and Evening

84 Vandyke: a deep-cut point or scallop to the border of a lace collar, as seen in Van Dyck's portraits.

Night and Darkness

85 The vast abyss, in Scandinavian mythology, between Niflheim (the region of fogs – see p 293), and Muspelheim (the region of intense heat). The Gap had no bounds, no night or day, and existed before heaven or earth.
86 See the account in *Exodus* XIII v21 of the Israelites' escape from Egypt

Moonlight

87 The ellipsis after 'queens' is Hardy's own.

Stars

88 e.g. "The Wind's Prophecy", p 39; "A Sign-Seeker", p 40; "Lying Awake",

p 43; "The Singing Lovers", p 143; "The Tree and the Lady", p 163; "Shut Out That Moon", p 215; "A Woman Driving", p 236; *FWL,* 10, 31, 253

Dawn and Sunrise

89 This passage is continued on p 41
90 See *Judges,* ch IV, v21
91 *Life,* 225

Sunlight

92 *Life,* 183

Skies and Clouds

93 See *FWL,* 105; (*Under the Greenwood Tree,* II ch 6)

Rain, Wind and Storm

94 See also "The Pedigree", p 216; and "Night in the Old Home", "Old Furniture", *FWL,* 32, 33
95 Gabriel, p 34; *The Trumpet-Major,* ch 2; *Tess of the d'Urbervilles,* ch 58
96 *The Return of the Native,* V ch 9; pp 195, 243, 271; *FWL* 182
97 Milton, *Paradise Lost,* Bk VI, 330-1
98 Translated from the Latin title (Magna Mater) given to Cybele the Many-Breasted, goddess of fertility
99 The dark valley (sometimes called Gehenna) where Jerusalem fired its rubbish, and where in the times of Jeremiah and Isaiah children were burnt as sacrifices to the idol Moloch

Fog

100 i.e. Death (cf. Congreve, *The Double Dealer:* 'Love, like death, a universal leveller of mankind.') Another picture of fog is on p 27

The Four Seasons

Winter

101 see pp 178-181
102 "Afterwards", *FWL,* 10; "Penance"

103 William Pritchard develops this in his essay 'Hardy's Anonymous Sincerity' (*Agenda,* TH Special Issue, Spring-Summer 1972, p 100-101)

Spring

104 *Tess of the d'Urbervilles,* III ch 16

Summer

105 See Ronald Marken's essay in *The Poetry of Thomas Hardy,* ed. Clements & Grindle, (London 1980); or my *A Journey into Thomas Hardy's Poetry,* (London 1989), 322-3

Sounds, Scents and Colours

106 *The Well-Beloved,* II ch 4, I ch 4; *The Mayor of Casterbridge,* ch 1; *Two on a Tower,* ch 15; *The Woodlanders,* ch 19, ch 42; *Two on a Tower,* ch 3; *A Pair of Blue Eyes,* ch 19; *Desperate Remedies,* ch 11 pt 6. See also *Desperate Remedies* VI 2, part of which is quoted on p 220; and, for example, *Two on a Tower,* ch 2, where the hidden Swithin deduces Parson Torkingham's arrival entirely from its sequence of sounds.
107 See for example p 51
108 "Night-Time in Mid-Fall", p 52
109 "Silences", *FWL,* 20; "The Five Students", 82
110 Similar 'acoustic perceptions' occur in 'A Tryst at an Ancient Earth-work', *FWL,* 290; see also Hardy's remarks about Stonehenge (p 7)
111 "Rome: Sala delle Muse". For more about the rank garden, see p 278
112 Lady Cynthia Asquith, in *Portrait of Barrie,* p 108, vividly describes Wessex, 'the most despotic dog' she had ever encountered, and how, at dinner, he was 'contesting with me every forkful of food on its way from plate to mouth'. Postmen were bitten; but with Hardy Wessex appears to have been totally docile.
113 Wm. Archer, *Real Conversations (FWL,* 277); *The Return of the Native,* III ch 2, (see p 23)

114 "Childhood Among The Ferns", *FWL*, 13; "I Found Her Out There", p 235; *The Woodlanders*, ch 28, *FWL*, 236; ch 25. See also other noting of scents on, for example, pp 62, 84, 96

115 *Life*, 47, 52

116 *The Trumpet-Major*, ch 166

117 p 98; p 39

Animals

Horses

118 In Hardy's monastic metaphor, the place where he dispensed charity and stayed for contemplation.

119 *Life*, 303

Dogs, Cats, and other Quadrupeds

120 *Life*, 434; *Tess of the d'Urbervilles*, ch 23; *Far from the Madding Crowd*, ch 40; *Jude the Obscure*, IV ch 2, I ch 10.

121 Florence Hardy to Alda, Lady Hoare, 9 December 1914 (MS in Wiltshire County Record Office, Trowbridge)

122 Legend tells how seven Christian youths from Ephesus, fleeing from Decius' persecution in 250 A.D., were walled up in a cave and slept for centuries. One version says their dog was welcomed in heaven because he neither moved, slept, drank nor ate while they were asleep.

123 Dennis Taylor, *Hardy's Poetry, 1860-1928*, 150

Insects, Reptiles, Worms

124 Hardy published this identical passage in *Desperate Remedies*, ch 12 pt 6, and in *The Return of the Native*, III ch 5.

125 *A Laodicean*, VI ch 1. See also "Last Week in October", p 84; and pp 172-8

126 *The Return of the Native*, I ch 3. See also "The Later Autumn", p 206, and "If It's Ever Spring Again", p 95

127 A red dessert apple (several spelling variants) popular in Wessex

128 Alluding to Newton's theory that gravitational attraction of different parts of the atmosphere to each other might have helped to form the universe.

Birds

129 *Life*, 400, 421

130 Powys, quoted in Blunden, *Thomas Hardy*, 159; W.H. Auden, 'A Literary Transference', *Southern Review*, (VI, 1940), also quoted in *Thomas Hardy: A Collection of Critical Essays*, ed. A.J. Guérard. Rosamund Tomson wrote in the New York *Independent*, 22 November 1894, of TH's 'most noticeable feature, bright, deep-set eyes, keen as a hawk's, but, for all their watchfulness, full of a quiet *bonhomie*. Indeed, there is something not un-hawk-like about his whole physiognomy, with the predatory expression left out; in no other human face have I seen such a still intensity of observation.' (More of her description is quoted in *Millgate*, 322)

131 J. Hutchins in his *History and Antiquities of Dorset* – favourite Hardy reading – tells how in 1853 the Earl of Ilchester had such a bird shot down. See C.J.P. Beatty, *Notes & Queries*, Vol. 206 p 99

132 See pp 87, 88, 91, 178, 188.

Trees, Leaves and Flowers

133 P 7

134 See TH's letter to R.D. Blackmore, p 3

135 "Afterwards", *FWL*, 10

136 p 33

137 See, for example, pp 94-100; "The Rambler", p 260; "Growth in May", p 94; "A Backward Spring", p 93; "The Milkmaid", p 146, etc. In "Panthera", a poem about the Crucifixion, TH can't resist introducing some of the local Palestinian flora.

138 *FWL*, 30

Rivers

139 pp 28-9; *FWL*, 68, 180-3

'The Never Speechless Sea'

140 Jack Ketch, notorious public executioner from about 1663-1686 (and who, incidentally, by 1702 was associated with the new Punch and Judy puppet play). See *FWL*, 77, and *Life*, 126

141 p 40; "A Dream or No". See also "I Found Her Out There", "After a Journey", "A Death-Day Recalled" (p 248); "The Phantom Horsewoman" (p. 242), "Where the Picnic Was" (p. 237), "The Voice of Things" (p 103), "The Wind's Prophecy" (p 39), "On the Esplanade" (p 223), "The Convergence of the Twain" (p 207), etc.

Hardy's Realism

142 *Life*, 377, 153
143 See p50
144 Similarly he described in a letter of 9 October 1908 to the absent Emma how their cat Kitsy had 'caught a leveret in the garden on Monday; and we have cooked and eaten it: she seemed quite willing to let us have it.'

III   HARDY'S NATURE IMAGERY

145 *The Well-Beloved*, first version, published serially in the *Illustrated London News* from 1 October 1892 (see p 215. Some of the original version is given in the New Wessex edition, Macmillan 1975.) *The Return of the Native*, Bk IV ch 7; *The Woodlanders*, ch 35; *Jude the Obscure*, II ch 1
146 *The Trumpet-Major*, ch 11
147 As seen for example, on pp 102, 116, 129
148 Hardy's understanding of history included deep feeling for individual human beings caught up in the political struggles of the powerful. In a letter of 31 January 1904 to Edmund Gosse, answering some queries about *The Dynasts*, he wrote: 'As for the title, it was the best & shortest inclusive one I could think of to express the rulers of Europe in their desperate struggle to maintain their dynasties rather than to benefit their peoples.'
149 A clear echo of TH's Sturminster Newton days, as also revealed in "On Sturminster Foot-Bridge", p 141, and "Overlooking the River Stour", p 127
150 A coracle-like boat peculiar to Portland Bill, particularly adapted to the difficulties of landing on the Chesil Beach
151 *Personal Notebooks*, 19 (on p 71) and 20 (p 71)
152 *Lit. Notes*, entries 63-5; *The Tempest*, IV 1; *Measure for Measure*, I 4
153 See pp 143, 142, 41, 82, 103; and many other instances
154 Absalom, rebellious son of King David, while riding on a mule through a wood, was caught by the head between two oak branches, 'and he was taken up between the heaven and the earth; and the mule that was under him went away.' (II Samuel, ch 18, King James version.) While thus caught he was killed. In his own copy Hardy marked several verses in this and neighbouring chapters, and in 1887 wrote that this chapter 'is the finest example of its kind that I know, showing beyond its power and pathos the highest artistic cunning.' (*Orel*, 107)
155 The temptations of St Anthony, a third-century anchorite of Upper Egypt, were a favourite subject with writers and artists (such as Flaubert and Breughel). The devils or tempters were often pictured as wild beasts.
156 "The Blow'; "The Old Gown", *FWL*, 127; "The Musical Box"; "The Curtains Now Are Drawn"; "The Pedestrian"; "By the Barrows"; "The Wanderer"; "An Experience"; "A Procession of Dead Days". This body imagery not only reflects the unity of all living things in Darwin's meaning, but also the way in which the human mind is locked with the world it inhabits.
157 'The poem "A January Night, 1879" in *Moments of Vision* relates to an incident of this new year (1879) which occurred here at Tooting, where they seemed to begin to feel that "there had past away a glory from the earth." And it was in this house that their troubles began.' *Life*, 124
158 When Tess was very wretched: 'The evening sun was now ugly to her, like a

great inflamed wound in the sky.' (Ch 21)
Other sunset images are on pp 47-50

Patterns

159 *Lit. Notes,* vol. II, 2359
160 See p 260
161 *Orel,* 214
162 ''A Young Man's Exhortation''
163 ''I Travel as a Phantom Now''
164 *Far From the Madding Crowd,* ch 2: see p 35
165 'Epeisodia'', see p 136
166 TH told Florence Henniker in a letter of 7 February 1918 that this poem was 'literally true'. The incident is echoed in the poem ''Great Things'' (*FWL,* 271)
167 ''Epeisodia'', p 136; ''Summer Schemes'', p 99
168 Similarly Grace and Fitzpiers were completely enclosed by boughs (p 135)
169 Newman Flower's own impression of TH after Emma's death: 'The little saplings he had planted around Max Gate when he built it were now vast inclosing trees. He was shut up in a prison of his own making. The future lay solitary before him, alone in this prison of trees. . . .' (*Just As It Happened,* 96)
170 In fact almost two years after their honeymoon. (TH's actual words may have been imperfectly remembered, although the gist sounds like him); *ibid,* 97

Lines

171 ''The Going'', p 165; ''The Darkling Thrush'', p 248; ''The Walk'', ''We Sat at the Window'', ''The Sunshade'', p 68; ''A House with a History'', ''The Pedigree'', p 216; e.g. ''His Heart'', ''In a Former Resort after Many Years''. TH's early study of Darwin's complex diagram of the Pedigree of Species also influenced him. The lines of experience on a human face cannot be explored here in a study of nature imagery, but are an important feature of his patterns: see 'Cold weather brings out upon the faces of people the written marks of their habits. . .' on p 285.
172 Nebuchadnezzar, king of Babylon, 'dreamed dreams, wherewith his spirit was troubled' until Daniel interpreted them. (*Daniel,* chs 2-4). The Swaffham tinker, one John Chapman, was a fifteenth-century pedlar, according to legend, who dreamed that a visit to London would bring him good fortune. There he met a man who told him of his own dream that treasure was buried under a pear tree belonging to a John Chapman of Swaffham. . .The pedlar returned home and found it true.

Webs

173 Ellen E. Titterington, *Materials,* No 4
174 Sails attached to the lower yards of a ship
175 ''The Dawn after the Dance''
176 *Hosea* ch 8 v7: 'For they have sown the wind, and they shall reap the whirlwind.'
177 See the explanation of the circumstances of this letter in *Orel,* 202-3
178 *The Woodlanders,* ch 1. See also p 123
179 See p 84
180 Dennis Taylor, *Hardy's Poetry 1860-1928,* 45
181 e.g. ''An Ancient to Ancients''; ''A Light Snowfall after Frost'', (p 174). See also ''A Hurried Meeting'' (p 191)
182 The poem in full is in *FWL,* 17

Frost

183 ''The Dead Man Walking'' (see p 228); ''Every Artemisia'', ''The Inscription''. See also *A Pair of Blue Eyes,* ch 29, where Knight's revelation to Elfride 'chilled her now like a frost'; and *Two on a Tower,* ch 38, where Lady Constantine suffers 'a fear as sharp as a frost.'
184 ''Welcome Home''
185 Psalm 101 in the Vulgate (used here for the epigraph) is Psalm 102 in the King James version Hardy knew so well: v 4 reads 'My heart is smitten, and withered like grass.'

Birds

186 ''At the Word 'Farewell' '', (p 164); ''He Revisits His First School''

187   "A Light Snow-Fall after Frost", (p 174); "Music in a Snowy Street"; "The Re-Enactment"; "A Kiss"; *The Return of the Native,* Bk V ch 7

188   The Bible is a likely source for the bird in this image. In *Isaiah* ch 14 v23, which begins 'I will also make it a possession for the bittern', TH marked in his copy a subsequent phrase. This is one of three Biblical references to bitterns, the others being in *Isaiah* ch 34 v11, and *Zephaniah* ch 2 v14. All suggest that bitterns will take possession of once-human desolate places. This novel was written in 1872-3; the pre-1871 Anglican lectionary ordained that the Isaiah 14 passage be read on the 1st December, and after 1871 on the evening of 27th November; the Zephaniah passage was, pre-1871, to be read on the evening of 16 September – any of which TH might have heard or read.

189   Something of a companion piece is the poem "The Caged Goldfinch"

190   See also "The Puzzled Game-Birds", one of four consecutive bird poems in *Poems of the Past & Present*

191   "Thoughts from Sophocles"

192   "Neutral Tones" (p 229)

193   See *FWL* 50-51

Insects

194   See p 5

Night and Darkness

195   "The Chosen"

196   "In the Vaulted Way", "God-Forgotten"

197   This poem is discussed by Isobel Grundy in her essay 'Hardy's Harshness' in *The Poetry of Thomas Hardy,* ed. Clements & Grindle.

198   The prophet Elijah, who challenged the prophets of Baal to a competition. When their god failed to perform as requested, 'Elijah mocked them, and said, Cry aloud; for he is a god; either he is talking, or he is pursuing, or he is in a journey, or peradventure he sleepeth, and must be awaked.' This story (I Kings, ch 18) precedes that of the 'still, small voice', TH's favourite Old Testament reading.

199   Bourbon roses, first grown on the island of that name in the Indian Ocean, and of course linked with the French royal family; lotus-eaters, as described by Homer in *The Odyssey* (and Tennyson), whose state of dreamy forgetfulness was induced by eating the (imaginary) lotus fruit; *Athalie,* the play by the great French tragedian Racine, for which Mendelssohn wrote incidental music, including 'The War March of the Priests'.

200   "The Going of the Battery"

201   "Night in the Old Home", *FWL* 32

202   "The Best She Could"

203   Egdon, p 36

204   p 57

205   *Job,* ch 12 v4, Vulgate. The King James translation, 'I am as one mocked of his neighbour', is underlined in TH's copy, with the marginal dates: '1868-71' – a time of great uncertainty and vulnerability for him as his first novel, *The Poor Man & the Lady,* was rejected, his love-affairs with the Nicholls sisters ended, that with Emma began, and his professional future remained unclear.

Light

206   *The Well-Beloved,* II ch 8

207   "Lament". "The Self-Unseeing" is in *FWL* 19

208   'An Indiscretion in the Life of an Heiress', II ch 1; "After the Visit" (see also p 1)

209   "The Musical Box"

210   eg "The Last Chrysanthemum", (p 274), "His Immortality", "The Two Rosalinds", "In Childbed", "Before Marching and After", (p 226), "I Looked Up From My Writing", "On a Discovered Curl of Hair", "Louie"; and the chapter title of *The Return of the Native,* V ch 1, from Job ch 30: 'Wherefore is Light given to him that is in Misery?'

211   See pp 250-1

212   "The Last Signal", p 66; "Once at Swanage", p 142; "Haunting Fingers". See also "The Two Soldiers", and the

lurid light of Tess and Angel's wedding-night on p 208.

Light and Shadows

213 *The Seven Lamps of Architecture,* ch III ¶ 24. The word 'dim' often has a metaphysical implication, as when Keats, at his death, 'passed to the dim.' (''At a House in Hampstead'')
214 'The Withered Arm', (*FWL* 51-3)

Changes in Light

215 *FWL,* 36

Fire

216 This poem is discussed by Dennis Taylor, *Hardy's Poetry 1860-1928,* 14, and in my *Journey into Thomas Hardy's Poetry,* 99-101
217 ''Logs on the Hearth'', *FWL* 30; ''Old Furniture'', *FWL* 33; ''Night in the Old Home'', *FWL* 32

The Moon

218 p 55
219 As usual with TH the message is in the rhyme and metre as well as the words' meaning. The 'imprisonment' is drama-tised in the tight and increased rhyming of the last verse. (See e.g. *A Journey into TH's Poetry,* 297-8, 300)
220 See e.g. J.H. Miller's introduction to *The Well-Beloved,* New Wessex edition, and Jon Stallworthy's essay in *The Poetry of TH, op. cit.*
221 Mary Jacobus, 'Hardy's Magian Retro-spect', *Essays in Criticism,* vol 32, 277
222 For the ominous significance of moths see ''Something Tapped'', (p 194), and *FWL,* 50-51
223 See ''After a Romantic Day'', p 258
224 Hardy seems to have had no intention (or, in this early work, understanding?) of this being a lesbian scene
225 'Her' is the moon, not Eustacia – see p 55
226 Horace's poem, *A Secular Hymn,* begins

with this line: 'O Phoebe, and Diana Queen of Forests!'
227 ''In Sherborne Abbey'' links the moon's illumination with the pattern of life and love of the two lovers who are hiding there from pursuit – but who in the end will become 'chiselled in frigid stone' like their recumbent neighbours on the tombs around them.

Colour Imagery in Nature

228 *FWL,* 75. The previous references are to ''Leipzig'', ''The Sick Battle-God'', ''The Peasant's Confession'', ''The Wound'' (p 158)
229 ''In the Days of Crinoline''. In a letter to Gosse of 5 June 1913 TH wrote: 'Our atmosphere here is crimson just now with murder cases, as you will have seen from the papers.'
230 ''The Lacking Sense'', p 269
231 ''Honeymoon Time at an Inn'', p 218; ''And There Was A Great Calm''.
232 ''The Dead and the Living One''. See also e.g. ''No Bell-Ringing'', ''Shut Out That Moon'' (p 215), ''An Anniversary''
233 ''One Who Married Above Him'', *FWL* 172
234 ''An Unkindly May'', p 94; Mayne, p 211; ''The Thing Planned'', *FWL* 149
235 ''A Commonplace Day'' (p 211), ''The Lack-ing Sense'' (p 269), ''The Wind's Prophecy'' (p 39, ''In a Whispering Gallery''
236 Metallic images are mentioned on p 111
237 *The Woodlanders* (quoted on p 174); ''The Minute Before Meeting''; ''Alike and Unlike'' (p 112); ''The Tree and the Lady'' (p 163). Hardy usually prefers 'gray' to 'grey' (as does Webster's dictionary); he may have differentiated according to the quotation from Field in the Oxford English Dictionary: 'Grey is composed only of black and white, the term gray is applied to any broken colour of a cool hue, and therefore belongs to the class of chromatic colours.'
238 ''The Seven Times'', ''Postponement'' (p 161); ''A Maiden's Pledge''. The laby-rinth image is discussed on pp 169-70

239 *FWL,* 19.
240 "My Cicely", "The Revisitation" (p 127); "Under the Waterfall", p 296
241 "The Children and Sir Nameless", "The Mother Mourns", (p 269); "Afterwards" (*FWL* 10); "June Leaves and Autumn", (p 85). See also "The Five Students", p 82.
242 "Middle-Age Enthusiasms", "Once at Swanage" (p 142; "At Moonrise and Onwards" (p 224); "The Pedigree" (p 216)
243 See "To Outer Nature"; "On a Fine Morning", p 204
244 From the Vulgate version of Isaiah ch 24 v16, translatable as 'My secret, mine'. (TH's use of this epigraph, a late addition, seems to have little connection with the meaning of the Isaiah apocalypse, whose drift is that any 'rejoicings are premature for further tribulation is still to come.' V 16, translated in the A.V. as 'My leanness!' is 'a figure for distress', really meaning something like 'I pine away'. (G.W. Wade, Westminster Commentary on *Isaiah.*)
245 See Donald Davie, 'Hardy's Virgilian Purples', *Agenda,* Spring 1972, 140
246 *Aeneid,* Bk VI, tr. E. Fairfax-Taylor, ls. 769-70

The Image of the Landscape

247 *FWL,* 218-20
248 "Drummer Hodge", p 61
249 pp 26, 75, 195, 269; *FWL,* 182
250 W.B. Yeats, '1919', Cf *Revelation,* ch 6 v8: 'And I looked, and behold a pale horse: and his name that sat on him was Death'; an image taken up by Carlyle in his *French Revolution,* describing the French National Convention as a 'black *Dream become real.* . .and from its bosom there went forth Death on the pale Horse.' (III, 2, i). See D. Taylor, *op. cit.,* 129
251 Ruskin, *Modern Painters,* vol. III, pt iv, ch 12; "Drinking Song"
252 It was then that 'the scene was engraved for years on the retina of Knight's eye' – see p 239
253 Apology to *Late Lyrics and Earlier.* See also the Preface to *Poems of the Past and Present,* TH's letter on p 295, and p 265
254 "The End of the Episode", p 201
255 *Life,* 307; Dennis Taylor, *op cit.,* 145
256 "The Voice of Things", p 103; "The Background and the Figure", p 137; "The Last Signal", p 66; "The Revisitation", pp 213, 225
257 p 208
258 pp 159*ff*
259 *A Pair of Blue Eyes,* ch 22
260 Tess and Marian, p 147, and more in *FWL* 218-9; Jude, *FWL* 296
261 See TH's note on p 34
262 Cytherea, p 244; *Two on a Tower,* ch 4
263 The rest of this passage is on p 37
264 Knight, *FWL* 222; *The Mayor of Casterbridge,* chs 11 & 43
265 "The Figure in the Scene", p 71
266 "The Roman Road", *FWL* 28
267 "The Roman Gravemounds"
268 p 244
269 p 233

HARDY'S 'IMPRESSIONS' OF NATURE

270 See e.g. Genesis ch 30 vv14-16; *Romeo and Juliet,* IV sc 3, *Antony and Cleopatra,* I sc 5. Newton in his *Herball to the Bible* says: 'It is supposed to be a creature having life, engendered under the earth of the seed of some dead person put to death for murder.'
271 p 120
272 Laocoön, Priam's son, was a Trojan priest who tried to dissuade the Trojans from taking in the treacherous Greek wooden horse. Two terrible serpents swam out of the sea and destroyed him and his two sons. The scene became famous through a fine marble sculpture of the 1st or 2nd century B.C. now in the Vatican.
273 *A Laodicean,* ch 5; *The Hand of Ethelberta,* ch 25
274 TH may have been referring to *Ecclesiastes* ch I v18: 'For in much wisdom is much grief; and he that increaseth knowledge increaseth sorrow.'
275 p 240

276 Wordsworth, 'Lines Written in Early Spring''

277 *Tess of the d'Urbervilles,* ch 19

278 This is Florence Hardy's interpolation after TH's death. The next parenthesis is TH's, quoting his own earlier note as he compiles the *Life,* 163

279 Jean Brooks, *Thomas Hardy: The Poetic Structure,* 44

280 *Romeo and Juliet,* Act II sc 6

281 ''The Later Autumn'', p 206; ''Yell'ham-Wood's Story'', p 275. It is an interesting question whether TH's orderly, reserved temperament and perhaps his buried 'fear of Aphrodite' contributed to his dislike of Nature's 'rank growths'. He complimented Anatole France on being 'a writer who is faithful to the principles that make for permanence, who never forgets the value of organic form and symmetry, the force of reserve, and the emphasis of understatement, even in his lighter works.' *Life,* 363

282 But cf 'Proof that earth was made for man', p 204

283 *FWL,* 113-4

284 *Tess of the d'Urbervilles,* II ch 14

285 ''Before and After Summer'', p 160. The returning field-folk, exalted by alcohol and rare relaxation, enjoyed feeling 'themselves and surrounding nature forming an organism of which all the parts harmoniously and joyously interpenetrated each other.' (*Tess of the d'Urbervilles,* I ch 10, *FWL,* 301)

286 *FWL,* 281

287 *FWL,* 304

288 ''Afterwards'', p 95, *FWL,* 10; ''Proud Songsters'', p 96

289 *FWL,* 18

290 ''Shortening Days at the Homestead'', *FWL,* 234

291 p 119

292 *FWL,* 162

293 *FWL,* 271

294 *FWL,* 274

295 p 10; *FWL,* 236

296 *The Woodlanders,* ch 46; p 146

297 His use of 'altruism', in letters above, is not quite the same as Dawkins' in *The Selfish Gene*

298 *FWL,* 240

299 'Literature as Context: Milton's *Lycidas',* in *Fables of Identity* (New York 1963), pp 119-20. I am indebted to David Lodge for this reference (See his introduction to the New Wessex edition of *The Woodlanders,* London 1974)

300 J.G. Frazer writes of the Adonis legend in *The Golden Bough,* chs XXIX-XXXIII. Visiting the source of the R. Adonis, (where 'Adonis was thought to have met Aphrodite, and to be buried') his glowing description of its 'wild, romantic wooded gorge', with 'tumbling water, green vegetation and brilliant sunset' would have delighted TH, who read at least part of the first edition. (Ch XXX, abridged edition, 1922)

301 Their failure throughout the book to comunicate with each other – a favourite Hardy theme – is here dramatised in the physical circumstances

302 See note 85

303 According to his housemaid and gardener, *op. cit.,* spring flowers were TH's own favourites

304 Roger Robinson, 'Hardy and Darwin', in *Thomas Hardy; A Writer and His Background,* ed. Norman Page

305 TH had long thought of the possibility of 'a limited God of goodness', 'One not Omnipotent, but hampered' (*Life,* 297) as a partial explanation for human life's problems. *The Dynasts* ended (1907) with the hope that 'the Will' might amend itself 'till It fashion all things fair!'; but the 1914-18 War made him say that 'he would probably not have ended *The Dynasts* as he did end it if he could have foreseen what was going to happen within a few years.' (*Life,* 368)

306 *A Journey into Thomas Hardy's Poetry,* ch 12

307 *op. cit.,* 16

308 *I Corinthians* ch 13

309 With some similarities to those of later existentialists like Albert Camus.

310 Prometheus, son of a Titan, stole fire from heaven and taught humans many useful arts. His punishment by Zeus was to be chained to a rock, where each day an eagle consumed his liver, (which was nightly

renewed). For more of this passage see
FWL, 72, 185

311   p 36
312   *Tess of the d'Urbervilles,* p 261 above;
      ''Julie-Jane'', *FWL,* 75; ''The Inquiry'',
      p 241

313   In a letter of 3 February 1909 to the editor
      of 'my old friend The Cornhill' who
      published it, TH wrote: 'When I had
      dispatched the MS to you I rewrote it, and
      have now corrected the proof accord-
      ingly'.

Index

317

171, 178, 197, 212–13, 220, 232, 238–40, 254, 285, 287, 293, 297, 301

Mendelssohn, Felix, 312

Mendip, 184

Messiah (Handel), 154

Metaphor, 2, 114, 169, 175, 183, 200, 209, 213, 250, 298, 309

Metre, 67, 313

Metternich, Prince, 188

Michael [Archangel], 75

Midsummer Eve, 134, 190, 293

Milky Way, 172

Miller, J.H., 313

Millgate, Michael, 306–7, 309

Milton, John, 308, 315

Mind/world relationship, 10–11, 59–60, 70, 74, 78, 158–60, 167–9, 173–4, 201, 206, 209, 222–3, 230, 237, 242–5, 253, 255–9, 261, 265, 273–4, 277, 287, 295, 298–9, 301, 310

Mirrors, 11, 43, 63, 98, 143–4, 180, 217–18, 299–300

Mist, 1, 8, 12, 28, 36, 40, 42, 48, 63, 72, 74, 81–3, 107, 111, 119, 126, 140, 153, 155, 173, 200–201, 232, 245, 252, 256, 271, 278, 293, 295

'Mistover Knap, 23, 86, 252

Moloch, 308

Monte Carlo, 173

Moon, 2, 9–11, 29, 34–5, 37, 42–4, 46, 49, 53–7, 62, 69, 76–7, 86, 113, 120, 140–44, 146, 171, 179, 190–92, 196, 211, 214–26, 228–9, 232–3, 243, 252, 258, 271, 313; *see* IMAGERY

Morality, 55, 291; *see* NATURE

Morgan, Charles, 2, 125

Morley, John; *Critical Miscellanies*, 257

Moschus (Greek poet), 293

Moscow, 89, 116, 129, 192

Moses, 171

Moths, 99, 119, 191, 218, 236, 313

'Mother, the Great' (Nature), 9, 76, 146, 180, 267, 269, 308

'Motoring with Thomas Hardy' (Voss), 306

Moule, Arthur, 305

Mountclere, Lord, 111, 187

Mumming, 53, 84

Music, 7, 29, 59, 64–5, 99, 104, 109, 125, 129–30, 134, 139, 143, 146, 154, 170, 178, 183, 189, 197, 203, 215, 219, 233, 246, 261, 278, 285, 288, 302

Muspelheim, 307

Myrrha, 293

'Nameless, Sir', 231

Napoleon, 89, 129, 155, 192, 252, 271; *see* WAR

National Gallery, London, 108

Nature, -& 'First Cause', 2, 12, 267–8; -& art, 11, 35, 160, 248, 250–1, 257, 267, 284–5; -& humanity, 1–2, 8–14, 16, 35–6, 46–7, 59, 61, 71, 78, 89, 97, 112–13, 115, 122, 128, 153, 157, 193–4, 205–6, 210, 225–6, 239–40, 243–5, 247–57, 259–61, 269, 272–4, 277–92, 295–6, 300–1, 315; -as Mystery, 257; -as setting, 8–10, 33, 51, 61, 70–71, 88, 137, 141, 144, 158–9, 164, 193–4, 225, 237–9, 242, 245, 249, 253, 257, 267, 269, 287, 293; 'continuous substitution' of, 160; defects of, 1, 11–13, 134, 148, 180, 186, 247–8, 267–74, 276–82, 285, 289, 292, 300, 306; distortions, 269–72; -hostile, 12–13, 187, 239, 251, 256, 260, 269, 280, 282, 298; -morality of, 13, 265, 278–9, 281; -qualities of, 1, 11, 59–60, 115, 141, 146, 257, 274, 283–4, 287–9, 293, 303; -'rank', 95, 97, 104, 138, 269, 277–8, 315; *see also* GROWTHS, IMAGERY, LAW, 'MOTHER', & *passim*

Nebuchadnezzar, 170, 311

Negatives, 204, 229, 277

Neigh, Alfred, 114

Neslon, Admiral, 129, 172

Neutral colours, 5, 42, 47, 79, 86, 91, 110, 112, 136, 147, 149, 158, 192–3, 205, 210, 212, 228–9, 232, 251, 256

New Jerusalem, 38

New York, 290; *Independent*, 309

Newberry, Mrs, 91

Newton, Sir Isaac, 309

Newton, Thomas: *Herball to the Bible*, 314

Nicholls, Elizabeth, 312; Jane, 40, 312

Nietzsche, 13, 279

Niflheim, 293, 307

Night, 6, 10, 23, 34–7, 40, 48, 50–53, 57, 60, 62, 73–4, 76–7, 79, 83, 92, 99, 104, 107, 115, 119, 136, 139, 141–2, 156–7, 165, 179, 181, 186, 190, 194, 197–8, 207, 209–10, 216, 220, 225, 255–6, 268, 271, 281, 286

Nighthawk/-jar, 95, 100, 125, 134, 190–92, 259

Noon, 36, 40, 42, 62, 68, 85, 98–100, 191, 194, 231, 233, 300

328

120, 143, 145, 234–6, 259

Purpose, 295

Putnam, George, 296

Quarrenden (apple), 124

Racine, Jean, 312

Rain, 1, 4, 7, 9, 12, 22, 26, 41, 43, 71–2, 74–6, 79, 91–2, 95, 97, 103–5, 109, 127–8, 134–6, 140, 145–6, 148, 156–8, 168, 171, 173, 194, 196, 212, 239–40, 243, 246, 250, 253, 255, 260, 262, 267, 271, 273, 281, 287, 292

Rainbarrows(s), 27–8, 53–4, 86, 243, 271

Rainbows, 8, 11, 129, 145, 170, 204, 232–4, 257

Rationalists, A Biographical Dictionary of Modern, 295

Raunham, Parson, 258, 301

Real Conversations (William Archer), 305, 308

Realism, 70, 114, 145–9

Reality, 1, 13, 145, 158–60, 167, 200, 203, 209, 220, 222, 236, 249, 257, 299; exploration of, 8, 237–8, 245

Reason, 15, 56, 204, 217, 222, 237, 269, 277, 289–91, 295; 'imaginative-', 146

Red, 28, 35, 38, 49, 53, 56, 62, 67, 78, 81, 84–5, 87, 91, 109–11, 120, 122, 128, 134, 137, 144, 146, 158, 165, 171, 208, 213–14, 225–8, 230, 239, 271, 273, 275, 288

Reddleman, 24–5, 62, 157

Reflections, 10, 41–3, 48, 53, 55–6, 65–6, 72, 77, 79, 84, 91, 98, 140, 143, 170, 208–9, 217, 229, 243, 246

Religious allusions, 56, 104, 293–5, 302–3, 315

Return, theme of, 27, 179, 227, 238, 240

Revelation (Bible), 28, 307, 314

Rhoda (Brook), 208, 213

Rhyme, 97, 132, 177, 213, 296–7, 313

Rhythm, 211, 213

Richard II, 158

'Ringsworth Shore', 143

Rivers, 8, 10, 28–9, 37, 43, 81, 87, 91, 101, 103–4, 116, 127, 129, 137, 139–41, 146–7, 184, 229, 240, 243, 252, 270; *see* WATER

Robinson, Roger, 315

Roman amphitheatre, 253; -arena, 102; -Baths, 173; -coin, 204; -remains, 253; -road, 254

Romantic pastoral lyric, the, 248

Rome, 204, 254

Romeo and Juliet, 314

Royal Academy, the, 41, 257

Royal Society for the Prevention of Cruelty to Animals, 115

Rushy Pond, 26

Ruskin, 206, 245; *Modern Painters*, 314

Russia, 90; Russian army, 90

Ruysdael/Ruisdael, Jacob van, 110

Salisbury, 56

Sallaert, Anthonis, 28

Sally (Hall), 250

Samuel, Book of (Bible), 310

'Sandbourne', 143, 240

'Sacrophagus College', 196

Satan, 75

Savile, Lucy, 154, 208

Scandinavian mythology, 40, 307

Scents, 6, 23, 28, 79, 84, 89, 96, 100, 104, 106–8, 140, 216, 278, 309

Schopenhauer, Arthur, 279

Sea, 6, 10, 37–41, 63, 70–71, 75, 85, 89, 100–101, 109–11, 118, 120, 137, 141–6, 157, 190, 197, 205, 208, 210, 212, 214, 223, 225, 234–5, 237, 242, 248, 250, 252; white-, 174

S, 122, 272, 275, 287, 300

Seasons, 9–10, 33, 40, 83, 87, 95, 97, 110, 122, 134, 226, 231, 239–40, 272, 275, 286–7, 300

Seaway, Anne, 54

Selene (moon goddess), 215

Selfish Gene, The (Dawkins), 292

Senlac, 72

Sennacherib, 195

Seven Lamps of Architecture, The (Ruskin), 312

Seven Sleepers, 118

Shadow, 6, 24, 29, 40–7, 49, 52, 54–5, 62–3, 65–8, 78, 81–2, 84, 97, 99, 109–10, 114, 122, 134–6, 158, 160, 163, 170, 172–3, 191–2, 195, 197, 204–9, 211, 221–2, 230; *see also* IMAGERY, PATTERNS

Shakespeare, William, 157, 182; -allusions, 256, 278, 294, 310, 314

Shelley, Percy Bysshe, 131, 215, 266, 293

Shiner, Mr, 124–5

Shoreham, 306

Simile, 58, 125, 181, 230

Sirius (star), 35, 58–9, 90

Skrymer (Norse god), 40

Sky, 1, 6, 10–11, 22, 34–5, 38–9, 41, 43, 50, 52, 54, 60, 62–4, 66, 69–71, 76–7, 79,

330